Community Without Unity

Post-Contemporary Interventions

Series Editors: Stanley Fish and Fredric Jameson

Community Without Unity

A Politics of Derridian Extravagance

William Corlett

Duke University Press   Durham and London 1989

Printed in the United States of America
on acid-free paper ∞
Library of Congress Cataloging-in-Publication Data
Corlett, William.
Community without unity : a politics of Derridian extravagance /
by William Corlett.
p.   cm.
Bibliography: p.
Includes index.
ISBN 0-8223-0732-4
1. State, The.   2. Community.   3. Collectivism.   4. Individualism.
5. Postmodernism.   I. Title.
JC325.C65   1989
320.2—dc 1989-1120

To my parents, Elsie Ross Corlett and William Southard Corlett

For me ideology is a kind of vast membrance enveloping everything. We have to know that this skin exists even if it encloses us like a net or like closed eyelids. We have to know that, to change the world, we must constantly try to scratch and tear it. We can never rip the whole thing off, but we must never let it stick or stop being suspicious of it. It grows back and you start again.—Hélène Cixous

Contents

Acknowledgments

To work for community while reading and writing from perspectives influenced by Derrida? Exploring and celebrating this possibility sometimes creates the impression that Derrida's extravagance is the best postmodernism, or that his work is a likely candidate for the next so-called paradigm in social and political theory. Readers should struggle to erase this mistaken impression: Derrida does not offer a new "paradigm," but reading his work can make worlds of difference. This book draws attention to the difference Derrida makes and suggests how theories of community might live through the extravagance of his criticism.

Of course, I write under the influence of other authors as well, two of whom double as my teachers. Tracy B. Strong led, watched, covered his eyes, etc., as my work took liberal, communitarian, and deconstructive turns over the past fifteen-odd years. Tracy directed my Ph.D. thesis in 1978, continued to read more pages than either of us can remember, and delivered a painfully close reading of the present manuscript. Four years ago I read Foucault and Charles Taylor with William E. Connolly in his NEH summer seminar, and my work still carries the imprint of his rigorous criticism. He has since then offered encouragement, sound advice, and more criticism, including a forceful reading of this manuscript. Perhaps having teachers I can never repay explains, in part, my effort to supplement notions of reciprocal exchange with free gift-giving.

Countless others have given time, advice, and encouragement during various phases of this project. Jane Bennett, John Chapman, Jean Bethke Elshtain, Rebecca Ann Graham, Douglas Hodgkin, James Malloy, John Nelson, Mark Okrent, J. D. Phaup, Michael Shapiro, and Michael J. Stevens are only the most memorable names. I learned the ins and outs of book production from Reynolds Smith and the staff at Duke University Press, and I benefited from the anonymous reviews Reynolds solicited. Preparation of the manuscript was assisted at Bates by Joyce Caron and Eban Mears.

Assistance also came in financial form. I must acknowledge the National Endowment for the Humanities for a 1980 Summer Stipend for Independent Research and also for the grant to attend the difficult Connolly seminar in 1984. At Bates, with the help and encouragement of Dean Carl B. Straub, I enjoyed a Roger Schmutz travel grant, a reduction in teaching for research, and a timely leave of absence in 1986–87. During that year I received generous support from Davidson College, where Dean Robert Williams and Dr. John Savarese transformed my one-term visit into a full-year stay.

Two parts of this book have appeared in other places. A similar version of chapter 4 was published as "Pocock, Foucault, Forces of Reassurance" in *Political Theory* (17:77–100). Parts of chapter 5 appeared as "The Political Significance of Lincoln's Epideictic Rhetoric" in the *Illinois Quarterly* (44:22–33). Thanking publishers for permission to reprint these articles in slightly different form is only a slightly different form of thanking those mentioned above for their permission to print in the first place. And in the first place, I was encouraged by my parents, to whom I dedicate this book.

Lewiston, Maine   William Corlett

I Subjugation

Postmodernism, a name associated with Foucault and Derrida, sometimes indicates the abandonment of structure, but this abandonment can be misleading. If used in the sense of deserting completely or giving up the notion of structure, *abandon* summons images of the nihilistic, the apolitical, the trivial, or worse. Names like Foucault and Derrida can, however, be drawn closer to political discourse by using *abandon* in the sense of losing self-control, or giving in to the accidental, chaotic aspect of any structure. Such usage permits postmodern critics to move closer to structures, to examine their binary oppositions for signs of play. Postmodern writing plays with abandon, then, by challenging uniformity, by searching for cracks in the foundations of political and social thinking.

Foucault is an important postmodern name because his work resists reducing human beings to patterns of subjectivity. Far from celebrating the death of all structured thinking, Foucault's resistance can be politicized to permit the cultivation of a self that exceeds the possibilities mapped out by contemporary political thinking. The political prospects for community, however, are not as clear; indeed, the shared oneness at the center of recent communitarian thinking cannot survive Foucauldian criticism.

But Derrida's work can also contribute to an affirmative politics. Rather than stressing—but by no means denigrating—resistance to the patterns of subjectivity, deconstruction refuses to act as if these patterns, such as man/woman, are ever fixed. Derrida seeks to affirm multiple sexual, cultural, racial differences in extravagant ways. Derridian extravagance is consistent with some usages of *community*. Extravagance and community both turn on the notion of free gift-giving.

While this book focuses on a politics of Derridian extravagance, it should not be read as an alternative to Foucauldian, or any other, politics. Postmodern writing does not deliver programs. To play with abandon—without abandoning all structure—is too accidental and irruptive to be a program. But in an age in which nearly everyone admits that the personal is the political, programs and alternatives and options are only a part of political possibility. By drawing attention to accident and chance in everyday practice, this book lends the force of extravagance to the struggle against individual and collective patterns of subjectivity.

The first part of the book studies Foucault's formulation of the problem of being shaped by social construction. The second part examines some of the many ways in which these patterns of subjectivity are reassuring. The third part turns toward the abandonment of structure, in its affirmative sense.

The chapters in the first part—subjugation—ask readers to consider the problem of being subjected to simultaneous pressures to be what the nineteenth century called "rugged individuals" and also, as individuals, to transmit messages about the collectivity—its prejudices, discipline, rules, etc.—into the twenty-first century. We are told that we, as individuals, are the center of discourse in a liberal age; such discourse is about us. And yet our traditions depend upon our ability to transmit their content to others across time. Thus we lie at the center of a discourse in which we cannot become fully implicated: we are the message that must be transmitted as well as the messenger: a "We" as well as an "I."

The first chapter is a general introduction to the problem of pursuing community while using language that reinforces domination. I announce my overall argument in this chapter. The second chapter reviews the ways in which theorists use the word *community*. The third chapter explains how Foucault poses a question that adds to the discussion of domination and exploitation—the question of subjugation—and reviews several well-known responses, including Derridian extravagance.

1 Mutual Service and the Language of Domination

This book attempts to celebrate both community and difference. I want to discuss our serving and defending one another without pretending that these communitarian practices bring unity to the global village or any other habitat. Bringing unity seems always to require silencing the so-called parts that do not fit the holistic vision, and I want no part of that. But avoiding community ignores the problem of lives of quiet desperation—shut-in singles, suicidal teenagers, homeless people—lives which are perhaps more desperate now than they were in Thoreau's time. I wish to attempt a Wolin-like stance toward the world—"taking care of people and things instead of using them up"—without relying on unity for a foundation.

Thoreau, who uses *community* to name such mutual service

and defense, fears its collectivistic consequences, and often prefers to be left alone. Bataille, who wants no part of unifying arguments, sees taking care of people as a form of dominating them and seeks that different kind of solitude—an "apotheosis of alcohol and flesh"—that celebrates a using up of people and things. My task is to show how overcoming the urge to say that human beings, or subsets of them, are all the same leads arguments neither back to the atomistic prejudice of nineteenth century individualism nor ahead to the solitary ecstasy of avant-garde eruptions.

Communitarian arguments pose a major threat to radical individualism, but many of these arguments illustrate how right Bataille, and perhaps Foucault, are to berate mutual service as a form of domination, or humiliation. The celebration of difference demands a rejection of what Connolly calls "attunement." Thus, contemporary political theory in the West seems to offer choices that range from a flat refusal to serve and defend other people to caring for people in ways that dominate and humiliate them.[1]

Thoreau refuses to serve others; Bataille exposes the domination of those who do not so refuse. Most people seem to embody both extremes: refusing and caring. We are caught in a bind between having to be individuals and having, as individuals, to care for the collectivity, or union. In other words, the state, which protects individuals as individual rights-bearers, requires them occasionally to make personal sacrifices for the collectivity. Government consequently fluctuates between refusing to provide services and providing services in ways that dominate and humiliate the recipients.

To illustrate this unhappy situation, I quote from an editorial in a Christian magazine.[2] The one-page article appears to be a straightforward comparison of a "cash merit system to reward citizens" for acts of social conscience—in this case, agreeing to live in a racially segregated, "woodsy Chicago suburb," Oak Park—and Habitat for Humanity, an organization whose volunteers build and sometimes live alongside houses for the marginally poor, in this case in segregated urban areas "where no one wants to live."

Habitat for Humanity grants no-interest loans to its new home-owners, who devote one thousand hours of labor to their houses and the houses of others (accumulating "sweat equity"). "People [who volunteer for Habitat for Humanity] don't receive cash bonuses; rather volunteers like Jimmy Carter work long hours without pay." In this particular project "committed Christian couples mostly from middle-class backgrounds move into the neighborhood [on Chicago's west side] offering role models for the poor and bringing a social stability to the area." This language seems to cast urban dwelling as a form of missionary work, if not as a mission for the National Guard.

The article is designed to underscore the difference between two news reports of a Carter visit to Chicago on behalf of Habitat for Humanity in 1986. One reports Carter swinging a hammer in the slums; the other reports him attending a "dress-up affair" in Oak Park, the suburb known for its cash merit system of integration. The following excerpt describes the two events in earthly and heavenly terms.

> Oak Park hopes to "fix" its society with a carefully controlled plan to change the environments, and, ultimately, the value systems of various minority groups. To accomplish that goal, they rely on a powerful motivator: human greed. Their plan is creative and rational—an example of the kingdom of this world at its best.
>
> Habitat for Humanity, in contrast, is working to produce a far more radical change among a smaller group of people. They desire to change not only the human environment, but the human heart. They believe it is not enough for people with resources to invite in well-screened representatives of minority groups.
>
> Rather, people of resources must go, voluntarily, to the places of need, and give their time, and their sweat, and their families, and their love. Even greed is not a strong enough motivator to accomplish that sacrifice. It requires instead the Christian commitment of people willing to take a risk with no prospect of reward in this life—in other words, the kingdom that is not of this world.

8 Subjugation

This "ironic juxtaposition" contains words that darken the illuminating distinction between the two kingdoms. One can sense Pauline traces of Rousseau or Augustine, for whom the two "kingdoms" commingle within us all, at least for the time being.

The surface distinction in these illuminating paragraphs draws a line between liberal reciprocity in a contracted universe (if you move in, then we will pay you fifteen hundred dollars) and the communion of saints in an expansive universe. These are the so-called two worlds of Jimmy Carter, a tension between greed and love. But notice that the greedy, rational side is described as "creative," a "plan to change the environment" toward racial integration. This is the power of greed on its best behavior, courting communitarian ends. And notice that the loving, committed side is a "risk" taken "voluntarily" with no prospect of "reward." This is the sacrifice of love couched in the language of liberalism. Given their attraction to one another, one might wonder if the relation of the two worlds is not rather like what Lewis Hyde calls a "lovers' quarrel."[3]

This quarrel is problematic because, apart from the bickering over whether to pay bigots to change their habitats or to hope that zealots will live like missionaries out of the goodness of their hearts, the marginally poor remain in the margins and spaces of the text. In the passage just cited one might compare two movements: "people with resources . . . invite in well-screened representatives of minority groups." and "people of resources . . . go [out] . . . to places of need." This contrast of having goods ("with resources") and being good ("of resources") is supposed to make the worldly approach seem like mere "safe conscience," while suggesting that the heavenly approach involves the risk of dirty hands, smashed thumbnails, and so on. But there is a disguised contrast which signals a resemblance between these two approaches. Those inhabiting the world of greed invite marginal people "in"; those inhabiting the world of love go out to meet the marginal people, to minister to their needs. In both cases the marginal people are out there, ripe for domination because their needs must be met from without by the resources of greedy middle-class folks or loving middle-class folks. This article somehow cannot accommodate the obvious facts that marginally poor people have infinite "resources" and middle-class folks have crying "needs" of their own, facts with which the author of this editorial would certainly agree. But these facts are neglected by the quarrel over which way to help the marginally poor from a socially distant point of view. The author's case is subverted by the terms of discourse used to make it.

The familiar this world/other world distinction seems to fuel a tension between feeling selfish when individualistic and feeling unrealistic or naive when collectivistic. The author can conclude only in cliché, wringing his hands, asking lame rhetorical questions:

> As I watched the ironic juxtaposition of the news reports of Carter's visits, I could not help wondering which approach gave him the most personal satisfaction. One thing troubled me, though: Why is it that when a former President comes to town to build houses for the poor, hundreds of people will pay $50 to dress up and hear him talk about it, but only a handful will take their hammers and join him?

This is the kind of question that cannot be defended very far outside the narrow boundaries of a Christian magazine. Why do more people not find "personal satisfaction" in taking a "risk" which has no "prospect of reward" in their lifetime? Even if one avoids all of the obvious answers, it is difficult not to address the troubles of the author. If acts of mutual service are versed in the language of domination, they cannot be mutual. If the good works of Habitat For Humanity boil down to the personal satisfaction of the outside volunteers, is it really surprising that most people opt for the more hedonistic delights of contemporary society? What good reasons can be given for rubbing shoulders with the poor and righting wrongs with blisters, dirty hands, and tired muscles, when one can more easily appease one's collective conscience by writing a check and arriving at the "dress-up affair" in time for cocktails?

Ironically, Augustine makes the same two-kingdom distinction when he contrasts mutual service and domination. He writes, "In the city of the world both the rulers themselves and the people they dominate are dominated by the lust for domination; whereas in the City of God all citizens serve one another in charity, whether they serve by the responsibility of office or by the duties of obedience."[4] From a postmodern perspective it is difficult to see the advantage of fighting the lust for domination only to win the duty of obedience. But that is a difficulty which cannot be addressed until one appreciates the irony of the article we have been reading. The author writes a story of citizens serving one another in charity, but his language tells a different story, a story of domination. My plan approaches the many good deeds performed each day in the name of community from a different perspective, one which draws attention to the give, or play, in the structures which underlie conventional thinking about political community.

My work might make a difference to current perspectives that are unable to avoid encouraging collective enterprises while leaving the question of such involvement up to each individual. Most political theorists make peace with either individualism or collectivism and then co-opt, rather than destroy, the enemy camp. For example, a theorist might stress the deeply rooted commonality that underlies the rightful diversity of each person, or s/he might stress the radical autonomy of persons, who are free to work out collective arrangements for their mutual benefit. There is also room, in conventional circles, for creative efforts to balance the interests of the autonomous person with the heteronomous demands of collective life. But these examples illustrate a stalemate faced by political theory: as people become collectivized they hunger for individualism and vice versa. The popular response to such situations, in which one cannot be right, is all too often apathy or a desperate effort to keep whatever order is at hand. Less popular, but more troublesome, are the efforts of critics, such as Bataille, to annihilate the stable subject of political discourse.

Postmodernism and Deconstruction

Deconstruction, as I use the word, is neither a method of analysis nor a synonym for dismantlement. Rather, deconstruction names what takes place during at least three overlapping ways of reading, or traversing, texts. One strategy notices how binary oppositions work to govern the sense that texts can make. These oppositions tend to produce hierarchies because it is difficult not to emphasize one side over the other. Another attempts to invert and dismantle the ruling oppositions. Mastering the negativity required to invert polarities must be attended by efforts to dismantle or neutralize the opposition altogether. All polar distinctions must be supplemented in the sense that they are shown not to be sovereign. And then there are strategies designed to preclude the emergence of new oppositions, of new hierarchies, of new synthetic ways of mutilating difference.[5]

To articulate this difficult ban, I shall borrow the notion of excess from Derrida, who borrows it from Bataille. That is, by making use of excess, I shall study mutual service without domination. This will involve reversing the benefit of the doubt and asking rational thrifty philosophers to give reasons for having to have reasons to ease up in the fight against flux.

Political theories can be thought of as providing order for the world(s) they seek to encounter. This is not to say that political theories impose these forms on the world; it is more accurate to see any imposition involved as an attempt at self-governance. Political theories, then, do not impose order on the world in the way, for example, a sculptor might give shape and vitality to un-formed clay. Rather, these theories govern themselves by giving themselves structure or orders. Ignoring any question of how the order of these theories is related to the world(s) they would encounter, there remains a question of how theories themselves are related to their order. That is, what do political theories *do* when they provide structure for the world(s) theorists seek to encounter? And what is the cost of their struggle?

To address these questions I shall use in the least orderly way possible the forms which political theories provide in the name of order. This means refusing the peace that lies within all understanding, turning my back on reassurance. To reject the reassurance political theory offers anyone who submits totally to the governance of its forms is to experiment with extrava-gance. An extravagant perspective uses reason and order in a provisional way while refusing to permit any form to become entrenched or to provide reassurance. This perspective is made possible by confessing that, in principle, the madness of not thinking along the lines of reason and order is never successfully straitjacketed or neutralized. Madness resides even in the order-giving text.[6]

Rehearsing the Argument

I am trying to look at the way in which political theories work: I am more concerned with what they *do*, than with their substantive content. I am not trying in this book to give yet another defense of community as a practice. Instead, I attempt to clear the way for my use of early Derridian texts and then to suggest that one can use *community* without teleology to supplement the liberal politics of our age. This is sufficient to remove *community* from the tired situation of being torn between individualism and collectivism.

I attempt to follow the political implications of some of Derrida's work. Briefly, Derrida's radical use of *play* can be used to supplement the double bind of individualism and collectivism. As long as this tension remains central to political theory, consequences will be as predictable as whether major parties win national elections in American politics. But if this tension were displaced in ways that permit an affirmative politics of community, some new consequences might follow. I shall try to show how Derrida's extravagant maneuvers can be used to displace the individual/collective tension.

First, I need to find some working space. I am not going to pretend to start my argument in the old-fashioned way of making a clearing, constructing a claim, and defending this claim against the outside threat of nonsense, illogic, ambiguity, and the like. Rather, I shall simply ask readers to admit that this romantic way of proceeding is now passé, if not embarrassing. Readers should join me in admitting that the clearing within which I will do my work is already infested with chance, accident, chaos; and in realizing that these silent, nonsensical forces help to constitute, by virtue of their difference, the sense one can make. This will take time. This part of the book is designed to distinguish between reassuring and extravagant—or radical—ways of thinking about subjectivity.

Part II shows why it is impossible to arrive at a radical notion of play without giving in to accident or chance. Chapter 4 develops a reassuring model of the development of order over time; this model shows how the breathtaking work of J. G. A. Pocock captures the structure and motion of most thinking about the creation and transmission of community. Traces of Pocock's model can be found even in the radical criticism of Michel Foucault, who has correctly diagnosed the problem I am addressing. I am not asking for a reversal of the priority of order over chaos. Rather, I want to encourage not choosing. Instead of asking why I bother with chaos, readers should grant me at least the benefit of the doubt. Allow me to ask: what is the cost of the old-fashioned way of building arguments, traditions and communities? What are the consequences of fighting the flux all the time?

Assuming that I receive the benefit of the doubt, but that many readers are still leery of refusing to choose between order and chaos, I shall provide two illustrations from everyday political life of the consequences of the old-fashioned choice of order over chaos. The remainder of part II shows how political life can cut life short in the name of felicity, beauty, and sobriety. These chapters apply Pocock's model on the creation and transmission of collective self-images across time. Chapter 5 reads Lincoln's contributions to political theory with an eye to his fear of the fullness of life. Chapter 6 turns to Burke's contributions and considers his fear of the madness of life. Creation and transmission, in Pocock's sense, are shown to exact the price of blind devotion and purblind prejudice in the name of communion. If this is all that community can be, perhaps we should join Foucault and others in dismissing it. By the end of part II most readers will be ready to admit that choosing order over chaos is at least costly, if not too expensive. If the price is too dear, perhaps there are other ways to read. And because I am not asking anyone to choose chaos, it seems most reasonable to refuse to choose. With that refusal I shall finally have gained my working space.

Second, I need to prepare for Derridian extravagance within this space where both chaos and order reside. Derrida's work promises to supplement conventional work in political theory by displacing the tensions that other work—from Rosenblum's chaste morals to Connolly's slack ones—learns to live with.

This displacement is a way around treating the yearning for communion and its impossibility as a paradox. Reading Derrida allows one to see how this paradox thrives only in orderly, perhaps multiple, worlds in which chaos is exiled to the fringe. Confessing that chaos is a constitutive element of order permits treating irrationality as if it were never exiled; Derrida brings a never-for-a-moment-exiled chaos to our attention in the spaces and margins of rational life by confessing that it always already resides here. Derrida forces us to reverse our thinking about irrationality and reason, but not in the usual ways. Does this place Derrida in the difficult position of having to speak the unspeakable? Part III shows how he lives with this difficulty.

My reading of Derridian extravagance proceeds in the following way. First, I announce the difference between his use of *difference* and that of Saussure. Chapter 7 might be read as an introduction to what Spivak (1976) calls "what comes close to becoming Derrida's master-concept" (xliii): différance. Second, I practice in chapter 8 the way in which Derrida shows how différance allows for an extravagance which makes radical play possible. Third, I show how acknowledging accident in everyday life is not best presented as practicing transgression. Rather, Derridian extravagance is silence, silence that he would conserve in speech rather than silence that he would deny speech by engaging in the ecstatic, solitary frenzy of Bataillean formation. Chapter 9 ends with reminders that any binary distinction is riddled with silent excess.

Part III carries a plea to politicize the excess Derrida would maintain in silence; the symmetrically arranged chapters of the book draw to a close there. Derrida opens new ground—a nonbasis of play upon which the history of meaning takes off —but it still may be unclear, in a practical way, exactly how his work does *not* rule out an affirmative politics of community.

To clarify this I have added a supplement to the book. There my argument loses its theoretical flavor and addresses the practice of everyday life. Perhaps everyday life is already overflowing with indications that Derridian extravagance may be all about us.

2 Reciprocity, Commonality, Mutual Service

"She is active in the community." How is the word *community* being used in this sentence? A member of a local chamber of commerce might answer that the word names a body of individuals in a geographical location, and leave it at that. This could cover possibilities that range from the local community to the interplanetary community. But political theorists speak of many states and qualities of community. Community is one of the best-loved terms in political discourse; even the "defense community" softens its image with the word. This chapter sorts out various usages. After attempting to come to terms with community, I shall examine two major usages—reciprocity and commonality—in terms of the assumptions they make about human subjectivity. The next chapter will expand upon these assumptions.

Some political theorists use *community* in its geographical sense, but only on the way to summoning images of commonality, perhaps human commonality. They speak of sharing qualities—ethnicity, respect for the law, love of God, duty to country—in common. Some philosophers point out that people must share the same usages of the word *sharing* to be able to communicate in their communities. Other political theorists, who also use *community* in its geographical sense, hesitate to emphasize the commonality we supposedly share. They wish instead to take charge of their self-definition; they consider it their right to be whomever they choose. These theorists would pursue community within their geographical communities as if it were the result of relations among rights-bearing people. Despite their disagreement—which we shall study in terms of the assumptions being made about human subjectivity—both groups of political theorists agree easily with a chamber-of-commerce usage: community names a geographical location.[1]

Political theorists tend, then, to take the geographical sense of community for granted. But even the most local community is an important part of the practice of their everyday lives. Before arriving at the offices in which they engage in discourse on community they might take the garbage out to the curb, walk the dog, drive a car, ride a bicycle, walk on a paved sidewalk, use electricity, register to vote, vote, rely on traffic lights, and so forth. Because these services are taken for granted, they overlap with other usages and get lost in the shuffle of political theory.

One common mistake is to equate *reciprocity* with the geographical usage of *community*. Anyone who has lived through a blackout, a power failure, a natural disaster, or chaos of some other sort, knows how nervous the people in both rich and poor neighborhoods feel. This nervousness should remind us that, while money may pay for superior services, it is not a service. No amount of money can buy services in a period of chaos. A foundation must exist before exchanges can materialize and payment can be made for services rendered. *Community* often names that foundation. The worst side of town and the fanciest require a foundation upon which agents of reciprocity can cut their deals.

But this foundation must not be confused with commonality. People with nothing in common can register their pets in city hall, drive on state highways, or be fingerprinted by the federal government. The chamber-of-commerce usage of community assists the business of perpetuating collective images across time. Political theories will come and go, atomistic and romantic possibilities will be explored—perhaps together—but the roads where I live will always need to be plowed, at least as long as the ozone layer survives.

Without getting caught in etymological tangles, it is possible to distinguish the roots of two different English words: community and communion. *Com* stands in for *with*; with what? is an important question. *Communis* is often cited as the root of *community*. If the final two syllables of *communis* are *unus*, one might combine them with *com* and say "with oneness or unity." This is how most so-called communitarian theorists answer the question, with what? But if *munus* follows *com* one might say "with gifts or service" instead. This is the everyday community most people take for granted; it is rather unusual to think about the municipality (*munia* + *capere*), the munificent (*munus* + *ficus*), and the munitions dump being close relatives. But when this is done one tends to regard such services as garbage removal and the defense industry with greater interest. The idea of communion, however, is more likely to lead one's thinking in the direction of human unity, of being brothers and sisters under the skin. There is a plausible distinction, then, between reading one *m* or two *m*s in *communis*: being one, or being obliged to serve.[2] If this distinction between community as unity and community as service holds water, then it is simple to figure out which side the reciprocity theorists occupy. Loathe to embrace unity, these theorists want to be free to come and go—to serve or not to serve—or to be immune (*im* + *munus*) to the vexations of municipal life if they so choose. They are interested in payment for services rendered. English has such a word for what they want: *remuneration* (*re* + *munus*). To advocate this kind of reciprocity, which is possible only after a community is founded, is to advocate what I shall call *remu-*

nity. Mutual service, reciprocity, and communion form three different ways of being communitarian.

Even if I may be stretching the grammar of *community* ever so slightly, I am not using these words just as I please; to keep my story straight I need to use them consistently. I shall reserve *community* to name the bodies of individuals that most people call communities; this should suffice to draw attention to the everyday sense of the word. I shall call what the so-called communitarians in the literature advocate communion, or community with unity. This will serve to remind readers that these communitarians value commonality, as opposed to mere service delivery. Rights-based theorists of communitarian individualism are, for the purposes of this book, advocates of remunity. One can never forget the importance of contracts to these arguments. Because I want my ideas on community without unity to stand in relation to others'—even if only to enhance the availability of my position—I need to show how works on remunity and communion draw attention away from mutual service and defense in the everyday sense.

Michael Taylor (1982) writes that, despite the "open-texture" quality of *community*, communities share to some degree three "core characteristics": (1) "persons who compose a community have beliefs and values in common" (26); (2) "relations between members should be direct [unmediated] and they should be many-sided" (27); and (3) "reciprocity" (28). Even Taylor's approach—looking for the core shared by all diverse examples—illustrates a need to establish unity. The first characteristic is the most common example of this prejudice in writing on community. The second and third characteristics are more closely related to an exchange mentality than they are to shared oneness.

If one gives maximum weight to the qualifier "to some degree" in Taylor's definition, the first and second characteristics need not necessarily conflict with using community to name mutual service. But the third characteristic is necessarily problematic. Taylor (1982:28) describes this characteristic of community: "Each individual acting in a system of reciprocity is *usually* characterized by a combination of what one might call short-term altruism and long-term self-interest: I help you out now in the (possibly vague, uncertain and uncalculating) expectation that you will help me out in the future." Even with most of its cost-benefit language removed, this contractarian way of thinking is inconsistent with the idea of service given freely. Taylor is actually describing a form of remuneration, not community. Substituting *re* for *com* in the word *community* transforms the idea of mutual service into just another form of exchange: citizens usually give in expectation of receiving something in return.

It is therefore not surprising that Taylor is unable to take love seriously as a form of community. Following the typology, one can read:

> There is much talk, among both admirers and detractors of community, of communitarian relations being "loving" or "emotional" or "intense." If it were stipulatively required of "community" that a person's relations with most or many of the other members of the community were of this sort, then very few communities would qualify and those which did would be found to be short-lived. (30–31)

By describing community as if it were a kind of exchange, Taylor drains its mystery. Of course the kind of intense, emotional encounter he describes is apt to be inconstant.[3] But conceiving such unity as the alternative to a contracted universe of remuneration is perhaps not the only way to think about the mysteries of love. Community and communion might be distinguished in ways which resist stark contrasts between a unitary love and the diversity of contracting parties.

Michael Sandel's way of distinguishing types of community permits greater complexity. "Instrumental community" covers the territory of reciprocity claimed by many liberals interested in community. "Sentimental community" is Sandel's expression for those bonds of affection which make such ridiculously easy targets for sporting liberal writers. But "constitutive community," while decidedly less vulnerable to liberal criticism, nevertheless requires more unity than is necessary for community as mutual service.

Unlike instrumental community—"where individuals regard social arrangements as a necessary burden and cooperate only for the sake of pursuing their private ends" (Sandel, 1982:148)

—sentimental community describes a situation in which participants "have certain 'shared final ends' and regard the scheme of cooperation as a good in itself" (Sandel, 1982:148, quoting Rawls, 1971).[4] Rawls claims, for example, that while all participants are free to be selfish, some (due to bonds of affection or sentiment) will choose to make sacrifices for other people.[5] The Sandel (1982:149) project advances a more intersubjective kind of community which "penetrates the self more profoundly than even the sentimental view permits." Sandel describes this constitutive community:

> On this strong view, to say that the members of a society are bound by a sense of community is not simply to say that a great many of them profess communitarian aims, but rather that they conceive their identity—the subject and not just the object of their feelings and aspirations—as defined to some extent by the community of which they are a part. (150)

Sandel clearly would not replace the self with constitutive community. The formulation above suggests only that persons can discover their identity "to some extent," an extent which must be allowed to vary, in the multiple communities by which they are constituted, to which they belong, and which they themselves constitute. It is important to notice that, for Sandel, constitutive community is not necessarily inconsistent with sentimental community. Whereas sentimental community describes unencumbered, altruistic subjects sharing common values—such as an interest in saving the atmosphere —constitutive community describes commonly situated subjects discovering their identity to some extent in the pursuit of shared values.[6] Instrumental community, however, is at odds with both sentimental and constitutive community because of the spirit of remuneration it engenders.

Even this brief consideration of how *community* is sometimes used in political theory shows how this word can indicate activities other than mutual service.[7] An obvious problem for those who would use *community* in this latter sense is the prejudice that their claims run counter to liberty, that to be free one must enjoy immunity from service and defense. From this perspective mutual service is just another name for a politics of domination. The often unwitting use of *community* to name shared oneness, or unity, reinforces this prejudice. From the perspective I wish to develop, the culprit is the underlying distinction between unity and diversity. Unity stands to the left of these polarities and remuneration to the right. It is a mistake to attempt to locate mutual service between these opposite extremes because such a move restricts the possibility of community to the field they govern; such a move forces community to toe the line of the continuum they form.

Drawing attention away from mutual service and defense in community life creates the impression that one is never fully implicated in the lives of others. Remunity experts advise that one is implicated only if a deal has been made. Communion worshippers promise warm feelings of solidarity for everyone in the parade of life, during which some are free to litter in full security that others will work overtime to clean up afterwards. Even—as we shall see in later chapters—those who seek to break out of the patterns of subjectivity that make remunity and communion possible do so as solitary beings. Community without unity cannot offer solitary escape from subjectivity because this would violate the duty of mutual service and defense. This mundane sense needs to be supplemented in ways that make it impossible for advocates of remunity and communion to accept: full implication in the infinite difference of fellow beings. A move in this direction requires examining which patterns of subjectivity are assumed by theories of remunity and communion.

The Communal Aspirations of Unencumbrance

The very different ways in which texts in political theory write on community can be explained in part by the yawning gap between their assumptions about subjectivity and attendant notions of agency.[8] To accommodate communitarian claims on intersubjectivity without disqualifying competing liberal claims, I shall for now use *subject* to indicate any being capable of maintaining continuity across time.[9] Accordingly, a (reasonably collected) person can be a subject, but so can a neighborhood or village.

The importance of assumptions about subjectivity to theories of community must not be taken lightly. If subjectivity is assumed to be removed from the thereby so-called external world, any theory of community that might follow would necessarily stress the priority of the part to the whole, in the sense of the individual being more important than the group. On the other hand, if subjectivity is viewed as being located in the world-as-lived, any theory of community that might follow would necessarily stress the priority of the whole to the part, in the sense of the group being a more fundamental consideration than the individual. Claims assuming a "We" that is even partially prior to an "I" sound exceedingly metaphysical to allegedly hard-nosed liberals, whose assumption of an "I" that is prior to a "We" sounds disgustingly positivistic, or worse, to allegedly soft hearted communitarians.[10] Despite losing ground to interpretive social science at the level of presupposition, this approach continues to take the priority of the individual part more seriously than the whole within which it can be said to be situated. Let us turn now to some representative liberal texts.

The liberal effort to insulate the modern subject from the flux of its worlds can be described, perhaps unfairly, as "atomistic." Atomistic prejudices begin with the assumption that all knowledge is a reconstruction of individually received impressions (Taylor, 1979a:52). This assumption rules out the possibility of subjects discovering life-plans and human bonds through knowledge of their contextuality. The possibility of a subjectivity which is wider and more vibrant than anonymous personhood is also ruled out because each "individual" enjoys, at least in principle, an antecedent unity or crystallization of self prior to being situated. The assumption of antecedent individuation requires a subject who can, in principle, stand outside all aims and attachments and choose a destiny (Sandel, 1982/1984:22/17).

If the popular language of atomistic prejudice is used when debating issues of community, the communitarian side is apt to appear threatening to privacy. This is a major reason why community is often associated with state domination, or the total control of private lives. Boone (1983:25) illustrates this kind of thinking: "In the absence of weighty reasons to the contrary, people ought to be free to choose when, in what way, and with whom they share access to those inner chambers in which personal existence is secured and celebrated." Such a claim implies that communitarians would crowd "inner chambers" with strangers and instruct everyone how to live; in this way community poses the threat of an invasion to privacy and its patron, liberty.

But liberalism is more complex than such rigid protection of privacy might suggest. S. I. Benn would allow liberal theory the possibility of "mutuality," which might be distinguished from "total community." Benn (1982:58) agrees that total community is an insult to Western civilization's interest in autonomy, but claims that mutuality—a kind of relationship which requires group participation in a process of the creation and development of autonomous personalities—is consistent with privacy and autonomy. Consider: "Unlike the total community, the object here is not to preserve an ideal pattern of unchanging relations; on the contrary, the enterprise is to keep the partnership moving, to make it a vehicle through which the personalities of the partners can develop autonomously, without destroying it." Benn concludes that some sense of community as mutuality is possible among "partners" within the confines of unencumbered liberalism, and he leaves open the question of whether liberal texts should be interested in including the quest for community in their filled spaces. Readers should notice for now that Benn sees community as a possible means of individual enrichment across time. This is a clear example of Sandel's "instrumental community" (1982:148).

The enterprise of making community safe for liberalism has flourished in the past decade. For example, Gutmann (1982: 221ff.) and Gaus (1983:176) would make the liberalism of Rawls and Chapman (respectively) sound less hostile to what they call community. And Hiskes (1982:23) pronounces community possible if it is pursued selectively among consenting adults. He shows, for example, that "concern for others" is not antithetical to liberalism: "In its most reduced form, community is generally conceived of as a relationship involving individual persons marked by sharing or at least by the holding in common of something by all members." By showing that excluding or perhaps even sharing is not a cardinal ideal of individualism, the Hiskes text begins to spill over into the territory of communion, beyond remunity.[11] And yet that the membership consists so clearly of "individual persons" suggests the lingering presence of atomistic prejudice, or unencumbered subjectivity. As such this text resembles a most serious project to save community from itself: the mediating structures project.

For over twenty years—from the sociology of Robert Nisbet (1962) to the Christian liberal theories of Cochran (1982) and Tinder (1980)—community has occasionally been dubbed a "tragic ideal." The ideal of perfect harmony of whole and part is so appealing, these detractors argue, that people who are not advised otherwise are likely to surrender valuable liberties to secure it. Totalitarian governments masquerading as saviors are able, they claim, to manipulate unwitting people into giving up their liberal birthright. Because this kind of sacrifice is unthinkable, the argument continues, a project was needed to develop social forms to mediate between the individual and the state. This resulted in, among other things, the "mediating structures" project described by Berger (1976)[12] and advertised by the adjectival community ("communitarian individualism") of Michael Novak. In Novak (1982:12), for example, one can read:

Undeniably, a large society faces problems that may overwhelm solitary individuals. Undeniably, the solutions to social problems must be social. It does not follow that the state is the only, or the most effective, or the cheapest, or the most sensitive social agency. Besides the state, there are many other social agencies, some already existing, and some perhaps yet to be imagined.

Some of the social agencies mentioned are the same mediating structures in the Nisbet text. "Among them are the churches, schools, unions, fraternals, neighborhood organizations, and other voluntary organizations of every sort" (Novak, 1982:14). The mediating structures project, then, would compensate for the liberal denial of political community by stressing the importance of alternative group activities. Those like Novak claim that such activities provide a buffer zone between the unencumbered self and the national state.

Siphoning off the quest for subjective unity beyond the antecedent unity of the unencumbered subject and yet allowing experimentation with forms of communion such as family, neighborhood, and church, this kind of argument pretends to protect the viability of contractual agreements between individuals and the national state which might otherwise be revealed as too harsh for insecure contemporaries. Mediating structures are designed to protect "instrumental community" from backsliding into the politics of "sentimental community" by injecting a limited apolitical dosage of communion; lives of immunity and remuneration are made more appealing when associated with the ideal of communion, especially if under the alias of community.[13]

Like Burke, Rosenblum would protect us against the radical ideas of the French, in the name of making the law more lovely. An alleged enemy of atomism, Rosenblum (1987:170), attracted to the "deep unity" of Walzer's spheres of justice, feels that community must be "beautiful to its members," but struggles to unload the metaphysical baggage signified by metaphors of depth. In the end the project of overcoming atomism is frustrated by the atomistic language of her text. When Walzer writes of a complex equality that "connects the strong and the weak, the lucky and the unlucky, the rich and the poor, creating a union that transcends difference of interest, drawing its strength from history, culture, religion, language and so on" (Rosenblum, 1987:169; Walzer, 1983:82–83), his claim depends upon a notion of situated subjectivity that most rights-based liberals cannot seem to comprehend. Rosenblum is no exception. The extended example below illustrates how language undermines her desire to co-opt interpretive communion. Rosenblum (1987:157) complains:

> Communitarianism tells us little about the character of membership if the quality of relationships in voluntary groups and other social structures is not analyzed. Michael Sandel, for example, regrets that people are "dislocated, roots unsettled, traditions undone"; he wants "situated selves." Roots and traditions are not identical to situatedness and attachments, though; the terms suggest distinctly diverse social milieus and psychological states. The sort of attachment he wants is not clear. Dislocated, frustrated selves "at sea in a world where common meanings have lost their

force" can be reconciled to tribes or democratic workplaces, traditional nuclear families or circles of friends. Communitarians must show whether their aims can be met by voluntary and perhaps temporary associations formed for limited purposes and capable of attaching only some of our loyalties, or whether it is necessary to be violently gripped by feelings of attachment.

I quote at length because this passage illustrates how atomistic prejudice can blind a writer to the difference between choosing or discovering one's situation. If discovering options is the way one faces life, then tradition, roots, place, and so on, constitute one's situations and attachments. But Rosenblum is a chooser; she wants to choose her own friends and ignore those relatives she cannot abide.

The passage above also offers a glimpse of the extent to which Rosenblum would chasten romanticism. The violent grip of feeling is at odds with the cold rationality of liberalism, but Rosenblum wants to order a little of each: "meaning the same thing while sitting face to face [read romanticism] across a table [read chastity], where common meaning is deeply affecting and the pleasure comes from the sharing" (183). Elsewhere she puts this rhetorical bundling into practice: "Yet these [romantic sensibilities] can be moderated and made compatible with respect for rights and the discipline of legalism. Chastened romanticism can make its peace. If romanticism can become liberal, it is also possible for liberalism to be romanticized" (188). Rosenblum seeks through rights and discipline to keep the world from becoming too passionate. She longs for communion, but not too much, and never on terms to which she has not consented. Arms-length relations in a contracted universe can be reformed, but one must not go too far; rights and discipline cannot be endangered. Just in case her readers are carried away by all of her intimations of communion— though it is difficult to imagine this—she brings the discussion back home: "Liberal political thought is uniquely attentive to boundaries, discipline, and constraints that create liberty and cooperation in a pluralistic society. Without these liberalism is nothing" (188). In a sober, concrete, chastened way, Rosenblum would import communion without accepting situated subjectivity. One senses that her citizens would always be free to leave those situations they no longer consider lovely.

As we now turn to the communitarians, I shall endeavor to keep Rosenblum's skepticism—"Embeddedness can mean being stuck."—ringing in the rafters, while removing the atomism in the foundation. For we shall see that the subject she is protecting from situated subjectivity is already constituted by situations, whether she likes it or not. Michael Sandel does not ask Senator Kennedy to sponsor legislation to situate American selves and then prepare to be asked by Congress what "sort of attachment he wants." And roots and traditions are inescapable even if we ignore them; to complicate matters, it is part of our tradition to ignore our roots.[14] Perhaps we must realize how we have no choice but to be "stuck," and then study how or where this situation can lead us to rethink the structure of systems that subject our bodies to such discipline.

The Tyranny of Situations

In "the acknowledged text for the principles of interpretive theory" (Schoolman, 1984:357), Charles Taylor claims that many social scientists necessarily misconstrue community because their assumptions preclude the kind of subjectivity that makes community possible. These social scientists, Taylor argues, cannot distinguish between discrete individuals sharing values—for example, Hiskes and other altruists (Barry, 1975) —and life in a common world in which the meaning of sharing is itself shared.[15] Taylor (1979b:52) explains that "the ontology of mainstream social science lacks" the conceptual categories necessary for "a subject who can be a 'We' as well as an 'I.' " "The exclusion of this possibility, of the communal, comes once again from the baleful influence of the epistemological tradition for which all knowledge has to be reconstructed from the impressions imprinted on the individual subject." We have just seen evidence of this influence.[16] By contrast, interpretive social scientists and their modernist critics agree that intersubjectivity, the fundamentally common life that makes the sharing of the sharing of values possible, supplies contexts that must be included in any interpretation of human activity. The idea of being caught in a (Weberian) "web of signification" is important to theories of community because it insists that community is prior to the question of individual identity and, therefore, liberty.

To understand the importance of distinguishing between choosing to join a group and discovering one's place in a context, one need only remember Taylor's (1977) distinction between two ways of looking at human agents: as "simple weighers" and as "strong evaluators." Simple weighers are unreflective and make trivial choices that do not require self-knowledge. Strong evaluators, on the other hand, are more reflective, learning through self-knowledge the conflicting values knitted into the fabric of their community; they do not choose but discover their situation. Strong evaluators become aware that these communal values shape or "constitute" their personal identities. "The notion of identity refers us to certain evaluations which are essential because they are the indispensable horizon or foundation out of which we reflect and evaluate as persons" [17] and "A self decides and acts out of certain fundamental evaluations" (Taylor, 1977:125). In other words, Taylor views the identity that liberals would celebrate in the ahistorical spirit of Kantian autonomy as more of an historical achievement. "We live . . . essentially related to a past that has helped define our identity, and a future that puts it again in question" (1984:180). Strong evaluators, then, do not pretend to choose their aims and attachments; rather, as "mature" and "cohesive" selves, they become aware of their situations. They realize that "identity is . . . defined by certain evaluations which are inseparable from ourselves as agents" (Taylor, 1977:124). According to this argument, found also in Sandel (1982), subjects enjoy no unity prior to their multiple contexts; subjects cannot be said to stand outside of their aims and attachments. To escape the "commonality of shared self-understanding" would be to "cease to be ourselves"; "we would break down as persons, be incapable of being persons in the full sense" (Taylor, 1977:125). Liberal theory, by sustaining a focus on free choice and the rights of unencumbered persons, cannot comprehend what Sandel (1982:182) calls our "deeper commonality."

Interpretive approaches allow one to view persons and situations in hermeneutical circularity.[18] Mary Hesse explains that for interpretive theory, "part cannot be understood without whole, which itself depends on the relation of its parts" (in Bernstein, 1982:32). This way of thinking about situated subjectivity is gradually replacing the atomism of liberalism. Indeed, the usual reaction from liberal theorists is not that situated subjectivity is wrong; rather, it is that these metaphysical considerations are irrelevant. Just as interpretive theorists defend themselves against postmodern claims by saying that at least they are not killing the subject altogether, so individualist theorists defend themselves against interpretive critics by saying that at least they are not situating subjects in ways that kill freedom altogether. In both cases the opposition is oversimplified. Gutmann and Rosenblum chide Taylor and Sandel for claiming that the self is only partially constituted, wholly missing the point that an important aspect of the modern subject is negative freedom, freedom from having to acknowledge one's heritage. Gutmann and Rosenblum, who illustrate passivity to that tradition, act as if we all got together one day and chose liberalism: this may explain why liberalism is so anxious about whether its so-called contract will be renewed.

To show how the situated subject leads those making such assumptions toward communion, toward sharing (regardless of what kinds of deals they can make sitting face-to-face across a table) I wish next to glimpse—perhaps through a glass darkly —Heideggerian and Hegelian efforts to keep God, or at least Nature, alive in the name of common unity.

Following Kohak's (1984:140) Christian approach is very close to accepting uncritically that human beings are equally situated in God's creation. For Kohak, who believes that "Truth is present in the fallen world, and can shine through it," the web of significance within which we are caught is not one which we ourselves have spun. "In the busyness of our days, amid our artifacts and constructs, we can indeed lose the sense of God's presence behind the veil of our god-constructs" (187).[19] Kohak is capable of writing: "What is good, insofar as it is good, cannot perish: it is forever inscribed an eternity. Only when humans know the eternity that intersects each moment of time can they live with the knowledge of finitude, at peace with the horizon of history" (162). In fact, Kohak's entire thesis would draw humans closer to the home he feels they share equally and communally in God's nature.[20]

Taylor and Sandel are less direct about cosmological unity, but have not forsaken a twentieth century effort to reconcile nature and human freedom. Taylor (1979a:167–68) realizes that "because nature cannot be for us . . . an expression of spiritual powers" the "syntheses" of the nineteenth century "can no longer command our attention." He supports, however, attempts to "situate subjectivity by relating it to our life as embodied and social beings, without reducing it to a function of objectified nature" (167). According to Taylor, the "attempt to situate freedom is the attempt to gain a conception of man in which free action is the response to what we are—or to a call that comes to us, from nature alone or from a God who is also beyond nature (the debate will never cease)" (168–69).

Taylor, then, is more likely to treat the Christian will as an achievement of modernity; that is, he takes history too seriously to see the self situated in the goodness of an eternal order.

Sandel applies Taylor's voluntarist ("simple weigher")-cognitivist ("strong evaluator") distinction to liberalism in general and Rawls (1971) in particular. His major theme is that Rawlsian justice "fails to take seriously our commonality." Sandel (1982:174) explains: "In regarding the bounds of the self as prior, fixed once and for all, it [justice as fairness] relegates our commonality to an aspect of the good and relegates the good to a mere contingency, a product of indiscriminate wants and desires 'not relevant from a moral standpoint.'" Sandel, like Taylor, wishes to restore the good's good name by holding open the "possibility that when politics goes well, we can know a good in common that we cannot know alone" (183). And he would agree with Schaar (1983:127) that "the self is not prior to, but constituted by, community"; in fact, as we have seen, Sandel contrasts others' versions of instrumental and sentimental community with a version he prefers: "constitutive community." The most striking feature of constitutive community is Sandel's refusal to restrict human subjectivity to the finite boundaries of the human body. But just when his work begins to resemble Kohak's, he carefully points out that he regards the situations which constitute the human subject as multiple and overlapping: "each of us moves in an indefinite number of communities" (Sandel, 1982:146). Sandel's work, then, is quite applicable at the local community level (see Sandel, 1984a), but can be adapted to include more sublime situations and resembles Taylor's work in its promise of admitting deeper discoveries.

The debate between interpretive and atomistic liberalism is not the debate for me. Charles Taylor is preparing new sacraments for communion every day, making his presence felt in faithful circles. The most common reaction to this shift from epistemology to ontology is the urge to balance communion, as communion leaves open the door to ever more sublime attunement, and remunity, as remunity is sufficiently pragmatic to convince people that isolation is not even in their interest. These balancing efforts serve mostly to draw attention away from the reaction I wish to articulate. My response is two-fold: first, I am concerned because of Foucault, to whom I turn next, with the way subjectivity forces bodies to become entities that are transmitted individually or collectively or both, across time. Second, I wish to erase the impression that to be so concerned is to lose interest in community, at least in the sense of mutual service and defense.

Questioning the Subject

Those who write about community in political theory usually go no further than to work with these great alternatives of free agency and collective unity. Citizens are said to be caught in the tension; some of the more sensitive theorists find ways to articulate this tension. We have seen that few theorists—at least of those considered here—advocate either radical free choice or total unity, though they may accuse each other of having these tendencies. Community is bandied about easily, in part because its sense of remuneration poses no threat to hard-nosed liberals who want to allow citizens to get their best deals: property taxes are high, but consider the loveliness of the tennis courts in the nice park. Another reason for the ease with which almost anyone can support community is that its sense of communion is always available to the softhearted brothers and sisters who dreaded the day that "We are the world" became a cliché for atomistic liberals.

But I have presented this tension in terms of assumptions about subjectivity: individuated subjects and collective subjects, both capable of maintaining continuity across time, sometimes at cross purposes. This manner of presentation permits a way to open up the time-honored relationship between the individual and the state.

Unencumbered forces treat the individuated subject as a given because they presuppose its presence outside of discourse. On the other hand, situated forces remind us all of our collective subjectivity, of the way we are implicated in discourse. But neither side in this individual/collective struggle worries enough about the price of being situated. The atomized liberals do not because they cannot see the extent to which they are embedded; their situated critics, who see the extent to which they are stuck, invent new ways to cope with this condition. But both sides are deaf to the remainder, the excess territory not covered by their defenses of the individual and collective aspects of life, and thus cannot sense the cost of keeping it out.

One could, without undue simplification, picture a continuum running from the individual extreme of an unencumbered self to the collective extreme of a being wholly situated in God's creation. At the center of the continuum lies the subject—an entity whose identity must be maintained across time. If the balance of this continuum is tipped in the direction of being God-like, the entity is collectivized and communion is out in the open. If the balance goes the other way, the entity is individuated and we are stuck with remunity. The modern person plays the role of a fulcrum, a center that is nevertheless somewhat immune from the struggle; the references to the self, or person, or man, refer to this real person (you or I or we) who is and is not the center of thinking. In Derridian words, "The center is not the center." That is, the subject lies at the center of discourse but does not wish to be fully implicated in discourse.

The problem with this picture of the structure of modern thinking about community is that it draws attention away from the problem of how the subject of consciousness achieves this central position. Michel Foucault is important these days because he struggles to ask such a dangerous question. In the next chapter I shall point out several features of one of his dangerous works and then consider his suggestion that modern political thought should add a new question to its repertoire: the question of the subject.

3 Opening Up the Dialogue Between Remunity and Communion

We have to imagine and to build up what we could be to get rid of this kind of political "double bind," which is the simultaneous individualization and totalization of modern power structures.—Foucault (1983:216)

Metaphor is not always easily noticed; but metaphor is never innocent. It orients research and fixes results. Without realizing that there is any other way to make sense, most theorists approach their work as modern day Robinson Crusoes, with industry and mastery, on the unfilled space of the empty page. Michel de Certeau (1984:154) reminds us, however, that Robinson did not feel masterful all of the time. "For a time, his enterprise was in fact interrupted, and haunted, by an absent other that returned to the shore of the island, by 'the print of a man's naked foot on the shore.' "[1] Defoe tells a story of resumed mastery—Friday is discovered and domesticated—but his story has become something of an embarrassment in a postcolonial age.

And yet Robinson Crusoe's approach to the virgin soil he inhabited is written all over late twentieth century life from shaping the youngest and ignoring the oldest citizens, to thoughtless waste disposal and wasteful farming practices. Even the way scholars write their books involves clearing empty space and keeping the cleared-out "other" out. Certeau (1984:135) shows how this way of thinking about subjectivity is reflected in approaches to writing.[2] He describes the island of the page in the following way: "The island of the page is a transitional place in which an industrial inversion is made: what comes in is something 'received,' what comes out is a 'product.' The things that go in are the indexes of a certain 'passivity' of the subject with respect to a tradition; those that come out, the marks of his power of fabricating objects." This "industrial inversion" is a most plausible metaphor. Most of us view the empty page as an island of work space: others' work is raw material that arrives periodically, reading and writing are the production process, and the argument is like the finished product. During the reading and writing stage, many simplifying assumptions have to be made just to get the job done; not everything can be said. This seems obvious.

But some theorists are more critical than others when making assumptions and presuppositions. Once their criticism is out in the open it is difficult to avoid. For example, it might still be exciting to set up shop around the tension between individual and collective subjects, studying the conflict between maintaining individual and collective identity across time, if producers like Michel Foucault and William Connolly were not already uncomfortable about some of the restrictions of situated subjectivity. Far from neglecting the tension between individual rights and collective enterprise, these works lead one to notice the violent side of the rather cozy assumptions of situated subjectivity. We are subjected, or subjugated, they argue, to forces that dominate life in ways that have hitherto gone undetected because we uncritically clean the factory of the page, eliminating all pieces that do not fit reasonable arguments. These critics force political theorists to consider the scrap material and junk that piles up around the production of a piece of writing. Bataille spends excessive time with this scrap material and his product deteriorates in the nihilistic frenzy that spooks safer theorists like Walzer, Taylor, and MacIntyre.

The Foucauldian critique of ignoring what is left out in order to produce intelligible arguments within discourse has changed political theory. It is no longer possible to use *subject* in the usual sense of identity without also using it in the sense of discipline. And the question of what we are not producing looms heavily overhead during the production of rational, orderly arguments.

But metaphor is never innocent. Connolly (1988) is showing that the days of mastery and attunement are numbered. Foucauldian criticism and the new line of products concerning domination and discipline makes criticism of the island metaphor of industrial inversion inevitable. These critics produce arguments that supplement conventional discourse by warning of the dangers of the forms of life some cherish most. They draw attention to the scraps, the fringe, the recalcitrant material that resists the production of reasonable discourse. Just as a raging storm outside reminds the person lucky enough to find shelter of how good it is to be safe and warm, so these radical critics work with the so-called prediscursive, inarticulate fringe in ways that might reassure some readers that reason and order still prevail within discourse. If the question of domination is to be articulated it must be said within reasonable, orderly discourse, but this point need not be reassuring. My work is an effort to keep the critique moving by supplementing the island metaphor.

Indeed, this is the kind of metaphor that those who endorse postmodern criticism of mastery and attunement need to reject: it smacks of the search-and-destroy mentality they seek to destroy. There is a subtle difference between speaking of what is left out when order is imposed, and admitting that order never manages to totally displace chaos. Both order and chaos must be maintained. Crusoe's presence makes Friday the absent other; but Crusoe's presence is itself problematic.

The metaphor of filling empty spaces within the limits of a frontier fixes the results of research by encouraging readers to use writing as if it were, in principle, governed by reason and order. As this chapter unfolds, readers should begin to notice another way of thinking about writing: the enemy of structure —namely, play—should be thought as radically as possible.

I begin by noting Foucault's contribution and three well-known responses: MacIntyre (1982,1988), Taylor (1986), and Connolly (1983, 1987, 1988). Then, we can attempt to introduce the radical play of extravagance not as an alternative but as a supplement.

Foucault on Subjugation

Perhaps political theorists such as Taylor (1984) and Walzer (1986) give Foucault's second lecture on power[3] undue attention because in it he sounds most like a colleague. All who read Hobbes for a living might read Foucault as his "other," construct an alternate political theory, admit (like Walzer) discarding the pieces that they do not understand, and then disagree. One must realize how Foucault is not Hobbes, but spending too much time reading this lecture risks missing the point that Foucault studies power relations for a perspective on subjectivity and not the other way around. I shall turn to the second lecture to sense the reversal of Hobbes's project, but then focus on an essay on subjectivity and power.

Foucault (1980:93) opens the second lecture by announcing his reversal of the usual approach modern political thought takes to power. Whereas the high and mighty metaphysicians in the discipline worry about how to discover truths they might then use to limit the rights of power, Foucault asks: "What rules of right are implemented by the relations of power in the production of discourses of truth." In other words, power institutionalizes, professionalizes, and rewards the pursuit of truth. Power stands at the apex of a Foucauldian triangle formed by power, right, and truth.[4] The destiny of the subject, then, is the underlying reason why Foucault studies power. The triad of power, right, and truth may be familiar, but he does unusual work with it. Most theorists seem to identify power with the state. Indeed, this tendency is encouraged by the individual/collective tension traced in my last chapter.

But Foucault, who is quite aware of our preoccupation, wishes to draw attention away from the state's exercise of power and to the factors that attempt to legitimate it, or render it reasonable. He writes: "The essential role of the theory of right, from medieval times onward, was to fix the legitimacy of power; that is the major problem around which the whole theory of right and sovereignty is organized." Many teachers and students of the history of modern thought can perhaps hear old lectures ringing in such passages as this. The rise of the modern nation-state is dependent upon convincing the people that they ought to obey the law. While those involved may well become "the people" through accidents that determine their status as subjects prior to law, there is nothing accidental about giving people good reasons for being orderly.[5] Foucault is well aware of this modern problem of obligation to the nation-state, but he reads the problem in a significantly different way.

To Foucault, the problem of obligation is an effort "to efface the domination intrinsic to power." Foucault's plan is to reverse this cover-up operation. This is how he explains it:

My general project . . . has been, in essence, to reverse the mode of analysis followed by the entire discourse of right . . . to invert it, to give due weight, that is, to the fact of domination, to expose both its latent nature and its brutality. I then wanted to show not only how right is, in a general way, the instrument of this domination—which scarcely needs saying—but also to show the extent to which, and the forms in which, right . . . transmits and puts in motion relations that are not relations of sovereignty, but of domination. (95–96)

Now Foucault's domination intrinsic to power is not "that solid and global kind of domination that one person exercises over another" (96).[6] He is concerned instead with the more insidious, because less visible, "manifold forms of domination that can be exercised within society" (96). The key word is *manifold*; Foucault is concerned with the multiple ways in which the state's domination is transmitted across time by the very subjects it obliges. That is, he is more concerned with the many disciplined ways that bossy and deferential people perpetuate their own domination than he is with the way the bossy person makes decisions for the deferential one.

This shift from questions of a subject's sovereignty and obedience to questions of domination and subjugation to power is difficult to accomplish, says Foucault, as he prepares some overlapping methodological reminders.[7]

First, to retain a focus on the hidden agenda of the state— the way in which it uses the dominated to transmit the forms of their domination—he avoids analyzing power in its central locations. Second, Foucault avoids analyzing anyone's conscious intention of exercising power. He is more concerned with how the peripheral subjects were pushed out of the centers of power, how they became by definition subject to the laws. "Well, rather than worry about the problem of the central spirit, I believe that we must attempt to study the myriad of bodies which are constituted as peripheral subjects as a result of the effects of power" (98). In other words, whereas Hobbes asks how to constitute sovereign power from disparate subjects and might study how the National Assembly controls the people, Foucault asks how subjects came to be peripheral and might study how the people discipline and punish one another. The third reminder underscores this point; the individual whom power constitutes is at the same time its vehicle.[8] His way of describing the flow of power sounds like Hyde's (1974) description of the gift.[9] Foucault writes: "Power must be analyzed as something that . . . only functions in the form of a chain." Foucault would hesitate, then, before viewing philanthropy as free gift-giving; he would view this practice instead as a possible example of how power is circulated. The fourth reminder cautions against moving from the top of society down in search of the circulation of power. Patterns of power are much more intricate on the periphery of society and tend to be missed if categories are established at the center. Finally, Foucault insists that he is not just talking about ideology. The domination he seeks to expose lies in the realm of all knowledge. Power is a form of knowledge. In summary, Foucault is concerned about not disguising the domination of the subject. Instead, he seeks to learn how such a disciplinary society came to pass.

These precautions indicate how taking Foucault seriously

may open up the dialogue between remunity and communion. His work challenges not only the assumptions of subjectivity, but also knowledge itself. Foucault issues explicit reminders that when the production of knowledge begins a great deal of life is exiled, and that this domination is too easily disguised. It may be possible to open up the dialogue between remunity and communion by coming to terms with the exiled elements that get lost in the constitution of the subject.

In "Why Study Power: The Question of the Subject," Foucault (1983:209) announces that his long-term objective "has been to create a history of the different modes by which, in our culture, human beings are made subjects." "Thus it is not power, but the subject, which is the general theme of my research." This is not to say that Foucault is disinterested in power: "It was . . . necessary to expand the dimensions of a definition of power if one wanted to use this definition in studying the objectivizing of the subject." He has the expansion of the game, not a shell game, on his agenda. Foucault examines the political implications of the Enlightenment, arguing that moderns seem to expect philosophy to keep watch over the excessive powers of political rationality. He feels that it is obvious that the advent of reason is attended by excesses of political power, excesses that can be expected to grow in fascistic or at least exceedingly bureaucratic directions. "But the problem is: what to do with such an evident fact?" (210).

Relying on Enlightenment philosophy to curb the modern state is like putting reason in charge of itself—trusting its capacity to reach for the truth. Foucault asks: "Shall we try reason? To my mind, nothing would be more sterile. First, because the field has nothing to do with guilt or innocence. Second, because it is senseless to refer to reason as the contrary entity to nonreason. Lastly, because such a trial would trap us into playing the arbitrary and boring part of either the rationalist or the irrationalist" (210). This passage illustrates Foucault's agenda. He is at once unwilling to remain situated in the dominion of reason and unable to subvert its commands. He feels one is compelled to give reasons—to avoid being arbitrary—for siding with nonreason. Either outrationalizing Kant or exploring the silent excesses of irrationality are bound to be boring or to become arbitrary. Instead he proposes examining the less commonly visited regions of the kingdom of rationality in an effort to resist reason's rules.

Foucault announces with the confidence of a tank commander that he will rearrange Kant by moving from the high ground of metaphysical inquiry down to patrol the low road of everyday struggle, where he locates the play of domination. That is to say: "Rather than analyzing power from the point of view of its internal rationality, it consists of analyzing power relations through the antagonism of strategies" (211).

To illustrate this antagonism Foucault mentions recent opposition to the power of men over women, of parents over children, of psychiatry over the mentally ill, of medicine over the population, and so on, and asks what they have in common. He is most interested in the following: "They are struggles which question the status of the individual: on the one hand, they assert the right to be different and they underline everything which makes individuals truly individual. On the other hand, they attack everything which separates the individual, breaks his ties with others, splits up community life, forces the individual back on himself and ties him to his own identity in a constraining way" (211–12). It is hard to miss the ambivalence of this situation: celebrating the right to be truly individual is attended by attacking the forces that make individuals separate entities. For example, women can now celebrate their right to vote but must, at least for the time being, endure such questions as "how do you feel, as a woman, about the Equal Rights Amendment?"

These forces are as firmly entrenched as reason itself, rooted in the privileges of knowledge; thus these antagonisms question the relation of knowledge and power. Foucault calls the power of the prevailing régime du savoir into question. He writes: "To sum up, the main objective of these struggles is to attack not so much 'such or such' an institution of power, or group, or elite, or class, but rather a technique, a form of power" (212). Within the language of rationality, Foucault studies how the knowledge industry has totally infiltrated our everyday lives. This leads him to two uses of the word *subject*.

I have been using *subject* to name those entities that maintain identity and unity across time. Foucault uses it that way too, but he is most concerned with another usage: "subject to someone else by control and dependence." This reminder of the grammar of *subject* allows Foucault to add an additional struggle to those usually found in political theory. But keep in mind that he is adding questions, not replacing them.

The usual struggles in political theory include the struggle against ethnic, social, or religious domination and the struggle against the exploitation that cuts people off from what they produce. The liberal writers mentioned above tend to mobilize remunity against the domination of the state. The communitarians have good ammunition against exploitation, though their neo-Hegelianism leads many of them to talk more about families than factories. To these struggles Foucault adds struggling "against that which ties the individual to himself and submits him to others in this way" (212). The literature of remunity and communion is overflowing with examples of how the individuated subject might either come to terms with collective attachments, or reject these terms. But this is wishful thinking: no one is immune to collective attachments—modern power structures are totalizing—but each person is forced to become a "one" referent—modern power structures are also individuating. Persons have no choice but to be cut off from the attachments that define them.

Foucault does not wish to replace rights or collective will as issues in political theory; rather he remarks that today the question of the subject, in both senses, is more important than it used to be. He discusses how this third struggle came to pass:

> The reason this kind of struggle tends to prevail in our society is due to the fact that since the sixteenth century a new political form of power has been continuously developing. This new political structure, as everybody knows, is the state. But most of the time, the state is envisioned as a kind of political power which ignores individuals, looking only at the interests of totality or, should I say, of a class, or a group among the citizens. (213)

Foucault does not dispute or deny the accuracy of this vision; he wants only to show how it is dominating modern lives. Whereas many political theorists are accustomed to viewing the state as a threat to individual liberty—and thus speak of the tension between the individual and the state—Foucault uses his dual treatment of *subject* to make and add the point that the state looks after the interest of the totality and *at the same time* individuates the subjects, carves them out of an amorphous mass. Just as the Roman Catholic church concocts pastoral power by allowing people to discover souls (which gives the church access to their innermost lives), so the modern state exercises pastoral power by allowing people to develop an individuality (which requires state interference for protection). In devising this "tricky combination" of being "both an individualizing and a totalizing form of power" the state has accomplished a most subtle domination. And, according to Foucault, the practice of everyday life unknowingly conspires.

Consider the options available to the person who wants to celebrate difference, to avoid being subjugated to others. This person can become conspicuous by breaking rules and asserting uniqueness, thereby falling under the watchful gaze of disciplinary forces—school officials, the law, peer pressure, and so on—or this person can blend in by exercising self-discipline and becoming free of outside intrusion, thereby serving as its agent against wayward friends and neighbors. Connolly (1983b) provides good examples from everyday life of what Foucault calls this "double bind, which is the simultaneous individualization and totalization of modern power structures." Citizens are either sufficiently obedient to pay taxes or sufficiently disobedient to cheat. Those who pay are more likely to discipline others. Those who cheat are more likely to be obedient in other situations. No matter what happens, the forces of discipline prevail.

Before considering three responses from contemporary theorists to Foucault's question of subjugation, I wish to call attention to what is at stake. Conventional wisdom tells us that the relationship of individualism and collectivism is stable in the sense that these forces are engaged in a perennial struggle: as soon as one side piles up victories the other works to regain lost ground. The pendulum moves back and forth over time as it does between Tory and Labour parties in the United Kingdom and Northern Ireland. The rhythm of opposition is much more reassuring than the motion of difference.

Foucault forces us to see that the structure created by the opposition of remunity and communion is a power play in its own right. The subject lies at the center of the structure. This subject is forcibly cut off from those aims and attachments s/he discovers everyday while acting as a vehicle of this subtle power. You may see how atomistic prejudice and situated subjectivity are at odds with each other, but Foucault points out that we embody this double bind. Thus even the most rugged individuals are subjugated to forces that define their individuality. There is no escape from post-Enlightenment techniques of power.

Furthermore, we are not necessarily talking about government; rather, the hegemon is the régime du savoir. We are forced by language, by all that can be said, to be individuals and to face each other as individuals when posing problems of communion: we commune as individuals with something in common. Rosenblum's chastened romanticism is an intriguing response because she loves those aspects of unity that fit with the cold rationality of liberalism and manages to draw the line there. But her splendid work draws attention away from the fact that the structure of individualism and collectivism can only stay alive by denying the subject at its center those aspects of life that do not fit. The state integrates individuals only on the condition that they become chastened, that they beat back the urges and whims, that might upset the balance between individual and collectivism. Rosenblum's is only one of many balancing acts. Others write in the name of community while protecting the rights of the subject. All balances reinforce the visibility of their so-called extremes. And so when Bellah et al. (1985:270) write that "the tension between private interest and the public good is never completely resolved in any society" and encourage us to "mitigate the tension and render it manageable," they are reinforcing the status of being individual and being collective, as if saluting the régime du savoir.

Foucault's third question—on subjugation—forces us to examine the subject (individual and collective) as a double bind, rather than to start with some limited version of the subject and go on to balance it with, or defend it against, its opposite. His work raises the question of resisting our doubly bound subjectivity, instead of restricting one's gaze to all that lies between the two extremes.

When faced with Foucault's third question, rational theorists might survey the history of metaphysical thought to see where the West went wrong. More romantic theorists might be inclined to make the best of not yet having reconciled nature and human freedom. Those with a feel for genealogy might continue his work by neutralizing the effects of the double bind, by resisting or countering its effort to control the subject. These are the three most germane responses: rational mastery, expressive attunement, and genealogical resistance.[10]

Rationality, Expressivism, Genealogy

Foucault forces political theory to pay attention to its uncritical reliance on post-Enlightenment rationality. This reliance leads toward a politics of totalization, in the sense that all the mysteries of life are scheduled to be solved by rational experts. When less critical theorists, such as Barber, Unger, Elshtain, or Bellah et al., warn against the excess of collective control in politics, their very projects strengthen the hold of rationality.[11] The politics of totalization is served by the way these theorists reduce political possibility to competing positions on the individual/collective continuum. These solid interpretive projects are designed to balance the excesses of liberal individualism with the defects of collective control. But, at the same time, these projects force individuals and collectivities to perpetuate themselves as unities of subjectivity across time. The subject, as viewed by most interpretive authors, lies at the center of the all-consuming continuum. Elshtain's speaking woman, Barber's arguing citizen, Unger's context-breaking person, and Bellah's concerned neighbor all balance individual rights and collective attachments in ways that force the subject to act as a fulcrum.

Reading these authors allows us to feel better about our discontinuous lives. Distinctions such as public man and private woman, unitary and weak democracy, and so on, are reasonable and orderly because the modern subject lies in the middle at all times. We can be said to embody these authors' distinctions in ways that give structure to our lives and bring us peace. But we are most secure when we realize that we can put down their books and make up our own minds about the relevance of their binary distinctions. As long as we continue seeing ourselves as the center of all the balancing projects, including time's "it was" and "is going to be," we can rest assured that the world is not coming apart at the seams. The play of absence or presence of civic-mindedness and the proper balance between their competing forces can be exhausting. But, at bottom, these texts also provide a reassuring certitude, which itself is beyond the reach of play. We can stand back from our central location. And on the basis of this certitude anxiety can be mastered, for anxiety is invariably the result of a certain mode of being implicated in the game. It is important, then, to realize the difference between being implicated in the pluralist, overlapping games of interest group politics and being implicated, inescapably, in the binary world of post-Enlightenment rationality. Less critical theorists would implicate everyone in the former, thereby saving them from the anxiety of the latter.

Rational Mastery

One ought not to implicate Alasdair MacIntyre in post-Enlightenment rationality—indeed he is one of its most resolute critics —but any reasonable person is apt to agree that he is nevertheless a most orderly, sensible theorist. MacIntyre is quite concerned about the status of the thinking subject. He is exercised by the arbitrary nature of a world that has lost track of its foundations. And he bemoans the assault on moral unities, with its implication that transmitting collective messages across time is becoming obsolete.

Whereas Sandel and (especially) Taylor can be described as neo-Hegelian in their effort to reconcile freedom and nature, MacIntyre advances a teleological argument which makes him sound like a modern-day Thomist. MacIntyre agrees with Sandel on the role of self-knowledge in discovering one's aims and attachments. Both reject the alternative (liberal) notion of discrete agents choosing aims and attachments (MacIntyre, 1981: 30). MacIntyre also resembles Taylor (1977) in the manner in which he rejects Sartrean radical choice (MacIntyre, 1981:33). All three theorists agree that human lives are lived out within *ultimately* purposive orders, but MacIntyre has a rather different teleology in mind: he contrasts Nietzsche with Aristotle, not Hegel.

MacIntyre admires Nietzsche's courage and honesty about what he agrees are the failures of the Enlightenment, but rejects Nietzsche's absence of faith in ultimate moral unity. I hasten to add, however, that MacIntyre's revision of Aristotle is sufficiently drastic to avoid the most toxic traces of Thomism. MacIntyre (1981:183) explains that although his "account of the virtues is teleological, it does not require the identification of any teleology in nature, and hence it does not require any allegiance to Aristotle's metaphysical biology." [12] While the scope of my project does not permit a complete analysis of MacIntyre's "logical development" (174ff.) of the concept of virtue, I must at least show the three stages of this development, because doing so illustrates yet another way in which the self can be said to be situated. Ranging from particularistic to universal, each successive stage presupposes the earlier one.

The most particularistic, a "practice," designates any human activity that can be described as possessing an internal good which can only be realized by practitioners trying to achieve excellence at the practice. Chess is a practice, for example, while tic-tac-toe is not.

Any single human life includes multiple practices organized in a unified "narrative" order, according to MacIntyre. This second stage of logical development of the concept of virtue allows him to summon a "concept of a self whose unity resides in the unity of a narrative which links birth to death as narrative beginning to middle to end" (191). The point, which we have already seen, is that the idea of the *antecedent* unity of the subject is a liberal pretense. Conflict is not ruled out for MacIntyre because "someone may discover (or not discover) that he or she is a character in a number of narratives at the same time, some of them embedded in others" (198). Or what at one point in time may have seemed to have been an intelligible narrative in which one was playing a part may be "transformed wholly or partly into a story of unintelligible episodes" (198). In fact, MacIntyre endorses at this second stage the "Sophoclean insight" that "it is through conflict and sometimes only through conflict that we learn what our ends and purposes are" (153). The idea of multiple, embedded narratives makes self-knowledge at once difficult and of central importance to questions of identity; ends and purposes are discovered, not chosen, amidst the conflict of a world that does not necessarily make sense at the time. But in principle, for MacIntyre, ultimate ends and purposes can be located; for this reason he needs a more universal situation, a third stage of development: living moral tradition (207).

This third stage is universal but not timeless. MacIntyre uses the term *universal* to signify comprehensiveness, adding an historical dimension to his concept of virtue. He views tradition as:

> an historically extended, socially embodied argument, and an argument precisely in part about the goods which constitute that tradition. Within a tradition the pursuit of goods extends through generations, sometimes through many generations. Hence the individual's search for his or her good is generally and characteristically conducted within a context defined by those traditions of which the individual's life is a part, and this is true both of those goods which are internal to practices and of the goods of a single life. (207)

Thus, the concept of tradition supplies a context for the different narratives of human practices; in this sense it is the ultimate situation. MacIntyre, who rejects Sandel's and Taylor's notion of extending subjectivity beyond the finite boundaries of the human body, would nevertheless situate subjectivity in "living" moral traditions. All selves are, for MacIntyre, encumbered to the extent that they are situated (in practices which are situated in narratives which are situated) in a moral tradition; moreover, these contexts cannot be freely chosen but must be discovered.

MacIntyre is not claiming that our "culture of bureaucratic individualism" realizes its situation; rather he claims that "the kind of understanding of social life which the tradition of the virtues requires" is "very different" from popular culture (209). As an alternative he suggests: "Modern systematic politics, whether liberal, conservative, radical, or socialist, simply has to be rejected from a standpoint that owes genuine allegiance to the tradition of the virtues; for modern politics itself expresses in its institutional form a systematic rejection of that tradition"

(237). Notice that MacIntyre does not argue that the tradition of the virtues is lost; instead, he pleas for contemporary politics to get out of its way. This illustrates clearly the claim that situation is prior to identity.

Alasdair MacIntyre's (1988) recent work is a courageous effort to address what anyone less committed to scholastic revival might call the problem of identity and difference. He is viciously opposed to what he describes as the relativism of a world of difference and seeks absolutism without pretending ever to stand outside tradition. MacIntyre's courage lies in his challenge that some traditions are more rational than others.

Against those who would celebrate letting differences be, he suggests that moral traditions are not yet totally bankrupt. In fact, he says, we borrow from them all the time. The problem is that people do so in haphazard, unreasonable, disorderly ways. We have become arbitrary and are growing accustomed to bumping along from one irreconcilable difficulty to another. We have lost any sense of being masters of our destiny. This plays into the hands of the bureaucrats and other experts, who are quite willing to impose their version of reason and order. So MacIntyre can agree that the modern subject is subjugated in the many ways that concern Foucault; but he cannot pin the blame on the entire region of knowledge.

MacIntyre's most recent solution to the flux of postmodern life is a return to a Thomist synthesis of faith and reason, a synthesis that might remind us of a Straussian turn. Yes, rationality has destroyed all semblance of unity in the world except for a bland pseudo-neutrality, says MacIntyre, but if we return to faith and reason we can avoid going to the dogs. It is interesting, in light of the resurgence of Islamic fundamentalism, that Christians are finding their way back to Thomas's Aristotle. One senses that this will continue, among believers, as the foundations of modern rationality are shown to be rather arbitrary.

Islamic and Christian readings of Aristotle resemble each other in their conviction that human reason must be supplemented by faith, if not revelation, to address the complexity of human life. The result is a totalizing system that cannot be constructed by human beings alone, and therefore cannot be undermined by them. In fact, these readings question whether people are sufficiently rational to comprehend the divine order.

Expressive Attunement

Charles Taylor's position on situated subjectivity, as we have seen, is quite consistent with the communion typified by his more practical student, Michael Sandel. Common ground is a metaphor for the shared unity people can discover when they seek their aims and attachments. And yet it would be an exaggeration to insist that Taylor would unify at the expense of human rights. Pluralism attempts to save the day when both Taylor and Sandel turn their attention to neighborhood, family, and a less comprehensive sort of tradition than MacIntyre has in mind.

And yet Taylor speaks of purpose in nature in a most suggestive way. He cannot part with teleology when making assumptions about our existence. For this reason he finds it necessary to defend his ontology against Foucauldian attack. Interestingly, his blind spots help to illustrate the importance of the Foucauldian critique. Taylor, ultimately loathe to defend the modern subject, claims nonetheless that we are progressing in terms of truth and freedom and cannot see the point of spoiling that progress—sacrificing truth—in the namelessness of the unknown.

That Taylor has learned to love his captor, while acknowledging its faults, owes largely to his teleological assumptions about existence. As staunch a critic of objective neutrality as MacIntyre, he takes his cues from an expressivist reading of Hegel instead of reading Aristotle rationally. Thus Taylor (1985:379) can raise questions such as this one: "Can we move to a higher and fuller schema that will bring some hitherto smothered voices to speech, without suppressing some that we now can hear?" Taylor can lean in this affirmative direction because, as far as he is concerned, oppositions sometimes have happy endings and difference is opposition. His response to the question above is that it is too soon to rule out progress.[13] He has yet to retract his earlier neo-Hegelian hope for reconciliation of freedom and nature and is still searching for attunement, in the sense of discovering linkage between existence in general and individual self-understanding. We must avoid pigeonholing his teleological commitment. His words are important, if only for their historical significance:

> For what is meant by a "teleological philosophy"? If we mean some inescapable design at work inexorably in history, à la Hegel, then of course I am not committed to it. But if we mean by this expression that there is a distinction between distorted and authentic self-understanding, that the latter can in a sense be said to follow a direction in being, I do indeed espouse such a view. And that makes a big part of my "ontology" of the human person. (384–85)

So Taylor insists—after confronting the Foucauldian attack on his assumptions—upon defending the possibility of being a strong evaluator. As such, he is a powerful ally for less critical advocates of communion; it makes sense that he is cited by them often. His final questions for Foucault shortly after Foucault died are: can we just refuse who we are? Even if we could, can we know that it is worth it to destroy the subject?

MacIntyre's recent work shows how it is possible to write a history of the subject at the center of contradictory forces that form different tensions at different times: successively, and in a regulated fashion, the center receives different forms or names. MacIntyre wants to learn from such mistakes of the Enlightenment as the Cartesian pure subject of consciousness and to produce a form of subjectivity such as the Christian soul that is more attuned to the reason and order of the universe. This leads him into the light of an earlier Paris.

Perhaps Charles Taylor has abandoned projects of totalization, but he still looks toward connecting self-understanding and human existence: authentic selves discover these connections. He is ready to admit that the modern subject is not a natural entity and is instead a product of the Enlightenment; but he is too Hegelian not to build from there on. He does not back up in time, drop the subject, or declare history to be always already over. History is for Taylor resumed at the end of each present form of subjectivity. In this sense history acts as his ally, as a detour between two presences. We are still living out the Christian notion of the will, according to Taylor. We must, as discursive creatures, send some message about ourselves in some code across time; and Taylor is not finished transmitting messages about what we now take ourselves to be. Taylor is unable to extend infinitely the domain of the play of signification because he is still holding on to what might be called a transcendental signified: that is, he refers to a human being at the center of his thinking, who through authenticity might achieve full presence. His thinking has structure because his transmissions are about a person, like you; Taylor does not think in terms of signs that defer the presence of a person, such as the anachronistic sign *man*. His rhetorical strategy is to force readers to choose to keep the self-understanding they have now and possibly to connect it to a more authentic meaning of existence, or to throw it away for unknown worlds of bodies, for inchoate feelings, and for not a shred of truth.

So whereas MacIntyre might rescholasticize Paris for another try at totalization, Taylor rejects totalization but dreams of the subject being fully present as an authentic part of a whole that is too large to understand. At present, there is too much, more than one can say.

Forsaking efforts to master the universe and instead seeking attunement with it permits radicals such as Foucault to attempt to replace Taylor's unified, if necessarily mysterious, *outside* with a monstrously discontinuous *outside*. But both work to reassure us that the subject is present, though not fully, at the center of the field of oppositions within discourse. They are talking about us. The point of contention is whether one brings in authenticity from the outside through discoveries in history (like suffrage) or lets the subject transgress the limits of reason.

Genealogical Resistance

Connolly distinguishes his reading of genealogy from more subject-centered approaches such as MacIntyre's and Taylor's. Genealogy helped spark a widespread movement to replace the subject with discursive formations. That is, instead of being concerned about the Christian will at the center of an introspective moment in time, one is concerned with the achievement of unity at the center of a structure, keeping in mind that this unity is made possible by "deflected, ignored, excluded" elements that do not fit. Connolly (1987:155) for this reason likes to call the subject an "ambiguous achievement," and wants to retain its unity while mobilizing the lost remainder to counter prevailing patterns. In this sense he remains true to subject-centered approaches but seeks to spare the subject the "designer's urge" he finds in other theories.

Despite the ways in which his work is part of the moment when language invaded the universal problematic, when in a manner of speaking, everything became discourse, Connolly's response to Foucault avoids treating the subject of consciousness as a mere signifier whose meaning is dependent upon its difference from other arbitrary signifiers. As Connolly (1983: 243) once wrote: "To show the subject to be a construction is not to render its deconstruction imperative." [14] I wish to show how this genealogical approach both resembles and differs from the work of Taylor and MacIntyre.

The difficulty with being sympathetic to Foucault on subjugation is that of explicitly and systematically posing the problem of the status of a discourse which borrows from a heritage the resources necessary for the deconstruction of that heritage itself. Connolly shares much of MacIntyre's indictment of post-Enlightenment rationality but urges him, in a review of *After Virtue*, to reject teleological alternatives more completely. As we have seen, MacIntyre (1982) rejects the Aristotelian telos in nature, but retains the possibility of discovering a unity of tradition. Connolly (1987:135) holds that unity of tradition can never be reconciled with human endeavor. He writes:

It is possible, after the self-destruction of strong teleological doctrines, to defend a much weaker version of the idea, in which telos, while drained from the cosmos, nature, and even to a significant degree from human bodies, is located in human projects. But the material deployed to realize these projects, because it can no longer be assumed to tend toward a natural harmony, also generates resistance and recalcitrance to their realization.

This leads Connolly to the ambiguity of the subject and MacIntyre back to an earlier drawing board. Connolly (1988) is moving to surpass liberalism. But MacIntyre (1988:403) is moving back to rethink the predecessors of liberalism, back to the point of suggesting that Thomism is the most reasonable tradition in terms of the "adequacy and explanatory power" of its history. Thus the latter theorist is as inclined to agree with rational projects of totalization as the former is to pronounce them hazardous to one's health.

Connolly reads Taylor as someone who is preoccupied with the attunement of self, others, and nature. And he advises that this is also a hazard to the health of the subject. Connolly (1987: 151) implies that the "direction of being" Taylor would discover insinuates "a fictional ideal into discourse which can be actualized only through containment of that which deviates from it." In other words, for Connolly the need for attunement is a wish to disambiguate human subjectivity—to discover authenticity —and the political ramifications of this are unduly restrictive.

Of the three theorists, Connolly owes Foucault the greatest debt. Connolly (1988:157) is quite aware of the doubleness of being subject and being a subject. Echoing Foucault, he writes: "To be a subject is to have a unity imposed on the self which stirs up resistance and struggle within the self (the unconscious, insanity, perversity, depression, etc.) and which insulates the self from connecting these effects to its own form of being." Connolly argues that this situation cannot be reasoned away or solved by discovering attunement. While Taylor holds open the possibility that our ability to discover a direction in "being" will improve, Connolly seems to be saying that there will always be too much, more than one can say, a remainder, an excess. Connolly (1983:241) imposes this:

> Every way of life imposes some sort of order on the chaos and multiplicity which would otherwise prevail, and every way of life must therefore develop some means of setting and enforcing limits. The development of a subject-centered morality may turn out, when compared to other conceivable alternatives, to be the most salutary way to foster order through the consent and endorsement of participants.

It is useless to attempt total mastery or even partial attunement because something is always left out, but what harm does it do, according to Connolly? Connolly (1988:173) claims that the mastery willed by reasonable men and the attunement yearned for by alert strong evaluators are actually "self-destructive" because they increase the misery of the subject. His description of the subject at odds with itself sounds like Nietzsche:

> The modern subject carries around too much rancor against that in itself which resists subjectivity and that in others which deviates from its standards. That is the principal objection to it. To be a subject is to be too predisposed to punishment (of self or others) or too predisposed to help (self or others) to measure up to its standard. It converts difference into otherness, into a form of deviation which must be improved, excluded, punished, or conquered. (158)

This passage is very important. I join Connolly in an attempt to avoid reducing difference to opposition. But I do not stress resisting patterned subjectivity. While others work on resistance, I wish to call attention to the flaws in the patterns of our subjectivity. There is, of course, no reason to choose between these approaches to a celebration of difference. But a politics of extravagance is less obvious than a politics of resistance.

According to Connolly, this rancor can extend into a general resentment toward life without purpose and without equality: an existential and civic resentment. Connolly's politics—a radically liberal form of social democracy—addresses civic resentment in the hope of clearing ground to expose existential resentment. And here—with existential resentment—he hints of the possibility that "the struggle between affirmation and resentment," because it is universal, might open "each self potentially to bonds of identification with others who are also implicated in this interior strife" (1988:172). Connolly reworks the self/other tension into a tension between identity and difference; he does this by giving the self more room for difference and by giving others room to discover that their common fate is not politically directed. But the tension lies in the "interior strife" of the subject at the center of either tension. And the realization of a common fate would, at best, lead us back into communion.

The provisional position Connolly has staked out by predicting MacIntyre's need for mastery and flushing out Taylor's desire for attunement is no less affirmative than those he criticizes. He feels that the desire to make modernity less confusing results in a politics of resentment. Facing the same world(s) of multiple overlapping interpretations, and agreeing on the inability of positivist social science to make the world less confusing, these three authors disagree on how to overcome what Foucault calls subjugation. Connolly wants to import the pieces that do not fit by sacrificing aspects of what is now judged reasonable; MacIntyre wants to organize all the pieces, known and unknown, in the most reasonable way possible; and Taylor wants both to bring in new pieces and to avoid sacrificing what is now reasonable. All are unhappy with the results of post-Enlightenment reason and order. Their conflict and consensus promises to open up the remunity/communion dialogue. There is no need for me to take sides here—though I am most obviously following the Connolly line—because I am developing an additional line of argument.

The Excentricity of Extravagance

The last section contains readings of both totalizing and nontotalizing projects. Totalizing projects such as MacIntyre's (1988) aspire to total mastery of incoherence, and nontotalizing projects such as Taylor's or Connolly's cope within overall incoherence. All three projects can agree that aspects of life that do not fit within the structures of reason and order lie outside the zone of subject-centered discourse; they, of course, disagree about how to treat the excess. The result of this consensus is that advocates of reassuring politics seem to be on solid ground when they oppose their relatively secure visions with the nihilist urge to go paddling out to the seas of monstrous excess that supposedly surround discourse in the frenzy of annihilation that Bataille, following Nietzsche too closely, calls "joy before death." For example, Connolly may well have to agree with Taylor (1985:172) when the latter writes: "There not only can be but must be something between total subjectivism, on the one hand, holding that there are no undesigned patterns in history, and the strange Schopenhauerianism-without-the-will in which Foucault leaves us." And Connolly (1988) might, despite his avoidance of mastery and attunement, even show sympathy to MacIntyre's rejection of Derrida's allegedly pathological choice between tearing social life apart from within and floundering without it. MacIntyre (1988:369) writes contemptuously of the presupposition of "Derrida's choice between remaining 'within,' although a stranger to, the already constructed social and intellectual edifice, but only in order to deconstruct it from within, or brutally placing oneself outside in a condition of rupture and discontinuity." But this convenient dismissal of deconstruction—by portraying it as a synonym for dismantlement—blurs a critical distinction between two interpretations of *interpretation*: reassurance and extravagance.

The safe, reassuring way of being interpretive is to imagine being part of a web of signification that we ourselves have spun. This is the interpretive way that is being mobilized against positivist, or designative, social science and the way that inspires such advocates of communion as Bowles and Gintis, Barber, Elshtain, and Bellah et al., among others. Interpretive approaches deny liberalism the possibility of a subject that can escape being attached to discourse, or the play of signification. MacIntyre, Taylor, and Connolly are all engaged in projects designed to pick up the pieces that were created when everything became discourse.

These theorists show how much political possibility is lost in the contracted universe of atomistic liberalism, but they severely limit what might be gained. For there is a sure play: that which is limited to the substitution of given and existing, present pieces. Thus the defeated become victorious, women become men, they who humble themselves are exalted, and life goes on. The tension between individual and collective subjectivity has yielded many intriguing possibilities for the modern subject; but there is no way out of the Foucauldian dilemma of escaping the discipline of power only by turning it against oneself and others, or of becoming disciplined and an agent of discipline. Connolly (1987, 1988) resists the limits of reasonable discourse by giving presence to what is now absent, realizing that this will require making absent some of what is now present. But this must not create the impression that reason and order govern discourse so completely that irrationality is exiled.

Play is always play of absence and presence, but if it is to be thought radically, play must be conceived of before the alternative of presence and absence. To conceive of play before the binary opposition is to declare totalization not merely useless but impossible in principle, because there is no structure capable of covering a field that does not respect the limits and discipline of binary logic. One can either reason with a person who eschews binary logic or one cannot.

To treat discontinuity as the "other" of continuity gives continuity more credit than it deserves. In addition to calling the "designer's urge" useless because finite discourse cannot cover an infinite field, is it not possible to call totalization impossible because there is something missing from the field? What could be missing? Perhaps a center which (arrests and) grounds the play of signification. The reassuring, safe interpretations have succeeded in removing such ground from the atomistic liberals, but the commitment to rationality or attunement keeps the hope of gaining it back alive. Genealogy, to the extent it relies on history and binary logic, threatens to assist this finding of new ground for the modern subject.

The extravagant interpretation of interpretation holds, then, that the rugged individual of the atomistic liberals, the situated strong evaluator of the collectivists, and the ambiguous subject of their genealogical critics can never achieve absolute presence outside of what we are calling discourse (a system of differences). In addition to transgressing the limits of discourse, one can write and speak about the absence of a "real person" to speak and write about. And the absence of such a transcendental signified extends the domain and the play of signification infinitely.[15]

This extravagant interpretation of interpretation is no longer turned toward the origin, affirms play and tries to pass beyond man and humanism, the name of man being the name of that being who, throughout the entire history of metaphysics has dreamed of full presence, the reassuring foundations, the origin and the end of play. According to this interpretation, the Christian will that Taylor cannot fathom stepping outside of is always already riddled with monstrous irrationality: the "alternative" he condemns is not an alternative at all. And Foucault's resistance to patterned subjectivity is reassuring in the sense, and to the extent, that he takes those patterns seriously.

We are all aware that play is the barely natural enemy of structure and the standpoint of play teeters on the edge of gibberish, of the unspeakable, of having nothing to say. But just because one agrees that no project of cosmic unity can succeed does not mean that one cannot use metaphysical language. There is no sense in doing without the concepts of metaphysics (God, man, consciousness) in order to shake metaphysics. All of the habits of the mind left over from the days of distinguishing intelligible minds from sensible bodies cannot be broken at once. The quality and fecundity of a discourse are perhaps measured by the critical rigor with which this relation to the history of metaphysics and to inherited concepts is thought. To think one's relation to the logic and concepts of metaphysics must not, then, be confused with refuting the modern subject. I want simply to emphasize that the passage beyond philosophy does not consist in turning the page of philosophy (which usually amounts to philosophizing badly), but in continuing to read philosophers in a certain way. That is, one can traverse texts in ways that highlight the extent to which they are governed by metaphysical oppositions; these oppositions can be displaced, and one can struggle to avoid replacing them with new hierarchies.

While these two interpretations of interpretation are absolutely irreconcilable, even if we live them simultaneously, I do not believe that today there is any question of choosing. I should hope that we have learned enough from Taylor that the category of choice seems particularly trivial. But it is my highest priority to conceive of the common ground and the disparity between two such different notions of play as extravagance and reassurance. But I must insist that extravagance defers the presence of a being that can be thought immune to the play of difference, or discourse.

While much work needs to be done before such extravagance can be articulated, the obvious place to begin to conceive of common ground, and upon which so much is written, is the body. As we struggle to substitute embodied signs for the Cartesian cogito, we fight against the urge to turn our eyes away when faced by the as yet unnamable which is proclaiming itself and which can do so, as is necessary whenever a birth is in the offing, only under the species of nonspecies, in the formless, mute, infant, and terrifying form of monstrosity. At this point I ask only that the distinction between reassurance and extravagance be introduced.

From Paradise to Inscription

The last two chapters have shown how this book is related to other books that use the word *community*. Most of these books encourage remunity, communion, or both, in the name of community. These authors are concerned with Foucault's first two questions: those of domination and exploitation. Atomistic and collectivistic authors regularly accuse each other of these vices. This book is an attempt to use *community* while struggling with Foucault's third question: subjugation.

My plan is to add another dimension to the debate between Foucault and his critics. While there is much disagreement on how to relate discourse to that which cannot be said, none of the authors cited in this chapter, with the notable exception of Derrida and Certeau, reject the metaphor of clearing space, filling it, and defending against or welcoming in what is necessarily excluded. While MacIntyre still manages faith in reason within the space filled by discourse and the horizons beyond, Taylor seeks unified direction in what he agrees appears to be a sea of monstrosity outside discourse. And Connolly resists the security of an island paradise in ways that reassure us of its possibility. Even Foucault, who is often read in contradictory ways on the subject, has been described as placing the subject in one of the folds of the shoreline of the outlying sea of monstrosity (Deleuze, 1988:120–23), sparing him the walk to the beach and the paddling out on the day of annihilation, drawing him close to Bataille's interior experience.

Certeau (1984:152) is perhaps ahead of political theory on this score. "The time is thus over in which the 'real' appeared to come into the text to be manufactured and exported. The time is over when writing seemed to make love with the violence of things and place them in a rational order." In the place of Robinson Crusoe's island paradise attuned with the Great Clockmaker, Certeau finds that "The blank page is only a pane of glass by which representation is attracted by that which it excluded; the written text, closed on itself, loses the referent that authorized it . . . Writing has become an 'inscription island' . . . a laborious dream, occupied by this 'impossible' to which or about which it thinks it 'speaks'." The extravagant critic must look for ways to clear space for writing, ways that do not extinguish what Derrida calls the dark and barely natural rays of irrationality, ways that also do not deny political theory access to the safe play of reassurance.

In discussing the rationalist, expressivist, and genealogical reactions to Foucault, I do not always use my own words. There are voices other than my own and I can now identify the most persistent one: Derrida.[16] As I show in chapter 9, Derrida is not another name for Bataille. Derrida notices the crack in the foundation of Western thought and follows it all the way to the center of subjectivity, which he then decenters by treating the subject as a function of substitutions of signs while acknowledging our need for the subject also to be a form. After Derrida, one does not pretend to close off the sea of monsters; one notices the trace of violence left over when each page is cut into, to break silence. Silence is the body of the world which is violated by discourse. These metaphors are no less innocent, but they orient a different kind of research.

Derrida's "Structure, Sign, and Play in the Discourse of the Human Sciences" (1978:278–94), from which I have been quoting freely since presenting Foucault above, moves from a depiction of totalization to an account of how some (although still under its sway) call totalization useless, to an admission of the impossibility of such projects of mastery and attunement. This admission permits an introduction of Derridian extravagance. Derridian extravagance carries two tensions into modern political theory that are usually not noticed, even by many radical critics.

The extravagant critic, following Derrida (1978:291–93), listens to the remunity/communion dialogue, but also explores tensions between history and play and between presence and play. History must be viewed as an accomplice of metaphysics, not a liberator. The notion of linear time that history takes for granted is obviously an integral part of transmitting messages across time. And the presence of the subject at the center of binary oppositions must be exposed to as much play (or should I say brainy rearrangements?) as it can stand. The presence of a centered subject gives structure to existence and lies between birth and death, but any structure must give or fall to the "pathology" MacIntyre misreads in Derrida.

Derridian extravagance explores these tensions, along with others in political theory, in an effort to maintain silence in discourse, rather than to force us to treat the silence of irrationality and chaos as exiles, outside discourse. Connolly is right to call our attention to silent monstrosity; this must be maintained as a constitutive element of discourse because silence is always already discursive. If history is always already over, and absence/presence distinctions are never finally differentiated, then writers are always already adrift in seas of silent monstrosity, in glass-bottom boats that attempt to break the silent waves. The islands of Defoe are boggish islands of inscription, penal colonies: the days of industrial inversion on dry land are over.

To avoid the problem of being left with "writing given over to its . . . solitary erections," the combination and separation of radical play and safe play must be politicized. The main attraction of this extravagant extension of what Connolly calls the discordant lodged in the concordant tissue of life, this "joyous affirmation of the play of the world and of the innocence of becoming" (Derrida, 1968:292), is that it adds a surplus even while shaking down illusions of a subject one can write to or about. Deconstruction is not just a shakedown operation. But this surplus must be politicized if double agents who practice deconstruction alongside resistance are to avoid becoming bogged down in the endless wordplay and punning—or substitution of signs—that their ways of reading and writing make possible.

II Reassurance

The next three chapters address the forces of reassurance, the reluctance to let go of the subject at the center of discourse. Such reluctance might be stated positively as a desire for foundations; a desire to escape the play of the world and stay at home for the night; a desire found in the sighs of relief one hears, for example, when municipal services restore electricity after a blackout. This desire is found in these chapters in attempts to develop the subject so fully as to perpetuate it—whether as personality or collectivity or both—across time: the desire to overcome time's relentless "it was."

First, I shall present a model borrowed from J. G. A. Pocock, a model which is sufficiently general to explain even the structure of Foucauldian resistance to patterned subjectivity. Then I will be able to illustrate the model of creation and transmission of self-images across time by reading the more practical work of the renowned statesmen, Lincoln and Burke.

But alongside this rather structural accounting of the forces of reassurance lies a critique of their power. One can notice how the next three chapters anticipate forces of extravagance. Chapter 4 can be read as an argument for the benefits of doubting reassurance. Do I propose to abandon reassurance? Heavens no! But even reassured theorists can loosen the subject at the center of discourse and stop fighting flux all the time. Chapter 5—on Lincoln—illustrates how the refusal of extravagance can, in the name of reason, cripple the experience of being human. Chapter 6—on Burke—illustrates how it is possible to sense the extravagance of what Bataille calls "joy before death" and beat it back into the boundaries and patterns of subjectivity we call "being normal."

4 Pocock, Foucault, Forces of Reassurance

One cannot step twice into the same river, nor can one grasp any mortal substance in a stable condition, but it scatters and again gathers; it forms and dissolves, and approaches and departs.—Heraclitus

Play is always play of absence and presence, but if one wishes to think it radically, one must think it before the alternative of presence and absence; it is necessary to think of Being as presence or absence from the possibility of play on, and not the other way around.—Derrida

Michel Foucault comes dangerously close to addressing the problem of domination—total hegemony—by merely pluralizing the situations in which one side can lord power over the other. Foucault (1988:12) wishes to distinguish the unlimited violence of controlling the other from the practice of making power relations "changeable, reversible and unstable." In such situations both sides gain a sense of freedom. For example, during the construction of a Habitat-for-Humanity house, a poor person might on occasion feel more powerful than a middle-class person. I am concerned with this pluralizing of hegemonic situations—now I'm master, now I'm slave—because it does not criticize the principle of domination as much as it spreads it around. And as long as the principle of a balance of power occupies thinking, mutual service in its extravagant sense of giving free gifts is impossible. Free gifts degenerate into mere reciprocity in the presence of strong/weak oppositions, the oppositions of power.

The principle of hegemony is a continual source of political conversations which do not seem to lead anywhere. Dead-end conversations about power relations usually reduce political possibility to one side lording its victories over the other, at least for the time being. That is, to conserve the more powerful cultures, states, classes, groups, and persons is to continue the subjection of their weaker counterparts, some of which may in time aspire only to reverse the balance of power in question. This chapter suggests how one might, by assuming a critical perspective, supplement conservative and some radical theories during the moments at which they disagree about which hegemonic patterns to maintain across time. I wish, for example, to supplement such positions as those which urge nation-states to conserve their traditions in the name of national security, and the bourgeois subject to invest in political forms of life insurance.

Instead of being supplemented by new experiments in language, such conservative pattern-maintenance is often only countered by competing alternatives. Popular examples of this include the attempt to disrupt continuity in history by criticizing traditionalism or even by dismantling the subject of consciousness. But the politics of "now" generations and "sub-individuals" often represents little more than shifts in overlapping balances of power. While critical of facing the malice of time with collective strength at the expense of individual diversity (or individual strength at the expense of sub-individualistic multiplicity), alternative theories, and even radical theories, are usually content to attempt mere reversals: to face the malice of time with the "other" of the conservative formulation.

But whether a text in political theory reminds one of the work of a Burke or of a Foucault is a question that does not begin to criticize the principle of hegemony which underlies the idea of balancing power. Supplementing conversations across conservative and radical perspectives requires asking how it is possible to think in binary terms in the first place.

To reduce political possibility to binary opposition requires faith in the existence of unity beneath the rich diversity of everyday life. The persistence of unity in any form reassures those who take it seriously, in that it permits sufficient order for one to think solely in terms of polar opposites. This is because thinking solely in terms of polar opposites requires that one allow the extremes of continua to signify the ranges of political possibility. This assumption allows one to forget about the forces of madness, oblivion, delusion, accident, or chaos because these elements of irrationality cannot find places along the lines of any continuum. Once reassured by this assumption, the principle of hegemony is simply a matter of taking sides near one extreme, the other, or both. A political discourse seeking to supplement conservatism, without posing merely as its opposite, cannot rely even on temporal unity, cannot continue to reassure practitioners of its natural rightness, must instead create its own possibilities. At least this is the pretense I wish to entertain here.

Any politics which is unencumbered by weighty metaphysical concerns must postpone questions of pure ideality, transcendental deductions, absolute truth, etc., but this need not include stopping to make sense. I wish to suggest only that while engaging in sufficient de facto sense-making to survive, one must also confess that in principle "the fairest order in the world is a heap of random sweepings." [1] Giving in to the play of the world might "supplement" its various orders, but this might happen only if such extravagance is not posed as the opposite of reason and order. One must, it seems, either reject the reassurance of thinking along the lines of continua or continue the habit of thinking in binary terms.

Norman Jacobson, perhaps playing to its worst inclinations, once described political theory as a "vocation worthy of giants" who rescue human subjects (and sometimes each other) from their most abysmal thoughts, or at least from facing them alone.[2] Deploying a continuum is a tried-and-true rescue maneuver.[3] The most reassuring feature of *continuum* is that it names a "series."[4] There are at least three approaches to the continuum: to declare continuity moot in a pure world of immutable ideality;[5] to declare continuity possible in worlds reassured by immanence;[6] and to declare continuity impossible in the chaotic world of flux.[7] It is as difficult to adopt either the first or third approach uncritically as it is tempting to adopt the second uncritically. The presumption of immanence is a habit of the mind, especially in our time. This chapter is an attempt to draw attention to the subtle influence of the continuum, as illustrated by one of the most persistent unities: the notion of linear time.[8] My attempt will indicate how the first and third approaches to the continuum do not constitute extreme opposites.

The terms immanence and transcendence circulate widely in political discourse and can be used to distinguish various perspectives on social time. The principle of transcendence, when used to signify the divorce of universals and particulars, can never lead to the establishment of elapsing time continua. Wholly particularistic moments share nothing in common. *Immanence*, however, can name a unity of universals and particulars, a unity which allows all moments on an elapsing time continuum to share temporality (more or less elapsed time).[9] Saying that all points on an elapsing time continuum share temporality, or more or less elapsed time, requires making two different theoretical moves: reducing all of infinite mystery to being either wholly timeless (transcendent above particulars) or immanent; and eliminating the wholly timeless from consideration. This reduction and elimination permit the reassurance that time elapses, or flows like a river from past to future.[10] My task in this chapter is to show how this theoretical motion does its work in typical texts in political theory.

First, to illustrate the widespread influence of this theoretical motion, I shall attempt to establish its presence in a well-known model drawn from the history of political thought. The model is the work of J. G. A. Pocock, whose writing on politics, language, and time lends structure to the radical divorce of universals and particulars. I want to work with Pocock because of his breathtaking generality. His work accounts for many radical and conservative perspectives. Pocock's model of traditionalism and its critics can explain so many approaches to social time because he juxtaposes the radical creation of political possibilities with the usual transmission of political principles. But even though these forces help to explain how historical continuities can be broken as well as maintained, Pocock's model is limited by his presupposition of an elapsing time continuum.[11]

Second, I shall illustrate how a text which works conscientiously, in an outright rejection of metaphysics, to undermine continuity can embrace the continuity of elapsing time. I wish to work with Foucault because his name is often associated with postmodern rejection of the work Pocock's model helps to explain. Foucault's work experiments with disruption, dismantling, discontinuity. The essay (1971/1977) I wish to examine —"Nietzsche, Genealogy, History"—is in many senses a condemnation of continuity. One might expect Foucault's essay to deploy ranks of counter-memory against conventional forms of time: "It is a question of giving history a counter-memory,— and consequently of unfolding in it a wholly other form of time" (1971:167, 1977:160). These words draw a new form of time into their sights, but the text nevertheless reassures because it also contains words that betray any intention to disrupt. This is perhaps best shown by using the language of Pocock's model to trace the movement of Foucault's claim. After studying how these rather diverse theorists sometimes resemble each other, I shall consider how their work might be supplemented.

The Language of Pocock's Model

To cover as many cases of traditionalism and its alternatives as possible, Pocock builds his model by experimenting with what he calls "paralanguage."[12] Pocock describes this model as a matrix within which traditions are given form and then pushed out into the world as history (239-40).[13] The following sentence is especially clear about the structure and motion of the text:

> A society's institutions, it is clear, may be either consolidated or discrete, homogeneous or various; it may *inherit* dialogue, dialectic or conflict between its traditions, and the impulse

to replace tradition, first with another image of normative action and secondly with history as the vision of interplay between modes of action, may arise *from within the inheritance.* (241, emphasis added)

After the ways in which institutions may vary (all words to the left of the semicolon) are stated, four possibilities appear: societies transmit pure-and-simple traditions (237–41); societies "inherit" competing traditions and nontraditions (ideologies) (241–53); from within "inheritance" there arises an impulse to replace tradition with another image of normative action (pure, objective historiography) (253–69); and from within "inheritance," but only after the antitraditionalist voices are singing, there arises an impulse to replace tradition with history (253–72). These possibilities are developed systematically in a series of movements. Pocock begins by rejecting pure-and-simple tradition as the prototype of traditionalism. He uses it instead as a place to begin raising the issue of transmitting an inheritance across time. The crucial maneuver requires forcing a binary opposition between timebound and timeless considerations. With this distinction firmly in place, Pocock next eliminates wholly nonsecular items from his agenda by granting hegemony to the timebound "side." Finally, this one-sidedness is made manifest by the birth of history.

Step 1: Rejecting Pure Tradition

In its pure-and-simple usage *tradition* names "an indefinite series of repetitions of an action" (237). Each particular repetition is attended by "the knowledge, or the assumption, of previous performance" (237). Because previous performance need only be "assumed" and because the series of repetitions is "indefinite" the question of origin is never raised. Rather, simple traditions are "immemorial." Pocock provides a hypothetical example of a simple kinship society in which everything is learned from the "fathers" before the shrines of vague ancestors. The mode of action, or characteristic practice, embedded in this kind of traditionalism is "transmission" (239). Transmission is, even at this early stage, one of the model's twin forces of reassurance. This will not change.

But Pocock is interested in pure-and-simple tradition only

as a starting point, a seed to place in the "matrix" awaiting the "conceptualization" of tradition. He wants to show "what happens when a society forms an image of itself as a constant transmission of ways of living and behaving" (239) and, more complexly, he is curious about when this image is and is not a strictly traditional form.[14]

Step 2: Forcing the Timebound/Timeless Distinction

The logic of the model's development is related to language. Pocock presents the process of giving a tradition conceptual form—"conceptualization"—as a process which has "a logic of its own . . ." (241).[15] He wishes to show how ideas about time follow "causally" from the way language is used.[16] His text stresses that "images and concepts of a non-traditionalist kind may arise from causes lying within the process of giving a tradition conceptual form" (241). That is, within the process of forming tradition as a concept there are "causes" which result in nontraditional concepts.

The major cause of nontraditional concepts within the logic of conceptualization is a timebound/timeless polarity. The text forces this distinction upon the reader. Pocock first notes that not all societies consider inheritance from an immemorial past to be their sole mode of reception.[17] Some societies, after all, are not content to "presume" continuity and actually seek to establish continuity with the past by locating a mythical or sacred "origin" there. Still other societies place this origin altogether outside of time.[18] Pocock could treat the notions of being out of time altogether, of having sacred origins, and of immemorial continuity as indications respectively of being timebound, of timelessness being sacred, and of being out of time. But instead he writes the following:

> To describe a timeless existence, a sacred origin or an immemorial continuity, are all ways of conceptualising the continuous existence of society. The *more precisely* we imagine society as a *series* of concrete human actions in time, and time in terms of the *sequence* of such actions, the more we seem to *move away* from imagining society in terms of the sacred, as our use of the words "temporal" and "secular" indicates. (242, emphasis added)

We must not miss that the out-of-time/timeless distinction has been collapsed, and both elements are now called timeless in the sacred sense. This sacred imagining is then contrasted with the secular idea of being timebound. In other words, immanence has now been distinguished from transcendence.[19]

The time/timeless polarity permits Pocock to distinguish institutional (immanent) from sacred (transcendent) time. Locating an origin for a tradition is, by definition, locating an authority *without* an antecedent tradition. Hence the timeless side of time-consciousness leads thought away from tradition and toward what Pocock wishes to call "charisma."[20] If time is viewed in the institutional way, the charismatic is simply outside tradition and is worshiped as a sacred origin. But time can also be viewed as a "sequence" of charismatic acts, in which case "a new vision of time may be constructed in terms of moments of creation rather than moments of transmission" (243). This is how the timeless side of time-consciousness causes a vision of time as creation, rather than as the transmission caused by the timebound side. Creation, then, joins transmission (the first force of reassurance) as the second force of reassurance. In Pocock's model they constitute a dialectic—caused by the arbitrary imposition of a timebound/timeless distinction—which grows over time into a complex view of history, and thereby retains elements of both.

One effect, then, of the dualistic time-consciousness embedded in the conceptualization process is that the form given to tradition is divided against itself. "Within tradition there will be a dialogue between the non-traditionalist and traditionalist voices with which it speaks" (244). Pocock feels that this "dialogue" might also appear as "conflict" or "contradiction" and continues following the "logic" of conceptualization he has started by mapping some of its complexity.[21]

Step 3: Eliminating Transcendence

Pocock opens the third movement hinting that eventually he will present history as a criticism of tradition, but this does not happen during this movement. Instead, "conversation" within tradition builds up to a complexity sufficient to allow disagreement about the relation of past to present. Of course, for conversation to be possible all parties must share common meanings made possible by literacy.[22] But because the elapsing time continuum is not yet sufficiently entrenched, because some moments—such as myth, charisma, sacred stories—cannot be discussed in terms of elapsed time, not all parties are yet talking in terms of institutional time. This section of Pocock's essay works to entrench the elapsing time continuum and then builds complexity into the secular conversation.

Pocock remarks that the voices which would perpetuate the authority of the present are not likely to welcome the classicist's "definitive" version of past texts. This is because written words are politically unreliable. Words "cut across the processes of transmission and create new patterns of social time; they speak direct to remote generations, whose interpretation of them may differ from that of intervening transmitters of the tradition they express" (255).[23] In other words, because no writer can control the meaning of words in those texts s/he undersigns, every reader is a potential radical (255).

The critical question is whether information about the past ought to be collected and agreed upon independently of its impact on the authority of the present. Pocock's point is that the impulse to do so can arise among radicals and classicists only within a literate tradition. He is now prepared to show that, in literate society, the transmission/creation polarity of the first two movements undergoes a sort of metamorphosis. Recall that its origin in the timeless-timebound distinction led Pocock to juxtapose transmission with charisma to emphasize the sacredness of the timeless. Being out of time altogether was eliminated arbitrarily. Now, in literate societies, even the sacred timelessness of charisma (which is defined in terms of its other), or transcendence, is completely eclipsed. The transmission/creation distinction lives on, however, in a different form. Pocock writes: "Since what we are concerned with is history, the light in question must be that of a *common temporal context*,[24] and it should therefore seem—at least prima facie—that it will be hard to construct a historiography where the dominant mode of authority is and remains sacred" (258, emphasis added). With this development, time as a continuum (elapsing time) becomes firmly entrenched. First immanence was distinguished from transcendence as primordial chaos was banished arbitrarily, now transcendence is eclipsed. This state of affairs moves the elapsing time continuum (with its presupposition of immanence) to a position of hegemony. Conversation is now forced to move along a continuum of elapsed time, but does so in such a variety of ways that discontinuity is the name of the game. The pages which immediately follow in Pocock's text illustrate some of the play possible.

Step 4: Giving Birth to History

Readers may recall that earlier in the text Pocock promised that history would emerge from his matrix: "history as the vision of interplay between modes of action [transmission and creation] may arise from within the inheritance" (241). Well, the text is about to come into its inheritance. History is the conservative's strategy for saving face in the presence of the classicist and the radical. One could resemble Oakeshott, and venerate history without demanding that it make sense. Pocock prefers to take the play of complex overlap more seriously and to treat history as another "self" which is perpetually explored.[25] Some theorists find inspiration in this plea to have a past.[26] Pocock's point is that this other self emerges from an inheritance within the form which gives the secular (timebound) world hegemony over the timeless.[27]

Pocock's model of historic growth over time can be reduced (with no negligible violence) to the difference between maintaining the authority of the past over the present (conservatism) and questioning it (radicalism). The absence or presence of a coherent understanding of the past plays an integral role in this difference. In many cases in literate societies "speech-acts" in favor of maintaining the authority of the present are attended by a denial of the relevance of a detailed past. These voices "presume" that the past authorizes the present and do not ask that it make sense. On the other hand, in many other cases in literate societies, speech-acts in favor of questioning the authority of the present are attended by an insistence on the relevance of a detailed past. These voices show how memory can undermine the present. In Pocock's memorable words, "The radical reconstructs the past in order to authorize the future;

he historicises the present in order to deprive it of authority" (261).

That Pocock presumes time's continuous passage is most easily shown by applying his model to the text which presents it. That is, Pocock delivers a model which can describe both the transmission and creation of traditions, but his text is preoccupied with the transmission of elapsing time. Pocock's model—from the originary time/timeless distinction, to the primitive transmission/creation distinction, to the metamorphosed transmission/creation distinction—culminates by locating within history the binary opposition between traditional and antitraditional voices. Using paralanguage, Pocock is saying that history is both tradition and its other (criticism of it).[28] But if one attempts a more general perspective and applies the Pocock model to his text, it becomes clear that Pocock considers time only as an inheritance from the past. Put simply, he is not concerned with creative experimentation with the language of time.[29]

Pocock's labors do not include facing the excess which is eclipsed arbitrarily in the name of polar distinctions at the level of paralanguage. In the language of Pocock's model his text, which can explain both "presumptive tradition and radical denial of the relevance of the past," represents "presumptive tradition" exclusively when coming to terms with the passage of time. This representation is so subtle that it is nearly invisible. While telling the story of how immanence gained hegemony in its relation to transcendence, Pocock draws the reader's attention away from aboriginal dreams, Heraclitean flux, and Ovidian chaos, etc., as if to erase (or at least to cast into oblivion) any element which cannot be classified in terms of universals and particulars. By exercising the silent power of presumption, his work permits the forces of reassurance to become entrenched.

Foucault on Temporalization

In a well-known essay Derrida explains a sense in which Foucault is naive about temporalization.[30] Foucault, he claims, does not work at a sufficiently general level of analysis to escape uncritically presupposing the continuity of time. That is, he cannot imagine excesses which cannot in principle be captured by the time/timeless distinction. Instead of joining in the play of the paradox, "the time before first,"[31] Foucault plays a safer role—as creator—in the reassuring model of the transmission and creation of principles along a line of time.[32] He assumes this role in a celebrated essay, "Nietzsche, Genealogy, History."[33]

To use the paralanguage of Pocock's model, Foucault's essay rejects pure-and-simple traditions (section one); distinguishes timeless and timebound approaches (section two); eliminates transcendence (sections three and four); and advances a view of history which resembles the "radical" strain of Pocock's more complex variety of history (sections five through seven). Concentrating on the third step of the Pocock model—the elimination of transcendence—I show how Foucault also reassures readers of unity by presupposing that all timebound events share the universal quality of temporality. This presumption of immanence gives Foucault an elapsing time continuum that ranges from an elapsed past to a present, and surges forth into the not-yet-spent future; in other words, time is conceived as a series of events.[34]

Step 1: Rejecting Pure Tradition

According to Foucault, genealogy must avoid studying events as if they came into being in a linear fashion ("genèses linéaires" [145/139]) and instead must record each outcome in its singularity ("la singularité des événements" [145/139]). Even areas of life which seem to be without history, or outside time (such as love, conscience, or instincts), are timebound events, or outcomes, for Foucault. Saying that events do not come into being linearly does not, then, commit him to abandoning the timebound notion. But this does require that genealogy oppose itself to investigating the so-called genesis of "origins" (146/140). Foucault places *origine* in quotes because his second section attempts to recover a (less haughty) usage consistent with genealogy.

Step 2: Forcing the Timebound/Timeless Distinction

Section two imposes the same timebound/timeless distinction that Pocock's model relies upon to distinguish two different kinds of origins, "haut" and "bas." High and mighty (haut) origins come before the world and time: "avant le monde et le temps" (149/143).[35] But Foucault does not imagine a primordial chaos without bounds and timeless/timebound polarities; rather, like Pocock, he assumes such polarities and equates being before time with timelessness being sacred. Hence, the "haughty" origin which comes before time is forced to be sacred—"est du côté des dieux" (149/143)—because it is not profane.[36] On the other hand, of course, the historical debut—"le commencement historique"—is lowly, base, vile (bas).[37]

Genealogists, then, focus on the opposite "side"—the other–"side" of the ideality of the origin. Their research worlds are wholly particularistic, allegedly devoid of continuity. They use *history* to signify becoming. We must read carefully here because the text comes close to describing history as a Heraclitean state of flux, as if to avoid the immanence presupposed by linear time after all.[38] Consider the next-to-the-last sentence in section two: "History, with its intensities, lapses of memory, secret furies, feverish, syncopated restlessness, is the very body of becoming" (150-51/145). History is the very body of becoming. While the notion of coming before time has been called sacred and is therefore anathema for genealogists, there is no evidence in the first two sections that genealogy is committed to facing the chaos of Heraclitean flux.[39] One must ask, then, how is history "becoming" for Foucault? How chaotic—or reassuring—is timebound life? Sections three and four of his essay offer at least preliminary responses to these questions.

Step 3: Eliminating Transcendence

Section three examines the first aspect of the lowly origins studied by genealogy: "la provenance," or source (151/145).[40] Foucault as genealogist uncovers base and vile ancestors many of us would like to forget. My reading of this section focuses on the extent to which this past is earlier, in the sense of elapsed time, than the forgetful present. I am also interested in how completely this continuum is entrenched.

According to the text, genealogy locates, within individuals, sentiments, ideas, and the hint of a chaotic network which is difficult to sort out. Foucault describes the work of a genealogist as being a question of: "pinpointing the many subtle, singular, subindividual markings which can crisscross in them [individuals, sentiments, ideas] and form a network which is difficult to unravel" (151/145).[41] Only a high-and-mighty metaphysician would attempt to find unity in these multiple, crisscrossing, entangled "markings." The lowly origins sought by genealogy allegedly permit only discontinuity; lowly origins permit only the separation of each entangled marking, the destruction, not the reconstruction, of the network. And yet in describing this destruction Foucault switches verbs from "démêler" to "débrouiller," the latter which can be used in the double sense of to unravel that which was crisscrossed and to draw order out of chaos.[42] This doubleness never leaves the text.

Later in the same paragraph we learn that, because genealogy has unravelled the entangled markers, swarms of hitherto lost, and now stirred-up, outcomes ("événements") begin to multiply in profusion. Foucault is consistent, if arbitrary, to associate "marque" and "événement" in this way; recall his assertion in section one that all individuals, sentiments, and ideas upon which markings are inscribed are "outcomes." To continue, these outcomes are themselves now making historic debuts. In other words, the origins sought by genealogy are comings out ("des commencements") which are themselves outcomes ("mille événements").[43] In addition to stirring up lost events, then, genealogy can pinpoint ("repérer") the earlier proliferation of events which formed them. This movement back in time to earlier outcomes is not intended to be continuous and in many senses is not, but a close reading of Foucault's account of its discontinuity suggests a presupposition of the elapsing time continuum which superintends even his rejection of linear history. Consider:

> To follow the complex channels back to where we came from, is rather to allow that which took place in the original disper-

sion to endure: this is to pinpoint the accidents, the most vile acts of deviance—or on the contrary the complete reversals —the mistakes, the lapses in judgement, the bad calculations which gave birth to that which continues to exist and have value for us; this is to discover that, not truth and being, but the foreignness of accident is at the root of what we know and are. (152/146)

To say that there is an unevenness which is foreign to us at the "root" of what we are is unsettling to readers who still long for homes in the world; but to say that much time has elapsed since our lowly, blood-spattered, ancestors crept out of the sea is reassuring—we need not face immediately the monstrosity of sliding back in.[44] Please notice two different critical movements here. First, the violence of nonmeaning has been neutralized by making the question of our so-called roots the most critical item on the agenda. Second, within the worlds of meaning which can be traced to these roots, the lowly accidents have been sequestered as the other, allowing the metaphysical pretense of the hour. Foucault calls genealogy critical because it draws out the other (the mad, the vile, the base), making "veneration" of the past impossible. We are dishonorable all the way back to our roots.

But—and here is the point—the first critical movement is eclipsed by the uncritical acceptance of elapsed time. In this text the question of neutralizing nonmeaning is immune to criticism: the questions of what kind of territory the time-bound/timeless distinction is imposed upon or of why anyone should rest assured that such imposition is sufficiently totalitarian for time to be a river within which one can splash about, for events to pass by as if in a series, or for there to be a "root" ("racine") to unearth, are never on Foucault's agenda. Foucault's text is governed by that nondecision: to deny the past veneration is, among other things, to presuppose having a past. Only this presupposition can give the genealogist the time it takes to step into the river of time ("débrouiller") more than once.

The root of the problem is that the unevenness exterior to human knowledge and being is, according to Foucault, merely an earlier point on a continuum of elapsing time. The passage last cited above moves from original dispersion to the birth of reality to contemporary hypocrisy (Nietzschean forgetfulness). Such reliance on an elapsing time continuum is quite a different matter than reliance on continuous linear history. In the remainder of this section Foucault uses the reassuring language of elapsing time to warn against embracing even bodily continuity when writing history.

According to Foucault—or should I say Pocock?—our heritage is dangerous in the sense that it is neither venerable nor unitary. "Dangereux héritage que celui qui nous est transmis par une telle provenance" (152/146). Having a history offers no stability; in fact, it undoes most of the security people rely upon.[45] But while this paragraph challenges the security of foundations, it is filled with reassuring (elapsing time) words "héritier" and "ancêtres" (152–53/146–47).

The final two paragraphs in this section show how serious Foucault is about discontinuity. If what has been established in the text so far is extended, not even the body can exist as a continuity. Foucault, as might be expected from his reputation, feeds bodies to the disremembering facilities of "la provenance." The body carries the stigma of past outcomes, which we have learned must include all of the least-honorable markings. But, assuming the other Janus-faced role, the body also carries all desires, moral failings and errors into the world. In the absence of continuity the body must endure the insurmountable conflict of our dangerous inheritance. Genealogy, writing where we really come from, tells a story of history ruining the body (154/148).

By now it should be evident that genealogy must read literally the passage cited in the second section, "history is the very body of becoming." History inscribes interpretations of the past on bodies in markings which the genealogist must make sense of.[46] Of course none of this marking/remarking (fathering/re-fathering?) is possible without a flowing river of elapsing time. The more time elapses, the more inscriptions accumulate. But how totally is humanity dominated by its heritage? How total is the eclipse of Heraclitean flux when this text eliminates transcendence?

If section three can, without willful distortion, represent the analysis of " événements passés"—every event to the left of NOW on the elapsing time continuum—then section four can represent the coming into view, or surging forth, of events, everything to the right of NOW on the elapsing time continuum.[47] "L'emergence" is for Foucault the second sense of the lowly origins studied by genealogy. We can expect to find an emphasis on discontinuity but must keep both eyes open for evidence of the serenity of lapsing time. For an early indication, the text juxtaposes the uninterrupted continuity denied by "la provenance" with only the impossibility of finality ("le term fin"), rather than with any continuity whatsoever. More seriously, perhaps, on the same topic of "le fin" Foucault uses *série* to describe the events studied by genealogy ("série d'asservissements" (154/148). My task is to examine the extent to which such language of reassurance is present in this text.

Here again the argument contrasts lowly genealogy and high-and-mighty metaphysics. Whereas metaphysics pretends to discover continuity in the meaning of human history, genealogy seeks only to reestablish ("rétablit") multiple systems of subjection.[48] In other words, genealogy studies the play of domination.[49] The way the text works with play resembles the way Pocock's model maps conversations between radical speech-acts and others. In both texts the presence of systems of subjection ("les divers systèmes d'asservissement") precedes the play of domination.[50] But waiting in the wings lies the unmistakable presence of an elapsing time continuum. The diverse systems of bondage are retrieved by genealogy. They are re-established.[51]

Just as Foucault's verb "débrouiller" indicates both the discontinuity of criticism and the drawing of order out of chaos, so he continues in this section rejecting continuity in history while using words that reassure readers about the continuity of time's passage. Another example comes in a passage which contrasts "la provenance" and "l'emergence" as the difference between designating the quality of an inscribed heritage and designating the space within which one either dominates or is dominated. A contrast is drawn between having been inscribed upon by past events and participating now in an indefinite repetition of domination and its other (156/150).[52]

We next encounter a general form of the same point. The passage cited below shows that Foucault is prepared to apply the past/now/future continuum of elapsing time to the development of all humanity. To honor elapsing time is to become human. Read for reassurance: "Humanity does not progress slowly from struggle to struggle until reaching a universal harmony in which laws are substituted once and for all for war; she installs each of these abuses of force in a system of laws, and advances in this fashion from domination to domination."[53] This passage illustrates Foucault's claim that there is no final destination to human history; this is the "surging forth" ("l'emergence") element of the "where did we come from" ("la provenance") claim that there is no ultimate origin of origins. But this passage also illustrates my claim that Foucault assumes the continuity of time. Human history does not "progress" ("progresser") from primordial chaos to universal reciprocity, but the struggles for domination which mark human history "advance" ("aller"), one after the other, as if in a series. The presumption of immanence underlying the elapsing time continuum helps to set the stage for the play of domination.

But surely one must read too much into the word "va" to find solace in such an unsettling, violent passage as this. Would it not be unfair to attribute the adjective *serene* to this emergence? Such an interpretation is hard to resist, however, because the text is still surging forth with generality about becoming human ("le devenir de l'humanité" [158/151]). Foucault—who has already decided that "history . . . is the very body of becoming"—now shows in one clause how the continuity of human history can be rejected in the language of the continuity of (elapsing) time: "becoming human is a *series* of interpretations" (emphasis added).[54]

While it is indisputable that Foucault distinguishes the timeless from the timebound and then eliminates any idea owing to transcendence (divorcing particulars from universals), the same text carries evidence of uncritical reliance on a universal quality shared by all "événements." This unmentioned quality is temporality; without presupposing it Foucault would be unable to contrast "l'emergence" and "la provenance," unable to write of bloodied ancestors and their unhappy heirs, and unable to use *series* to describe the movement of domination. The doubleness of "débrouiller" is driven home by the presumption of immanence.

Step 4: Emerging Radical History

Sections five and seven can be read as a summation of this doubleness. Section six is a mere illustration of genealogy. The tension between voices of metaphysical continuity and genealogical discontinuity illustrates the two forces of reassurance in Pocock's model. To see how they reassure—because there are many ways in which genealogy is unsettling—one need only move alongside the intentional alliance between Foucault and Nietzsche to the superintending motion in the text. We have been reading the serenity of a primordial "débrouillement" which banishes chaos in the name of polarities (such as the distinction between the highly and mightily metaphysical and the profanely, politically radical). Foucault's creative rewriting of the past, using the ploy of counter-memory, is radical in that it undermines the authority of the present, but is reassuring in that it accepts uncritically the totality of this banishing act. Before rejecting contemporary turns in political theory, then, one must dissociate such work from certain residua of metaphysical inquiry, such as the elapsing time continuum. That is to say, a problem with much of postmodern theory is, perhaps, that it is insufficiently postmodern.

Reading *Everything* Carefully

Even the casual reader has by now acquired a sense of what lies in excess of the model I impose on the rich texts of Foucault and Pocock. I hope I have shown that both texts illustrate the reduction of possible worlds to immanence and transcendence and the elimination of transcendence necessary to enjoy the reassuring forces of transmission and creation. I have also shown that Pocock explains how these reassuring forces can interact and that Foucault sides with the forces of creation at the expense of the forces of transmission. But my focus obscures other features of these texts, many of which are unknown to me. Some of what I have left out is perhaps analogous to the general excess which attends any form, including all continua and including the elapsing time continuum. Ignoring this general excess may stifle political possibility, so I wish now to turn toward the problem of supplementing worlds governed by forces of reassurance.

The elapsing time continuum is so completely entrenched in political discourse that one is often reduced to silence when asked what the absence of the continuity of time might be like. Such a question implies that the continuous time series stands in opposition to temporal discontinuity. This implication cannot be allowed here because it would merely substitute a continuous/discontinuous opposition for a past/future binary opposition. And yet one cannot pretend immunity to the question lurking behind the implication. So what if Pocock, Foucault, and countless others accept uncritically the idea of a line of time?

I cannot begin to respond to this question without facing the problem of articulating the notion of flux. *Accident, perpetual becoming*, or *chaos* can name the formless monstrosity of flux, but any account of flux must necessarily rely on the reason and order of language, which thrive at the expense of formlessness. It is beside the point, then, to propose that one choose between linear time and perpetual becoming.[55] But perhaps this suggestion can be directed to both sides of the impossible divide. Those who approach politics as an imposition of form on a chaotic world can be said, after all, to have chosen order over chaos. Critics of linear time might ask instead how those who presume linear time find it possible and feel compelled to make such choices. They might also wish to assess the cost of this "decision," a decision which must be forced because it can never be made.

This reversal raises a different question: what are the implications of fighting flux, of resisting a supplement which has never *not* been available?[56] Any discussion of the linear flow of time is bound to be affected by a transfer of the benefit of the doubt from those who side with reason to those who refuse to choose between reason and flux. A refusal to presume that all events share a universal quality which allows them to lie along an elapsing time continuum is a way of insisting that wherever one finds a structure one finds an excess.[57] That is, unitary forms can be imposed only by sequestering the mysteries, accidents, and madness of flux. But while such forms—for example, the line of time—may "straitjacket"[58] nonmeaning, they cannot eradicate it. This is because flux works as a resource for writing in its most obvious sense, for drawing binary distinctions; closing out flux makes the familiar order of reason possible, and this order houses all of the familiar distinctions (man/woman, past/future, individual/collective, etc.) that structure political discourse. Because the imprisonment of flux makes such absent/present distinctions possible, one cannot speak reasonably about forcing it out completely. That the sleep of reason produces monsters is not a reassuring statement to the person who is not certain of ever being fully awake. Pretending such certainty by forgetting about all that necessarily exceeds structures can only restrict life's possibilities.

When facing such passages as this one by Nietzsche—"Zarathustra does not want to lose anything of mankind's past; he wants to pour everything into the mold"[59]—it is important, then, to read *everything* very carefully. This quotation is consistent with Pocock's project and Foucault's essay if *everything* names all outcomes along an elapsing time continuum, including those outcomes which dart playfully back and forth in time, ignoring historical continuity. But if *everything* must also signify those aspects of life which exceed any conceivable totality, then pouring "everything into the mold" must indicate an overflowing as well as a flow.

Before experimenting with the possibility of an overflow and before tracing its political implications, one ought to assess the costs of not doing so. At what price have republican myths been created? How expensive is it to transmit and conserve self-images across time? How much is saved by restricting political thinking to a tension between traditionalism and its critics? Perhaps there are stale problems in political theory which might look different if studied from a perspective which is not merely positive or negative. Answers to these questions, of course, exceed what can be said here.

But as political worlds continue writing, remarking, reprogramming, and making de facto sense of worlds which in principle defy reason and order, certain terms of political discourse are already implicated. If all order is in principle provisional, then in a cowering struggle against reassurance within binary force-fields it may well become increasingly difficult to defend, let alone to justify, hegemonic dominance in political life. It may become necessary to use the words *legitimacy*, *sovereignty*, or *powers-that-be* in a minimalist sense that allows one to admit that political forms are vulnerable and not merely reversible. Such confessions might lead away from either the entrenchment or the mere reversal of certain familiar hegemonic patterns. But to avoid the pitfalls of reassurance one must make sense of the advice that a critique of the principle of hegemony, if it is to be thought radically, must insist that it is the *give* in the structures of our worlds which makes power plays possible and not the other way around.

As this book continues one can expect to find cracks in the formulation of community. This is because community has not been designed to *give*, and in this it can symbolize many other theoretical treatments of the hour. The next section—chapters 4 and 5—study the cost of protecting ourselves from the murmurings of madness, of denying ourselves the heights and depths of pathos.

5 The Problem of Time in Lincolnian Political Religion

It must be considered that there is nothing more difficult to carry out, nor more doubtful of success, nor more dangerous to handle, than to initiate a new order of things.—Machiavelli (1950:21)

Let every American, every lover of liberty, every well wisher to his posterity, swear by the blood of the Revolution, never to violate in the least particular, the laws of the country; and never to tolerate their violation by others. As the patriots of seventy-six did to the support of the Declaration of Independence, so to the support of the Constitution and Laws, let every American pledge his life, his property, and his sacred honor; —let every man remember that to violate the law, is to trample on the blood of his father, and to tear the character [charter?] of his own, and his children's liberty. Let reverence for the laws . . . become the political religion of the nation.—Lincoln (1955–57:I:112)

If by humanism we mean a philosophy of the inner man which finds no difficulty in principle in his relationships with others, no opacity whatsoever in the functioning of society, and which replaces political cultivation by moral exhortation, Machiavelli is not a humanist. But if by humanism we mean a philosophy which confronts the relationship of man to man and the constitution of a common situation and a common history between men as a problem, then we have to say that Machiavelli formulated some of the conditions of any serious humanism.—
Merleau-Ponty (1964:223)

Many political theories, including those that criticize traditionalism, assume that time is a continuous line from past to present. This line of time reassures theorists by allowing the exclusion of anything that cannot either be plotted along it or viewed as its eternal "other." Much work in political theory illustrates a transition, analyzed by Pocock, from timeless to secular thinking. Those who are preoccupied with the line of time often do not take timeless principles, such as the elements of natural law, seriously. But Pocock has shown that even secular political leaders must ground traditions in a timeless zone if they are to write messages which can be transmitted. Pocock's work shows the need in statecraft for an origin which is not itself a point on the line of time.

The social construction of the world is a perilous task, in part because each generation cannot begin anew. The charter members, so to speak, must arrange for the preservation of their handiwork. According to Pocock, societies conserve images of themselves across time by creating myths larger than life and transmitting them from one generation to the next. What might otherwise be a neat and tidy operation is complicated, at least in literate societies, by the multiplicity of competing strategies and conflicting interpretations. A successful statecraft can emerge from this tangled web only when most of the citizenry agree on a signified worth signifying, a message worth transmitting. Over time, as Burke illustrates in the next chapter, transmission may become an end in itself.

The next two chapters, then, are practical in the sense that they read the work of actual statesmen concerned with the creation and transmission of traditions. Pocock has shown that there is no clear-cut line between these forces of reassurance.

Nevertheless, Lincoln's situation required him to find ways to assure that those generations that did not fight the British for independence would honor those generations that did by obeying their laws. This called for the creation of tradition. Lincoln could not attend Burke's preoccupation with transmission.

Lincoln faced the political problem of establishing the principles of the American Revolution as an order. A successful statecraft must require all citizens to perpetuate that order, even when the strongest among them may not see the point of doing so. For example, there may be cases when obeying laws violates an individual's perceived interests. As in any act of domestication, the problem is either to train the wild to be reasonable and orderly or to make it stay outside the bounds of public life. Either way, the passions are curbed.

Pathos names transient emotions which reflect the best and the worst of the human condition. A Greek-English dictionary from 1838 lists excitement, ecstasy, passion, rapture, and affection as possible synonyms for pathos, but it also lists distress of mind, perturbation, sorrow, disease, accident, unnatural desire, and lust as synonyms. This curious doubleness is really not so curious. The grammar of *pathos* suggests that people can live exciting lives only by drawing close to destruction. But the pursuit of pathos must not obscure the fact that a simple destruction/construction polarity is itself a construction, and it cannot become pleasurable until it is brought face-to-face with the "other" of form: flux, madness, accident.

Here is the problem. For a variety of reasons explored in this book, Western political thought—especially texts on community—protects us from flux, madness, accident, and the like. Following our principle, this denies us the pleasures of pathos. This helps to explain why most established Western democracies are plagued by social and political apathy. And where do we find pathos in its positive sense? We must look to nations and states struggling to establish themselves, fighting to create traditions. Nation-states appear to require pathos, which they later must deny. Let us join Lincoln at Gettysburg for a preliminary indication of what is at stake.

At Gettysburg, Lincoln delivered a plea for political religion, a plea which continues to find an audience. Lincoln's address is a plea delivered to living citizens, for civil religion. It places the deaths at Gettysburg in a larger context, one in which living citizens can participate. But this distinction between the larger context of a united nation (the whole) and the smaller event of the Civil War (a part) allows a twofold appreciation of civic virtue: one can either (re)create the whole or work to maintain an established whole. While Lincoln appears to find the former more honorable, he must publicize the honor of the latter. Lincoln must show that believing in an entrenched civil religion is as honorable as imposing a new form. But how can he do this without undermining the pathos of battlefield glory? Lincoln must somehow honor passivity if he is to preserve unity, and yet he is driven to believe that there is little honor in passivity, especially when compared to battlefield action.

Lincoln, then, must honor docile citizens while teaching them to honor their more active ancestors. With this in mind, the following becomes problematic: "It is for us the living, rather, to be dedicated here . . . to the great task remaining before us—that from these honored dead we take increased devotion to that cause for which they gave the last full measure of devotion . . ." (VII:23). Lincoln appears to be using *devotion* and *dedication* as rough synonyms. If these words were synonymous, his problem would disappear: if it were equally honorable to be dedicated and devoted, he could find pathos in docility after all. Lincoln's text creates just such an illusion by blurring the distinction between dedication and devotion. Lincoln writes:

> Fourscore and seven years ago our fathers brought forth on this continent, a new nation, conceived in Liberty, and dedicated to the proposition that all men are created equal. Now we are engaged in a great civil war, testing whether that nation, or any nation so conceived and so dedicated, can long endure. We are met on a great battle-field of that war. We have come to dedicate a portion of that field, as a final resting place for those who here gave their lives that that nation might live. It is altogether fitting and proper that we should do this. But, in a larger sense, we can not dedicate—we can not consecrate—we can not hallow—this ground. The brave men, living and dead, who struggled here have consecrated it, far above our poor power to add or detract. The world will

little note, nor long remember what we say here, but it can never forget what they did here. It is for us the living, rather, to be dedicated here to the unfinished work which they who fought here have thus far so nobly advanced. It is rather for us to be here dedicated to the great task remaining before us —that from these honored dead we take increased devotion to that cause for which they gave the last full measure of devotion—that we here highly resolve that these dead shall not have died in vain—that this nation, under God, shall have a new birth of freedom—and that government of the people, by the people, for the people, shall not perish from the earth. (VII:23)

First, notice that our "fathers" "conceived" and "brought forth" a "nation" which was "dedicated" to a proposition. There is honor in this provision of structure, according to Lincoln. He next acknowledges the problem of extending a nation "so conceived and so dedicated" across time. This is why a war is being fought. Lincoln's next usage of *dedicate* distinguishes between the legalistic sense of devoting something to public use and acts of actual consecration. He seems to admit being unable to do the latter, but he is not finished yet. "The brave men, living and dead, who struggled here have consecrated it [the ground] far above our poor power to add or detract." But what is there left to be done, other than construct war monuments? After admitting that people living with established forms cannot consecrate or dedicate, Lincoln proceeds to do so anyway by treating *dedication* and *devotion* as synonyms. In the passage noted above, he first brings the soldiers over to the side of devotion by speaking of being dedicated to the unfinished work of the (now) devoted soldier. Now, Lincoln is telling us that it is honorable merely to be devoted—soldiers are dedicated in the sense that they give all of their devotion to the cause. And so can we, says Lincoln. In fact, if we are not devoted, our honorable ancestors have died in vain. We are in this sense superior to them, in control of a past they can no longer influence.

But *devotion* and *dedication* are only somewhat synonymous and should not be used interchangeably. Lincoln's text succeeds to the extent that it draws attention away from the rough spots. Readers are led to equate dedication, consecration, and devotion. But it is more relevant to compare the Bible's Ruth and the Civil War's General Grant. Ruth was devoted; Grant was dedicated. Only by blurring the rather striking difference between being like Ruth and being ruthless can Lincoln extend the republic while honoring living citizens.

This conflict, which we can study in greater detail in Lincoln's other work, illustrates the reason for the creation component of Pocock's model. Principles must be placed out of reach of continual reinterpretation if they are to be transmitted. We shall see that Lincoln was not above ruthlessly using the authority of the state, if necessary, to develop the devoted population needed to withstand the silent artillery of time. His elegant statecraft has in this way contributed to the authoritarian reputation of *community*. I study his work to determine how a linear understanding of time (presented in chapter 4) might have helped to prepare Lincoln's agenda. I am particularly interested in his fascination with the imposition of form, because of the violence this does to wildness.

Reading Lincoln's Ceremonial Rhetoric

One must approach Lincoln's work in an unusual way because of its unusually fragmented consistency. Most of the work considered here appears in addresses and short lectures. His debates cannot be read in my project because they include others writing on Lincoln's discourse. I wish to study only Lincolnian statecraft. I cannot explore the relation between intended and indicated meaning in texts associated with multiple authors without risking a contribution to the myth of Lincoln.[1] I have another myth to study, the one about the "founding fathers" of the eighteenth century. Those who had lived in Lincoln's day (and knew better) were dying, and history needed to be spun as myth: I shall read selected texts for evidence of how this was done. In reading Lincoln's ceremonial rhetoric I have noticed several different themes which can be extracted to organize my observations. I plan to show how Lincoln's work illustrates some of the abstractions discussed in the first section of this book.

Aristotle calls the rhetoric with ceremonial ends "epideic-tic." If a speech "aims at proving" an historic or living figure "worthy of honor," or unworthy, it can be said to be a piece of epideictic rhetoric (1954:33). Considering the ways in which Lincoln praised historical figures, it is possible to locate at least three strains generally found in the statecraft associated with his name: ordinary administration, the management of national crises, and the creation of traditions. The first is found in his praise of Zachary Taylor, the second in his words on Henry Clay, and the third in a speech honoring Thomas Jeffer-son. Together, the three show how Lincoln insists upon both liberty and equality, but not in the paradoxical way Jaffa (1959) writes about. Rather than question how obviously unequal people can ever freely agree to give liberty to all, I read Lin-coln as an illustration of the bind between personal liberty and collective integrity (state and national). The former question is training for those who use *equality* to name "equal liberty" in the bankrupt language of unencumbrance. The latter read-ing illustrates how sovereign individuality must acknowledge, and cannot be reconciled with, the entrenchment of collective sovereignty (which is not equal liberty but the general will to moral equality in shared subjectivity).[2]

Ordinary Administration: Taylor as Caretaker

In 1848 Lincoln campaigned actively for Zachary Taylor to re-place Henry Clay as the Whig nominee for president. Lincoln urged his party to abandon what he took to be an emotional attachment to Clay and to realize that the younger Taylor was more electable. While his opposition within the party criti-cized Taylor for failing to clarify his position on issues such as the Wilmot Proviso, internal improvements, tariff laws, and the banking system, Lincoln defended Taylor's unwillingness to permit the chief executive to exercise legislative powers in matters of ordinary administration.

Taylor's approach, according to Lincoln, respected direct representation and separation of powers, so long as they worked. Consequently, Taylor represented only the most cir-cumspect exercise of the presidential veto. Before the U.S. House of Representatives in July 1848, Lincoln marked Taylor's words to make the following point: "The power given by the veto . . . should never be exercised except in cases of clear violation of the constitution, or manifest haste, and want of consideration by congress" (I:503). The same speech also asserts that to "transfer legislation [from Congress to the president] is clearly to take it from those who understand, with minuteness, the interests of the people, and give it to one who does not, and can not so well understand it" (I:504; see also I:454). This conservative view indicates what I call the strain of ordinary administration. Lincoln and Taylor would restrict the legislative powers of the president (proposing legislation and the veto) to moments of emergency; ordinary administration abhors flamboyance. But their similarity stops here. Lincoln's praise for the dead Zachary Taylor indicates that the almost mundane strain of statecraft is not fitting for all situations.

"Eulogy on Zachary Taylor" praises Taylor for having "sober and steady judgment" and a dispassionate "absence of excitement and absence of fear" (II:87). Accustomed to uphill battles, Taylor always approached military situations with a "dogged incapacity to understand that defeat was possible" (II:87).[3] Never defeated in battle, always "kind" to his soldiers, the unretreating Taylor marched through life with a "blunt business-like view of things" (II:86). He rose through the ranks to become General Taylor and was finally exalted with the presidency, "verifying the great truth, that 'he that humbleth himself, shall be exalted'" (II:90). Lincoln would have his live audience learn from Taylor about the eventual return (though these words indicate that one may need to wait for more than a lifetime) one can expect from an investment in duty: "It is *much* for the young to know, that treading the hard path of duty, as he trod it, *will* be noticed, and *will* lead to high places" (II:89). A more immediate virtue of duty is the order it permits; Taylor is praised for being as predictable "as the earth in its orbit" (II:89).

Aside from his unassailable devotion to public duty, what does this speech find praiseworthy in Taylor? Lincoln appears to hedge his remarks: "I will not pretend to believe that all the wisdom, or all the patriotism of the country, died with Gen. Taylor" (II:89). According to Lincoln, Taylor was adept at winning the "confidence and devotion of the people" (II:89) because he was harmless. That is, the devoted general never exerted his political will. Where Henry Clay would later be praised by Lincoln as a man of "indomitable will," Taylor conversed with Congress using the following phrases: "*Your* will, gentlemen, not *mine*"; "Just as you please"; "Say yourselves" (I:504). That Lincoln felt Taylor did nothing (remained passive) better than most other politicians becomes clear when he laments that the slavery question was not resolved during the administration of a President who would have gone along with most any proposal.[4] Such a connection between presidential passivity and public confidence—a relation between two devoted forces—signals the extent to which Lincoln praises Taylor for being a caretaker. Neither as wise as the mythologized Jefferson, nor as passionate as the indomitable Clay, Taylor was dutiful, sympathetic, and humbly devoted.

By praising only what Taylor could do during the normal operations of government, this eulogy indicates that Taylor was not a model for all aspects of statecraft. Though Taylor sought the presidency, he never sensed its significance and was not dedicated to its sovereignty. The need to secure victories against time was not burning in his blood. Lincoln closes by reading the poem, "Oh, Why Should the Spirit of Mortal Be Proud?" In the case of Taylor's devotion this is a ruthless question.

The Taylor style of leadership—deferring to the opinions of the people and their other representatives—is inconsistent with Lincoln's retaliation at Fort Sumter in 1861, or his hiring and paying pro-Union private agents in New York before Congress had approved the Civil War, or his arbitrary suspension of habeas corpus, or even his Emancipation Proclamation. The Taylor style is, however, consistent with the passivity of Lincolnian statecraft. Examples of that include Lincoln's practice of deferring to his generals for battle strategies, granting his cabinet considerable discretionary authority, and using the presidential veto only at the proper Jeffersonian moment.

Taylor is, then, only conditionally praised by Lincoln. The idea of founding a republic in the opinions of the people is inspirational for caretakers during ordinary times: other times, during crises for example, require more expedient measures. Crises in democratic polities demand rigid political enforcement of the will to moral equality. Only within such entrenched forms can opinions be tolerated.

The Management of National Crises: Henry Clay as Troubleshooter

Henry Clay was such a fixed symbol of the Whig party that one might expect Lincoln to praise him unconditionally. Lincoln's eulogy is filled with ceremonial praise, but the image of Clay which emerges is more that of a master of expedience than a charismatic leader whose truths can be mythologized by later generations. Lincoln seems to find Clay too practical to have reflected upon the ideals of the institutions he helped to perpetuate. Clay's political action was designed to preserve the Republic because he had great passion for its preservation, not because he understood the moral equality he was protecting.

One learns from Lincoln that Clay represented two types of politics in the forty-nine years he participated in American politics. "In times of peace and quiet" Clay had a flair for partisan politics, advancing the interests of his section and party (II:126). But when called upon in times of "national emergency"—such as the Missouri question, nullification, and the general slavery question—Clay became a "truly national man" (II:131). Just as Taylor was the best available caretaker, Clay was the best available troubleshooter. Lincoln writes of Clay: "although . . . the American people . . . have been opposed to him on questions of *ordinary administration*, he seems constantly to have been regarded by all, as *the* man for a *crisis*" (II: 129, my emphasis).

Lincoln honors three qualities in Clay which describe his "pre-eminence" as a statesman in critical times. First, "he was surpassingly eloquent": "The spell—the long enduring spell— with which the souls of men were bound to him, is a miracle" (II:125). Clay was an orator who could play an audience —one who "truly touches the chords of human sympathy"— creating moments of "deep pathos" (II:126). This was what Clay did best. That Clay was more apt, to Lincoln, to generate profound feeling than to pen immortal ideas becomes evident when reading about his second praiseworthy quality, his judgment.

Lincoln acknowledges readily that the Republic lost a measure of patriotism with Clay's death, but he is less willing to comment on how our stock of wisdom would be affected. Clay is never praised as a man of vision or probing intellect. He is credited for having "inventive genius" in the sense that "all his efforts were made for practical effect" (II:126). In fact, Lincoln explicitly avoids discussing the wisdom of Clay's political strategies;[5] instead, he has the good judgment to write that Clay's "judgment was excellent" (II:125). While a wise leader might invent axioms which the state could force all citizens to call immanent truths, a leader with good judgment is better equipped to read the currents of time, discover what is possible, and move with determination. Lincoln viewed Clay as the latter kind of leader: one of God's "instruments of safety and security" for troubled times (II:132).

To unsurpassed eloquence and excellent judgment, Lincoln adds "indomitable will" (II:125). The first quality indicates that patriotic Clay could inspire exaggerated feeling in others. The second quality indicates that Clay knew his way about the region of pragmatic politics, or when to play which audience. But the third quality, indomitable will, assures that Clay was a man of action. It is difficult to miss Lincoln's admiration for this no nonsense assurance of finding solutions to problems and making them work. The leader as troubleshooter needs the will to proceed as if right, regardless of the consequences.[6] Clay would not know how to connect the sound-images with the concepts in the sentence, "Your will, gentlemen, not mine."

Clay's will, judgment, and eloquence, according to Lincoln, were all employed in the cause of human liberty. Clay never approached this matter philosophically; instead, he championed the cause of liberty by saving the Union because he felt that the Union symbolized liberty. His efforts required political action more than philosophical reflection. Clay's commitment to liberty was "a primary and all controlling passion" (II:126).

Lincoln presents Henry Clay, then, as an active partisan politician during normal times and an active national man in times of peril. His passion led Clay to defend the Republic in the name of liberty against all threats. In a passage quoted by Lincoln perhaps more often than any other, Clay argues that the idea of slavery contradicts the spirit of the American Revolution (II: 131). Here Clay uses language which indicates the way in which a fixed set of principles must be accepted, not debated or analyzed philosophically, if the nation's institutions are to be allowed to extend across time. To embrace slavery justifiably (as opposed to allowing the institution to live out its last days), argues Clay, it would first be necessary to "muzzle the cannon which thunders [the] annual joyous return" to the "era of independence," to "blow out the moral lights around us" (II: 131). Finally, it would be necessary to "penetrate the human soul, and eradicate the light of reason, and the love of liberty" (II: 131). If the light of reason is extracted at its root, it is difficult to justify anything; Clay would shoot first and ask silly sophistical questions later.

The Creation of Traditions: Jefferson as Myth

Jefferson died too early (1824) for Lincoln to eulogize him, but Lincoln was quite concerned that the nation not forget him or the text associated with his name: the principles of the Declaration of Independence. The praise he extends to Jefferson provides evidence that Lincoln, like Clay, is more inclined to enforce the principles of liberty and equality he finds in the Declaration than to bother with the opinions of citizens who interpret them differently. More important, this provides a glimpse of a statesman attempting to establish a new order by creating a timeless origin to which all succeeding generations can be said to be, if not forced by law, attached. This takes us to the "heart" of politics: its forms of entrenchment. To see this as a departure from politics is to muzzle Machiavelli's message about the disaster of the Prince believing in the illusions s/he necessarily manipulates. Jefferson, whose body has long since passed away, must be praised for being lifeless so as to resist the passage of time. As Lincoln needs to bond future generations to this departed hero, one time-honored strategy is to claim that in our hearts we all agree with what Jefferson was fortunate enough to put on parchment, and then to stand unflinchingly by, to the death.[7] This politics of entrenchment is made possible by forcibly repulsing any competition, including the flow of time and other philosophical arguments, before that competition gains an advantage. It is very much like digging a trench and defending it come hell or high water. Let us read through Lincoln's denial of pathos.

In 1859 Lincoln was invited to attend a festival in Boston in celebration of Jefferson's birthday. The letter which indicates his regrets for being unable to attend contains praise for this dead forefather.[8] Such praise is not uncharacteristic; Lincoln was fond of pronouncing Jefferson's name in public. In 1854, during one of the Debates, Lincoln reportedly said that Jefferson "was, is, and perhaps will continue to be, the most distinguished politician of our history" (II:249). Jefferson symbolized what Lincoln reportedly calls "the pure fresh, free breath of the revolution" (II:249). Jefferson's most significant act, for Lincoln's purposes, was becoming "the great oracle and expounder" of republican faith by drafting the Declaration of Independence (III:124). The only problem is that the members of the Democratic party he founded "have nearly ceased to breathe his name everywhere" (III:375).

After saying that the Republican party must struggle to "save the principles of Jefferson from total overthrow in this nation" (III:375), this letter mentions how those who disagree with Jefferson ought to be treated:

> The principles of Jefferson are the definitions and axioms of free society. And yet they are denied, and evaded, with no small show of success. One dashingly calls them 'glittering generalities'; another bluntly calls them 'self evident lies'; and still others insidiously argue that they apply only to 'superior races.'
>
> These expressions, differing in form, are identical in object and effect—the supplanting the principles of free government, and restoring those of classification, caste, and legitimacy. They would delight a convocation of crowned heads, plotting against the people. They are the van-guard—the miners, and sappers—of returning despotism. We must repulse them, or they will subjugate us. (III:375)

And so Lincoln digs in. But what good is a trench without brothers- and sisters-in-arms (across generations)? WE MUST repulse THEM (in the name of personal liberty).

Lincoln praises three qualities in Jefferson which permitted him to draft the "immortal paper" he and others undersigned in 1776. Jefferson displays "capacity," not the "excellent judgment" of a Clay. Where Clay has "indomitable will," the more distinguished Jefferson has "forecast," or greater vision. Finally, Jefferson is praised for having "coolness"; recall that Clay was "passionate" and "eloquent."[9] Lincoln wishes to praise Jefferson's coolness in an effort to make his principles lifeless —that is to say rational—enough to be available to all living citizens in any age. These qualities—intellect, vision, and rationality—permit Jefferson to "embalm" the principle "liberty to all" which must be protected by the Union and the Constitution which stand in front of it.[10] This principle attaches citizens to their constitution in that it is entwined around the human heart *and* protected by the army. Citizens need not be cool, capacious visionaries. But neither are they in need of moral salvation. All they must do is remain attached in their hearts to the rational laws on the books, or be obedient, and as religiously so as eloquent, passionate leaders can make them.

Citizens must, then, be as devoted as Taylors, become zealous in the presence of Clays, and know that they are thereby perpetuating the words associated with the name Jefferson. Those who do not agree must be repulsed by whatever means necessary. My point in this section is not to claim that Lincoln honors these strains; rather I wish only to claim that the strains are distinguishable and judged praiseworthy by Lincoln. I do, however, expect Lincoln's more systematic writing to show signs of these strains as he struggles to create political tradition. The next two sections will examine some of this writing.

The Formation of a New Order: The Lyceum Address

On 27 January 1838 Lincoln wrote a remarkable address and delivered it to the Young Men's Lyceum of Springfield, Illinois. While this address is ostensibly about violence, it is also the only writing he signed which uses the words *political religion*. (The connection between violence and Lincoln's secular religion is also remarkable.) The Lyceum Address divides easily into five sections: an introduction; a statement of the problem of perpetuation in terms of the three strains identified in the above section; a presentation of political religion and tradition in response to the problem of perpetuation; an explanation of why his is the first generation to require being religious about tradition; and two concluding paragraphs. I wish now to read each section in turn.

Introducing the Lyceum Address

The word *perpetuation* in the title of this address—"The Perpetuation of our Political Institutions"—announces the importance of time's flow to the Lincoln born thirty-six years after 1776. From the beginning of his public life Lincoln was concerned about the vulnerability of the fledgling republic to time. Lincoln is concerned that the 1776 Revolution will turn out to have been a glorious experiment for the original revolutionaries and a distant memory for everyone else. But he has stronger measures in mind than remembrance.

Before analyzing the problem of perpetuation, Lincoln introduces the current situation, locating the Republic in space and time: "In the great journal of things happening under the sun, we, the American People, find our account running, under date of the nineteenth century of the Christian era" (I: 108).[11] Our "account," according to a remunity-sounding Lincoln, contains "blessings" of both a material and a moral variety. Original participants in the 1776 experiment, he says, worked hard to enter these blessings into our account, but the effect of their work will be erased unless today's citizens act to perpetuate it. The point is that we can no longer rely on them to do that. After all: "We toiled not in the acquirement or establishment of them [the "blessings"]—they are a legacy bequeathed us, by a *once* hardy, brave and patriotic, but *now* lamented and departed race of ancestors" (I: 108). That these material and moral blessings are bequeathed leads Lincoln, sending like Pocock, to claim that we have a duty to keep them in the family, to pass them along. Our duty is "to transmit" the "political edifice of liberty and equal rights" to the "latest generation," so as to keep these blessings "undecayed by the lapse of time" (I: 108). But how?

One obvious way to faithfully perform this duty to posterity is to fight against external enemies, but Lincoln says clearly that this is not our present danger. Our problem is more subtle and therefore more dangerous. "As a nation of freemen, we must live through all time, or die by suicide" (I:109). By "suicide" Lincoln means that the greatest obstacle to repaying the departed forefathers is the present generation dedicating itself to some other experiment instead of devoting itself to the inherited family business. This ends the introduction.

Taming the Wild and Furious Passions

As Lincoln's analysis opens, he considers ordinary politics—the world of particular will and political faction—commenting on an "ill-omen amongst us" (I:109). He is concerned about "the increasing disregard for law which pervades the country" (I:109). Some people are ignoring the rules of the game and instead are giving in to "wild and furious passions" (I:109). To illustrate this he offers two recent cases of mob violence which are "most dangerous in example, and revolting to humanity" (I:109). Drawing a rather bizarre parallel, Lincoln compares the many victims of the Mississippi lynchings to "the native Spanish moss," describing both "as a drapery of the forest" (I:110). He then mentions the very recent lynching of a mulatto man in St. Louis. These examples are not explored in detail; they are concrete cases of "the effects of mob law" which are "becoming more and more frequent" (I:110). Leaving decisions to the will of the people is not working. It is perilous when wildness has its way.

After offering concrete evidence of mob violence, Lincoln shows how this outrage is related to the perpetuation of institutions. He is not as concerned with the loss of human life ("comparatively speaking, but a small evil") as he is with what lynchings symbolize at the national level of politics. "Abstractly considered, the hanging . . . was of but little consequence" (I:110). The greater cause for alarm is the way these murderous acts symbolize national chaos: the rule of "mob law." In the confusion of mobocracy citizens cannot rely on, not to mention preserve, "the edifice of liberty and equal rights" they inherited. Read Lincoln at length:

> When men take it in their heads today, to hang gamblers, or burn murderers, they should recollect, that, in the con-

fusion usually attending such transactions, they will be as likely to hang or burn some one, who is neither a gambler or a murderer as one who is; and that, acting upon the example they set, the mob of tomorrow, may, and probably will, hang or burn some of them, by the very same mistake. And not only so; the violations of law in every shape, alike with the guilty, fall victims to the ravages of mob law; and thus it goes on, step by step, till all walls erected for the defence of the persons and property of individuals, are trodden down and disregarded. (I: 110–11)

The legalistic Lincoln's only argument against rule by mob law is that it is inexpedient, that it can backfire at the expense of innocent people. The fabric of law and order which mobocracy would unravel prevents this confusion.

Thus far Lincoln has established only that the national chaos implicit in mob violence is inconvenient. He is appealing to those who drape forests with bodies unless convinced that the next body might well be their own. These delinquent citizens obey laws only because they wish to avoid punishment, and break them whenever they think they can get away with it. One must, like Clay, speak the language of expedience to them. But Lincoln does not restrict himself to this language. The next sentence after the lengthy passage just cited reads: "But all this even, is not the full extent of the evil" (I: 111). Just as he moved from the ordinary case to the abstract level of national crisis, Lincoln now assesses the impact of mob violence on tradition.

At this cool level of capacious forecast, Lincoln deploys his distinction between virtuous citizens and delinquent ones who obey laws only for "dread of punishment" (I: 111). Virtuous citizens are aware of their inheritance, the traditional significance of law and order, and their duty to transmit these values: these are the "best citizens." Lincoln fears that in the confusion of mob law both kinds of citizen will become disengaged from law and order: the virtuous will lose heart while the corrupt will lose the fear of reprisal. This disengagement would, in effect, undermine the foundation of our political institutions: "Thus, then, by the operation of this mobocratic spirit . . . the strongest bulwark of a Government . . . may effectually be broken down and destroyed—I mean the *attachment* of the People" (I: 111).

Lincoln is emphatic about not threatening citizens' attachment (if not in the heart then at least in the mind) to the laws. He discusses this national resource and the way disregard for law would deplete it:

> I know the American People are *much* attached to their Government;—I know they would suffer much for its sake. . . . Yet, notwithstanding all this, if the laws be continually despised and disregarded . . . the alienation of their affections from the Government is the natural consequence; and to that, sooner or later, it must come. (I: 112)

This passage is written in the language of linear time with themes of virtue surviving in the future event of corruption; even the best citizens will become alienated if corruption sets in now. The hearts of the best citizens and the laws must be knitted together in a "fair fabric" so as to avoid the confusion of our wildest passions. Offering a glimpse of the scenario he paints at the end of the address, Lincoln speculates here about where this confusion might lead if the best citizens' affections are carried away by the winds of time. The fair fabric of liberty, knitted by citizens in the tradition of Jefferson, is the natural prey of those who wish to dominate, who burn with the desire to usurp rather than to perpetuate institutions: "men of sufficient talent and ambition will not be wanting to seize the opportunity, strike the blow, and overturn that fair fabric, which for the last half-century, has been the fondest hope, of the lovers of freedom, throughout the world" (I: 111–12). The predator whom we must fortify against shares our stock but would rob the Jeffersonian grave of its embalmed principles.

The greatest evil of mob violence, then, is neither the particular lives lost, nor the endangerment of personal safety; instead it is the alienation of popular "affections" in the hearts of the citizenry. Lost lives bring sorrow to particular families. The loss of personal safety places the entire nation in risk of confusion. But alienation, the last and greatest evil, marks the unraveling of that fair fabric it is our duty to keep "undecayed by lapse of time." Lincoln's political religion is a measure designed to prevent the alienation of popular affections from the government.

The third part of this address opens as Lincoln asks, "How shall we fortify ourselves" against the dangers represented by mob violence? Please recall that these dangers include the usurpation of a republic corrupted and crippled by alienated affections by "ambitious and talented" men. When citizens lose their affection for the law there will be no tradition or "public" available to frustrate emerging tyrants. Mobocracy, then, is very much on the side of the silent artillery of time. Only a secular act of reverence for law and order can prevent its victory. This is the context of his plea for political religion.

> The answer [to the fortification problem] is simple. Let every American, every lover of liberty, every well wisher to his posterity, swear by the blood of the Revolution, never to violate in the least particular, the laws of the country; and never to tolerate their violation by others. As the patriots of seventy-six did to the support of the Declaration of Independence, so to the support of the Constitution and Laws, let every American pledge his life, his property, and his sacred honor;—let every man remember that to violate the law, is to trample on the blood of his father, and to tear the character [charter?] of his own, and his children's liberty. Let reverence for the laws . . . become the political religion of the nation. (I:112)

The best citizens do not merely obey laws, they revere them in the memory of their origin, and in the anticipation of their future. Wrapping up the original founding of the nation, its present foundation, and its future in one politically religious moment of sovereignty, Lincoln hopes to avoid the chaotic side effects of the passage of time. Because popular affections are strong *today*, the Republic has survived; it is on the strength of devoted citizens that "every attempt to subvert our national freedom" might reasonably be overcome. Political religion, then, Lincolnian is a strategy in the name of Jefferson to avert the national crises Clay was so adept at addressing.

At the end of this section of the Lyceum Address it is still not clear why this plea for law and order necessarily requires a creation of tradition *now*, though Lincoln does seek to establish an interpretation of the past "out of time" as the origin for present authority (Pocock's definition of creating tradition.) But why create tradition *now* in Lincoln's generation? The next section of the address describes two hypothetical cases which suggest an answer to this question.

Why Create a Tradition Now?

Lincoln anticipates such a question: "But, it may be asked, why suppose danger to our political institutions? Have we not preserved them for more than fifty years? And why may we not for fifty times as long?" (I:113). He points out "that our government should have been maintained in its original form from its establishment until now, is not much to be wondered at" (I:113). Why? The experiment, because it was new, "had many props to support it through that period" (I:113). These props, however, are no longer available. What "props" are these? First, there once was the thrill of engaging in an undecided experiment. But it is no longer undecided. Second, one could pursue personal ends such as celebrity, fame, and distinction, by working to establish the "sacred" proposition: "the capability of a people to govern itself" (I:113). But such an "inseparable" link between personal ambition and public service is no longer possible now that the Republic is established. "This field of glory is harvested, and the crop is already appropriated" (I:113). The props that supported our ancestors "now are decayed, and crumbled away" (I:113). This is why it is necessary now to create and sustain new props, to create a traditional order. Hence the crying need for political religion.

Lincoln feels that a chief problem with the construction of a new set of props—political religion—is the historically established fact that "new reapers [of glory] will arise, and *they*, too, will seek a field" (I:113). He poses the problem in this way to those who would dispute it: "It is to deny, what the history of the world tells us is true, to suppose that men of ambition and talents will not continue to spring up amongst us. And, when they do, they will as naturally seek the gratification of their ruling passion, as others have done before them" (I:113). If these wild, passionate creatures can gratify their ruling passion by "supporting and maintaining an edifice that has been erected by others" (I:114), then they might not have to be domesticated; but Lincoln realizes that they would instead be dedicated to their own creations. Those who belong to "the family of the lion, or the tribe of the eagle" (I:114), hunger to see their own dominion, to conceive their own order, to make their own laws. "Towering genius disdains a beaten path"; "it thirsts and burns for distinction . . ." (I:114). Because the Republic cannot put the energies of such creatures to use, they must neutralize them.[12]

Lincoln uses this example of those who would emerge "boldly" to dismantle the Republic because there is "nothing left to be done in the way of building up" (I:114) to teach the need for a strong national defense, for a new set of props. Neutralizing a tyrant "will require the people to be united with each other, attached to the government and law, and generally intelligent, to successfully frustrate his designs" (I:114). The need for political religion is more pressing now than ever before because the Republic must now check the advances of ruthless members who would corrupt the Republic unless they are successfully "frustrated" by a politically religious, devoted following of citizens.

The new props differ from the old in that they are designed to support and maintain the edifice of liberty and equal rights, while the old were designed to erect it. If the new supports are not activated, we as a nation of free citizens will die by our own hand: one of our own will usurp the nation's foundation. Lincoln now moves to "another reason which *once was* [conducive to the health of the Republic]; but which, to the same extent, is now no more" (I:114).

It was once possible to enlist the passions of the people as an emotional prop for the republican experiment, but it is no longer possible to rely on these passions. Everyone, strong and weak alike, is to be neutralized, or domesticated. We must read closely to discover why. "Revolutionary" emotions were advantageous to the Republic during its conception and birth. "But this state of feeling must fade, is fading, has faded, with the circumstances that produced it" (I:115). Because it is subject to the flow of time, this emotional state is unreliable. Let Lincoln speak for himself:

The scenes of the revolution . . . must fade upon the memory of the world, and grow more and more dim by the lapse of time . . . their influence cannot be what it heretofore has been. . . . nearly every adult male had been a participator in some of its scenes. The consequence was . . . a living history was to be found in every family . . . in the limbs mangled, in the scars of wounds received. But *those* histories are gone. They *can* be read no more forever. They *were* a fortress of strength; but what invading foeman could *never do*, the silent artillery of time *has done* the levelling of its walls. They are gone. (I: 115)

Just as the first two "props"—the thrill of a new experiment and the gratification of ruling passion—are no longer available, so the emotional prop of participating in the rebellion is now gone. The silent artillery of time will defeat any order which relies solely on particularistic feeling, one generation at a time. Lincoln's generation must break this silence.[13]

Concluding the Lyceum Address

Two remaining paragraphs must be considered. Lincoln needs to show us how to replace the old props with some that can withstand the passage of time. He does this by connecting religious devotion (to laws) to the reason of logocentric order. Political religion is not a mindlessly passionate affair for Lincoln. Rather it is "hewn from the solid quarry of sober reason" (I: 115). We are again reminded that "passion has helped us but can do so no more" (I: 115). From now on a premium must be placed on the perpetuation of political institutions. "In particular," writes Lincoln, "unimpassioned reason" must "be moulded" into "a reverence for the constitution and laws" (I: 115). Only by neutralizing the passions with political religion can the Republic maintain the integrity of the "proud fabric of freedom."

Devotion, Citizenship, Temperance

Lincoln has "sober" reason in mind when he moves to neutralize the distempered passions. As we shall see, no citizen is immune from his invitation to join the traditional order.

The Lyceum Address shows the need for political religion but does not give a method of implementing it. The Temperance Address is a metaphorical statement whose central metaphor, alcohol, serves well to represent the now troublesome passions (I:271). Read in this way, this address sheds further light on how Lincoln would go about creating a new traditional order. While staying close to the text, I am presuming that alcohol is a metaphor.

This talk is given to the Washington Society on George Washington's birthday, providing Lincoln with a chance for political reminiscence. He addresses the need for a moral revolution to save our precious memories of 1776 from intemperate passions and the winds of time. This is an attempt to show how to implement the political religion he devises in the Lyceum Address.

Lincoln issues a reminder that our ancestors began the hope for a free society by establishing a foundation, but that it remains our task to perpetuate these institutions. Only our work can allow their inspiration its universal significance. Consider:

> Of our political revolution of '76, we all are justly proud. It has given us a degree of political freedom, far exceeding that of any other of the nations of the earth. In it the world has found a solution to that long mooted problem, as to the capability of man to govern himself. In it was the germ which has vegetated and still is to grow and expand into the universal liberty of mankind. (I:278)

An immediate question is how to interpret the organicism here. Will freedom grow naturally after its birth, or is it necessary to work hard at cultivating it? Is liberty found in the wild or in domestication? As we might expect, Lincoln has domestication on the agenda; he wishes to cultivate a moral influence which will keep passion out of politics.

Lincoln writes that the cause of rescuing original principles from temporal passions has come alive. It is breathing, and with an activated citizenry will breathe new life into those "prostrate in the chains of moral death." The new cause can be most effectively advanced by citizens recovering from passions of their own. These citizens are most likely to be sympathetic to the plight of their brothers and sisters. "Those who have suffered intemperance personally and have reformed are the most powerful and efficient instruments to push the reformation to ultimate success" (I:272). The strangeness of the metaphor is most pronounced here; imagine a zealous citizen recovering from a passionate devotion to a nation. But recall that Lincoln has no room for wild citizens or mobocracy. Note also the instrumentalism in Lincoln's approach; his moral revolution is the means to the perpetuation of political institutions.

Yet those who have not suffered also have a part to play in this dramatic domestication effort. The good of the whole requires that all citizens be politically religious: work for temperance. The newly reformed person needs "every moral support and influence . . . every moral prop" to guard against backsliding. The burden of sacrifice, that others might live morally free from intemperance, is shared; "all can give that will." The stakes are the survival of the Republic itself: "And who shall be excused that can and will not. Far around as human breath has ever blown, he [the Egyptian angel of death] keeps our fathers, our brothers, our sons, and our friends, prostrate in the chains of moral death" (I:278).

As the "noble ally" of the goal of political freedom, the moral revolution against the passions is expected to grant hegemony to "all-conquering mind." This victory of the mind over the body also signifies a defeat of the passage of time. Accordingly, such a victory would restore Washington (or the principles of 1776 which are for Lincoln better indicated by the name Jefferson)[14] to a position of "shining in deathless splendor." The wildness of the passions is banished in the name of deathless splendor.

Lincoln is explicit about this struggle against the lapse of time, and about the way he has been using alcohol mostly for metaphorical purposes, in the closing paragraphs of his address. We have seen that he feels it is necessary to immortalize the principles of the Union by overcoming passions which can no longer be diverted, by actively supporting moral temperance, and religiously obeying laws, thereby giving hope to all those who have not yet come over to the side of the mind.

Elsewhere Lincoln draws these threads together as he puts a significant twist on a familiar story. First read the familiar part:

It is said an Eastern monarch once charged his wise men to invent him a sentence, to be ever in view, and which should be true and appropriate in all times and situations. They presented him the words: "And this, too, shall pass away." How much it expresses! How chastening in the hour of pride! How consoling in the depths of affliction! "And this, too, shall pass away." (III:481–82)

If Lincoln had stopped here on the note of a limited politics, chastening those prideful Machiavellians who would work to extend the longevity of the regime, this story would pose serious difficulties to my interpretation of his statecraft. But his version of the story continues with a twist:

Let us hope, rather, that by the best cultivation of this physical world, beneath and around us; and the intellectual and moral world within us, we shall secure an individual, social and political prosperity and happiness, whose course shall be onward and upward, and which, while the earth endures, shall not pass away. (III:482)

The silent artillery of time can be answered only by our collective moral revolution, says Lincoln, in a curious appeal to the pocketbooks of his high-minded audience. Wildness is lost, and individual remunity couples awkwardly with collective communion, as if to maintain the deathless splendor of continuity across time.

From Creation to Transmission of Tradition

This chapter opens with Lincoln at Gettysburg saying words which the world has not long forgotten, telling heirs to the American Revolution of 1776 that the days of dedication are over, that it is high time for a large measure of devotion. This "ruthlike" devotion requires us to adopt the principles laid down by our ruthless forefathers. Political religion is designed to entrench a reasonable semblance of order so that the Republic can repulse threats to its longevity. Political religion is installed as passion's "other." Reading Lincoln permits an excellent illustration of the bind of modern liberalism: Lincoln grants clear hegemony to national interest because he has a crisis on his hands; we tend to grant hegemony to our personal lives because we live in times of ordinary administration. Foucault shows how disciplined we are in our so-called freedom. Lincoln would not flinch in his manly defense of national interest if it were ever threatened by civil disobedience. He could appear to embrace the spirit of forgiveness (as those who worship the Second Inaugural are fond of repeating), but he manages this only after victory is secured. Machiavelli would admire Lincolnian statecraft. It worked precisely because it was not what it appeared to be. People boarded the republican wagon of their own free will, under the banner of shining liberty, and not because their brothers and sisters who refused to still their distempered passions were gunned down. And once aboard they continued to embody the dilemma (of being parts responsible for the whole) associated with any struggle against time, the dilemma and struggle which Jaffa (1959) and Thurow (1976), but not Lincoln, would spare them. When not claiming outright immunity, they pay their debts to the forefathers (remunity) and dream of sharing a common humanity (communion). The idea of mutual defense and giving freely in the name of neutralizing oppositions—division of labor, North/ South, male/female, property a and property b—is completely foreign to this kind of republican politics. Difference is reduced to these oppositions.

The creation of a political tradition is, of course, only one of the forces of reassurance in the Pocock model. Transmission is the other. Neither creation nor transmission of traditions is possible without presupposing the reassuring passage of linear time. Lincoln opposed the flow of time by creating a religiously civic tradition which forced citizens to worship collective laws in the name of individual liberty. In the next chapter I examine Burke's preoccupation with extending a way of life, or a "fabric of states," across time, as opposed to the projects of his revolutionary colleagues who would defend the individual rights of man.

Pocock mentions Burke by name during the construction of his model of traditionalism. Burke is far less concerned with the actual origin of the system he fought to perpetuate than with maximizing continuity. Continuity is all the more crucial for Burke because he senses arbitrary or irrational elements at play in the world. He gives the impression of being prepared to go to almost any extreme, even to the "blindest prejudice," to avoid giving in to the irrational. And yet, Burke cannot seem to admit his deepest prejudice without undermining the traditionalism of his less fundamental prejudice.

This part of the book illustrates efforts to extend collective self-images across time. This chapter has attempted to show that Lincoln's work illustrates the innovative dimension of Pocock's model. To take issue with Lincoln's authoritarian plea for religious devotion to law usually means to stress the continuity of the individual. Individuals are asked in time of crisis to stand united. It comes as no surprise, then, that citizens who have been denied pathos for the sake of the Union should become apathetic.

The next chapter offers a reading of Edmund Burke's approach to the problem of time. Unlike Lincoln, Burke was more concerned with the transmission than the creation of traditions. Burke resembles Lincoln in his view that the passage of time can unravel the fabric of a national political system. And yet Burke seems more anxious. Whereas Lincoln presents life outside the political forms he perpetuates as dominated by foreign powers, Burke draws close to describing such life in terms of personal derangement and bewilderment. But Burke necessarily stops short of such an indictment. He cannot confess this danger without betraying his project of traditionalism. My task is to study how this sensitive writer, Burke, can gesture toward total derangement without confessing that it is always already at hand.

6 The Power of Fear in Burkean Traditionalism

The reassurance Burke would provide is, from my perspective, especially revealing because some of his writings come perilously close to the very absurdities, such as epistemological insanity, and ever-present primordial chaos, often associated with extravagant claims. While I do not wish to say that Burke was ahead of his time—whatever that might mean—reading his work allows me to show that sensitive work in political theory sometimes attempts to cover its tracks after it wanders near the edge of reason and order. Such a focus might help make sense of contemporary assaults on sense-making.

Edmund Burke lived his "missing years" on both sides of the edge of nervous collapse. During two of the worst years, in his early twenties, he received care in the home of a physician named Nugent; shortly thereafter he married Dr. Nugent's daughter, Jane. In a poem (hereafter called *Epistle*) young Burke describes himself meeting Nugent:

> 'Tis now two Autumns, since he chanc'd to find,
> A youth of Body broke, infirm of mind. (Burke, 1958–71,
>   I:117)[1]

The lines which immediately follow and continue his self-assessment offer a glimpse of his fearful nature.

Burke first reassures Nugent that he is recovering, though he admits being confused about what to do with his life. He appears to be ambivalent about wealth. Wealth would, he says, solve many of his problems but he cannot find the energy to pursue it.

> Mean time ten thousand cares distract my Life,
> And keep me always with myself at Strife;
> Too indolent on flying Wealth to seize,
> Of wealth too covetous to be at ease. (118)

Isaac Kramnick (1977:69–87) notices Burke's ambivalence to wealth, and extends the objects of Burke's ambivalence to include ambition and sexuality. But Kramnick becomes preoccupied with ambivalence and obscures the specific role of fear in Burke's early thought. I shall attempt to concentrate on the element of fear without ignoring his ambivalence.

The next lines in *Epistle* mention Burke's attraction to the heights of rational speculation (Kramnick interprets this as lofty social ambitions). Consider:

> I look at Wisdom, wonder, and Adore
> I look, I wonder, but I do no more. (118)

Standing alone, these lines might indicate that Burke is as ambivalent about "Wisdom" as he is about wealth, but they are better read as part of his announcement that he will shy away from the dizzying heights of rational speculation. Burke wishes, after all, to assure Nugent that recovery is imminent. But what is the relation of fear to this decision to keep his feet on the ground?

Burke tells us that he is wary of what certain of his enlightened contemporaries have called "Wisdom" because he fears for his health:

Timrous the Heights of every thing I fear,
Perhaps even Wisdom may be bought too Dear,
The Tortoise snatch'd aloft, to highest Air,
Was high 'tis true, but was not happy there. (118)

Whether one reads this as an allusion to Avianus, Aesop, or John Ogilby's (1668) paraphrase of Aesop—in which the tortoise cries, "Ah, must I creep, still as I were asleep!" and the eagle chides the tortoise before making him pay for venturing out of his depth, "Now for thy insolence I'll strip thee from thy shell/Cheaper thou might'st have seen the Gates of Hell (Ogilby, 1668/1965:133–34)—the tortoise was not only "not happy" when he aspired to a universal point of view, he was totally unable to cope. The price of the tortoise's Wisdom was, in all accounts of the fable, his being hurled to the ground.[2] Humans attempting to discover a correspondence between their world and the universe are similarly out of their element, according to the recovering Burke.[3]

Immediately after the Aesop allusion, Burke explains that he has no choice but to side with skepticism, to reject truth-seeking as an end in itself. To do otherwise would be, he feels, to pretend to the outside world that he can cope at the heights of speculation, to disguise his turmoil.

Shall I then vapour in a stoic strain,
Who, while I boast, must writhe myself for Pain. (118)

To avoid this, Burke decides to adopt a "creeping" lifestyle. That is, he rules out any rational style other than a healthy skepticism, substituting the practicality of prudence for the speculation of "Wisdom." While such a life-style may not be as glamorous as one of rational speculation, it does offer a certain security.

> Shall I, who grope my way with purblind Eyes,
> Shall such as I, pretend to dogmatise?
> Better in one low path secure to crawl,
> To Doubt of all things, and to Learn from all. (118)

While Burke retains an ambivalence to wealth, and his sexuality may well have been as complicated as Kramnick indicates, he is unequivocally opposed to speculation about connections between "Universal" and human order.[4] Indeed, he assures his future father-in-law that Jane will be happy with Burke firmly planted on the "ground"; "I will not wrong her in this creeping stile" (118).

I am not interested here in Burke's "missing years" from a biographical point of view, but I am intrigued by this early episode in his life because I shall later suggest that his treatment of traditionalism as prejudice, if it is to work as a theory, requires fearing a primordial derangement. Burke needs the silence of an absent ground so as to supply grounds (or break silence) with prejudice. But this requirement for the construction of prejudice, and all of the ambivalence it makes possible, is also the key to its deconstruction.

Burke on Constitutional Change

Burke's views on constitutional change over time are well-known. His *Reflections* advocates preserving any feature of a constitution which is working reasonably well, changing only the "peccant" parts. This arrangement is designed to maximize health and continuity across time. Burke writes:

> Our political system is placed in a just correspondence and symmetry with the order of the world, and with the mode of existence decreed to a permanent body composed of transitory parts; wherein, by the disposition of a stupendous wisdom, moulding together the great mysterious incorporation of the human race, the whole, at one time, is never old, or middle-aged, or young, but, in a condition of unchangeable constancy, moves on through the varied tenor of perpetual

decay, fall, renovation, and progression. Thus, by preserving the method of nature in the conduct of the state, in what we improve we are never wholly new, in what we retain, we are never wholly obsolete. (Burke, 1902, II:307)

Some readers might be tempted, if asked to offer an example of Burke's "permanent body composed of transitory parts," to think, for example, of the U.S. Senate requiring one-third of its members to stand for reelection every two years. But this example presupposes a constitutional stipulation, whereas Burke is describing constitutional stipulations in general. Notice that Burke is comparing politics and nature. How one reads him on political systems is bound to be influenced by how one imagines he views the "method" of nature. And this requires mentioning his relation to natural law.

Highly reassuring versions of natural law allow that human subjects are sufficiently reasonable to detect timeless principles which can then influence their behavior. Burke, however, seems to presume attunement with principles of natural law only after political order is established.[5] If nature has no fixed order, it is not reasonable to follow its order in the name of continuity. But Burke attributes to nature a "sure principle of transmission, without at all excluding a principle of improvement." Thus, when all is going well in politics, he can reasonably "presume" that nature's path is being followed.

The problem with such a presumption is that it does not offer guidance in times of turmoil. Thus Burke needs either to locate a guide or to risk new generations not learning the very principles he would perpetuate. There is a gap between the political order which, insofar as it works, can at best be presumed to follow nature's order, and the natural order which one cannot use as a guide. Until this gap is bridged, citizens and leaders are likely to be at a loss for guidance each time their population changes. Even status quo politics must face such problems as population shifts and recruitment of new leaders.

Burke's *Reflections* proposes to bridge the gap with national prejudice, a concept which he finds reassuring, or more time-resistant, than the more whimsical concept of human reason. Burke is fond of the metaphorical word *fabric*, which signifies a material that can be stretched, in his case, across generations to defend against the malice of time. When this fabric is torn, efforts must be made to repair it; but so long as it is whole, one can presume that it has been knitted in accordance with the laws of nature. Whatever happens, the "fabric of august states" must never be torn asunder, because this would open wide the gulf between the convention of human projects and the presumed world of nature.[6] Prejudice, then, works as a cohesive agent in Burke's thought. By maintaining national prejudice, making adjustments where necessary, his statecraft is designed to transmit political principles across time. This can be called *traditionalism.*

Some of the more effective strategies of statecraft involve diversionary tactics. One need not turn to Machiavelli to realize that, all other things being equal, armies preoccupied with fighting on one front are the least likely to notice movements on another front. Much of Burke's argument in *Reflections* can be read as just such a diversionary tactic. By creating an opposition between the high and low roads of nature, he succeeds in drawing the attention of armies of readers away from what is arguably his most haunting question: how are primordial chaos and human convention related? That is, the way Burke advocates blind prejudice in *Reflections* is itself a blind. Readers attempting to come to grips with the high-road versus the low-road debate may fail to notice that their attention is being drawn away from the more fundamental question of primordial chaos. In this way, even those who ultimately reject it are likely to be slowly settled by Burkean traditionalism. Perhaps this is part of the reason why conservative political theorists are not alone in their rejection of postmodern inquiry.

I shall read familiar passages from Burke's *Reflections* and attempt to explain how the argument on national prejudice works. Burke draws a line between the savagery of rational speculation and the enlightenment of blind prejudice, assumes his position on the so-called enlightened side, and puts all of his strength into supporting it. His moves can each be explained in the language of fear. As I read Burke's defense of traditionalism I shall explore the fears that are mobilized, sequestered, pushed out of all bounds whatsoever.

Burke's writing is filled with images of fear. These include the incapacitating fear of the consequenees of overheated imaginary voyages, but also the awe-inspiring fear of the more "exalted" ranks of society. His early *Vindication* and *Inquiry* illustrate these two aspects of fear. They are not opposite extremes in his early writings. Indeed, these aspects of fear have nothing whatsoever in common. The incapacitating fear insists that one turn away from rational speculation, while the awe-filled fear is caused by precisely such a turn as this. Just as it is misleading to place a condition which can vary—for example, a complicated written history—and its precondition—literacy—in a polar tension, so it makes little sense to speak of fear ranging from the negative connotation of naked, shivering savagery to the positive one of sublime astonishment.[7] Avoiding the negative connotation is a precondition of developing polar tensions in general; sequestering negative fear makes writing about positive fear possible.[8] Only after terrible fears are allayed can one begin to speak of the sublime. Mary Warnock (1976:59) has seen this: "The English writers on the sublime, and especially Burke, had called attention to the need, if we are to think of the grander aspects of nature as sublime rather than simply as horrifying, to contemplate them with a lively sense of their own security." I wish to study why Burke, in well-known sections of *Reflections*, attempts to present positive and negative fear as if they were opposites in a tension, instead of treating the suppression of the latter as an act which makes orderly tension possible. By concentrating on how his argument works, I attempt to gesture toward an aspect of fear which, I suggest, Burke was perhaps too terrified to encourage readers to detect. The power of this unmentionable fear lies in what theorists are forced to do to keep it out of their writing. In most cases the effort to perpetuate political forms is a fight against the flux of formlessness. But rather than face the problem of formlessness, theorists enlist our support in more-mentionable endeavors, such as perpetuating political institutions across time. These efforts draw attention away from the fact that certain forms, such as the line of time, are presupposed, or taken to be natural.

Getting followers to endorse uncritically one's position while asking them to decide another, less fundamental, position is a tried-and-true political strategy. Appreciating what Burke could not reveal openly is an important part of overcoming the hold that traditionalism, and conventional criticism of it, have on political thinking.

When I mention the power of fear in relation to traditionalism I wish to indicate three different, if overlapping, qualities: fear as a force Burke mobilizes to urge others to accept his claim; fear as a means of adorning everyday politics; and fear as an unmentionable terror dominating Burke's claim and forcing him to write an agenda of avoidance. I call these the three faces of the power of fear. The first, a fear of the consequences of asking too many fundamental questions, is a negative power Burke uses to threaten those who would undermine the status quo while it is still fundamentally healthy. This is akin to a fear of the unknown and it is powerful in that it can keep fairly satisfied people in line: its message is that things could be worse. The second, a fear of awesome powers-that-be, is a sublime feeling which, according to Burke, rewards those who learn to celebrate hierarchies of authority. This is also a fear of the unknown, but Burke finds it more reassuring because it is based on shared understanding. The third face of the power of fear is the fear which Burke refuses to confess. It refuses to be domesticated, bounded, or even pushed "outside." Burkean prejudice calls attention away from this powerful force by pretending to place positive and negative fear in a tension. But in principle nothing can defeat the unnamable fear because it has always already written the agenda of traditionalism. This agenda is designed to avoid the question of how to reconcile primordial chaos and political conventions.

The Problem of Burke's Ambivalence: An Overview

Much of Burke's writing is constructed in terms of polar tensions, for example, ambivalence or continua. Kramnick shows that in *Vindication* Burke is torn between radical indictment and conservative apologia. And in *Inquiry* the sublime ranges from astonishment to awe. But these polar tensions are possible only because Burke pushes out the undesirable aspects of life, where they are neglected, or silenced. In *Vindication*, Burke fluctuates between a defense of society and a denouncement of its practices in a way that presupposes the possibility of society. One can sense doubts about the foundations of society lurking in the margins of this skillfully designed text. But his fears of the consequences of relying on a natural foundation share nothing with his love/hate attachment to society and therefore cannot be plotted on the continuum occupied by these contradictory sentiments. Similarly, in *Inquiry*, the "simply terrible" is neglected, left out of the continuum of lower to higher forms of the sublime. The simply terrible—for example, being attacked by a wild dog—has nothing in common with the sublime and thus cannot participate with it. Worse, it can always reawaken and destroy the illusions which fuel the sublime. Only by exiling the fear of consequences and the simply terrible is it possible to form the orderly tensions which constitute Burke's thoughts on traditionalism.

Pocock (1973:237) uses *tradition* to name "an indefinite series of repetitions of an action." His works, especially his models, permit readers to sense the similarities in the various ways theorists like Burke attempt to transmit, intercept, and scramble messages across time. Pocock understands the importance to Burkean traditionalism of not asking too many fundamental questions. If a tradition is working, why spoil things by asking for a detailed account of it, especially of its origins? Prejudice, as you might expect, serves remarkably well the purpose of stressing the transmission (as opposed to the creation) of tradition. Blind prejudice, as a tool of statecraft, saves theorists from having to explain why the status quo is worth preserving, why hegemonic power relations are justified, why nondecisions remain in effect. Prejudice allows theorists to treat negative fear as if it were merely the absence of law and order. Whereas, without prejudice, negative fear can signify facing the terror or silent madness of the absence of positive/negative relations of any variety whatsoever.

But how is it possible to exclude the utter confusion of unbounded chaos? The simply terrible aspects of life must be forced outside the territory within which theorists like Burke construct traditionalism by defending prejudice. Here we can catch a glimpse of the formidable difficulty I am trying to illustrate. Burke needs an outside chaos to justify inside prejudice, but if chaos is as terrible as his defense of prejudice leads us to believe, the concept of prejudice itself becomes problematic. That is, if life outside bounds is simply terrible, it cannot be expected to obey the inside/outside bounds of a theoretical discussion. If the wolf at the door has never stopped huffing and puffing, the house is always already tumbling down. But if life outside bounds is not simply terrible, Burke's rationale for tolerating blind prejudice cannot work.[9]

Burke's *Reflections* ignores this difficulty and treats the positive and negative aspects of fear as polar opposites. This, of course, is like inviting the wolf at the door in for dinner in the hope of domesticating it. But, in principle, one can never domesticate what is wildly confusing beyond belief. To catch Burke in the act of pretending to domesticate the wildness he seems to fear, I wish to turn to the *Reflections* and to show how his work leads us to believe that negative fear and positive fear can work in tandem. This will eventually uncover a hidden prejudice about the fixed relation between thinking and forms of order and reason—such as the line of time—in Burkean traditionalism.

Placing Positive and Negative Fear in a Tension

Burke opens *Reflections* (1902, II:277–518) by refusing to follow a formal method because such reasoning cannot do justice to the tragicomedy of 1789 (284). "Astonished" by the French Revolution, he is uncertain whether to tremble in horror or to laugh derisively. Others in England are sympathetic to the Revolutionaries, however, and Burke decides first to show why their claims are deficient. This he does by reviewing three arguments defended by the sympathetic Revolution Society. Specifically, Burke wishes to dispense with the claims that France is only exercising its rights to choose a government to cashier its governors and to frame a government of its liking. At issue in this opening maneuver is not whether Burke agrees with Machiavelli's principle of purgation. Burke understands how to purge elements of the past by remaining silent about them.[10] Rather, Burke finds France's ruthless actions to be unnecessary because conditions do not yet, in his estimation, warrant a purge. The French act too swiftly, too soon, undermining their strengths while addressing their evils. Burke charges France with acting "as if you had never been moulded into civil society, and had everything to begin anew" (309). Beginning anew is tragicomic unless all order has eroded. According to Burke, France has sufficient order to preserve its traditions.

Burke next asks how, if conditions are not ripe for revolution, a violent purge can have taken place. He blames this "election of evil" on the composition of the National Assembly (313–18). While critical of the personal qualifications of many of the members of this democratic body, Burke is most exercised by the boundlessness of its power. "Nothing in heaven or upon earth can serve as a control on them" (318). Instead of viewing this situation as a state of sovereignty, Burke describes it as one of "unbounded power": "In such a state of unbounded power for undefined and undefinable purposes, the evil of a moral and almost physical inaptitude of the man to the function must be the greatest we can conceive to happen in the management of human affairs" (319). The evil of an "inaptitude of the man to the function" can be, for Burke, avoided by living in a bounded system. His famous "little platoon" metaphor is marshalled at this point in the text: "To be attached to the subdivision, to love the little platoon we belong to in society, is the first principle (the germ as it were) of public affections. It is the first link in the series by which we proceed towards a love to our country, and to mankind" (320). Burke is content neither with merely establishing a smoothly functioning system of platoons or subdivisions, nor with establishing a philosophical system of first and second principles. For Burke "art is man's nature." The attachment of persons to their local districts is a germ which might grow into public affection. The continuity signified by *series* is not, here, only a continuity over time, but also a continuity across space (from the geographical subdivision to the nation as a whole).[11]

The alternative to living this continuity is a chaos too horrible to anticipate. Burke describes how confusion is the enemy of any fixed order:

> Confounded by the complication of distempered passions, their reason is disturbed; their views become vast and perplexed, to others inexplicable; to themselves uncertain. They find, on all sides, bounds to their unprincipled ambition in any fixed order of things; but in the fog and haze of confusion all is enlarged, and appears without any limit. (320)

Thus Burke distinguishes between high and low natures, placing lives of discipline and control on the side of the high-and-mighty. He accuses the French of having "strayed out of the high road of nature" (325). And on this ground he firmly rejects their revolution.

But Burke does not spend most of his time in *Reflections* fluctuating in mock ambivalence between the tragic and comic aspects of the French experience. He soon moves to place the negative sense of fear in a tension with the positive sense. I find this tension most difficult because it introduces a face of power which Burke never manages to name, not to mention overcome.

The first step in fixing the high and low roads of nature as opposites is to establish both as forms of nature. Only when the two can share a common denominator can a continuum between them become possible. Burke does this by equating the two roads of nature with a more well-known distinction between rational speculation and empirical observation, and then associating the low road of nature with rational speculation.

Burke next turns to this point in a section on the dangers of applying metaphysical insights to political conventions. For Burke "the clumsy subtilty of . . . political metaphysics" (331) has no place in the world of politics. He writes: "If civil society be the offspring of convention, that convention must be its law. That convention must limit and modify all the descriptions of constitution which are formed under it. Every sort of . . . power are its creatures" (332). Burke is suspicious of beautiful, subtle arguments because they tend to disregard limits in general. Boundless speculation, he fears, can lead to chaos and bewilderment. This suggests that speculation may lead to the animalism of the low road of nature: being "subtilized into savagery." The high road of nature is conventional; a limited, repressed arena which curbs the bestial licentiousness of the low road. Metaphysical arguments about the rights of man are ultimately ruinous. Burke scorns them as folly but fears their effect.

According to Burke, the high road of nature made possible by convention is obviously preferable to the sophisticated animalism of the Revolution Society. The vicious manner in which he next attacks their endorsement of the French Revolution illustrates this. But Burke needs to show how convention and artifice are in any way natural. This passage is perhaps one of his more renowned, in part because of its passionate imagery. Here Burke contrasts the aristocratic status quo he would conserve with the brutish world defended by Dr. Price, a world characterized by the "dissoluteness of extravagant speculation." This passage establishes the natural quality of conventional ideas of tradition, limits and order. This is not contradictory of Burke because his point is that people by nature need to remove themselves from "wild and dangerous politics" (337).

It is now natural, according to Burke, to desire to escape the simple terror of one's animalism; it is natural to wish to improve one's condition. It is natural to clothe a naked, shivering nature with a fabric of some sort. In this sense it is natural to escape nature. The low road of nature is "savage and brutal" (352). With the least-common denominator, nature, intact, Burke can now place the high- and low-roads on a continuum and discuss how states become more or less elevated. At one extreme are empirical observations and elevated feelings of appropriately performing one's function; at the other extreme are the wild and dangerous French revolutionaries and the rational speculations of their bewildering friends.[12]

But if this maneuver to establish both roads as natural is to have any empirical content, Burke must describe more substantively the naturalness of political and natural order. He must bridge the gap between convention and nature in an equally obvious way. It is evident that political order cannot be portrayed as a realm of abstract ideas. Burke needs to show us what kind of fabric he would superimpose on the bestial human condition so as to render it less savage and brutal. The missing ingredient is prejudice, which Burke next introduces by showing how the French Revolution has insulted (higher) nature. Burke writes with assurance, if not reassurance: "We are generally men of untaught feelings: that instead of casting away all our old prejudices, we cherish them to a very considerable degree, and, to take more shame to ourselves, we cherish them because they are prejudices; and the longer they have lasted, and the more generally they have prevailed, the more we cherish them" (359). Most prejudice, at least "just prejudice," carries latent wisdom within it, according to Burke. To strip wisdom of its protective layering is dangerous from a strategic point of view. Prejudice is a boon to permanence because it is rooted in peoples' affections: "Prejudice renders a man's virtue his habit; and not a series of unconnected acts. Through just prejudice, his duty becomes a part of his nature" (359). Religion is the chief prejudice Burke wants to bring to our attention: "We know, and what is better, we feel inwardly, that religion is the basis of civil society, and the source of all good, and of all comfort. . . . We know, and it is our pride to know, that man is by his constitution a religious animal; that atheism is against, not only our reason, but our instincts; and that it cannot prevail long" (362–63). By the time Burke considers in detail the specific prejudice undergirding the British political system, he has become accustomed to viewing prejudice, or the conventional, as natural (in his "elevated" sense). God is presumably the almighty artificer, but man's handiwork, in imitation of the Divine, is most important in matters of statecraft. Naked reason is inadequate, though this does not rule out reason and order in a life of prejudice.

Employing the Positive/Negative Fear Distinction

The next passage in *Reflections* I consider is the one in which Burke employs the positive/negative tension. This passage is presented as an examination of prejudice, not a discourse on fear. Burke promises to examine four basic British prejudices— first and foremost, the church and, then, aristocracy, monarchy, and democracy. This promise is given up later when it becomes clear that his treatment of religious prejudice in England has become preoccupied with the French treatment of its clergy. I concentrate on the portion of this passage before it lapses into a critique of the French experience. This early portion is versed quite extensively in the language of fear.

The first paragraph offers an appropriate introduction. The Church Establishment is introduced as being "first, and last, and midst in our minds." And yet Burke will never mention the substance of the theological principles; what matters is that believers acknowledge the limits of a deity and thereby act reasonably and orderly. The opening lines of this passage are clear about the strategic significance of the Church Establishment. Consider: "For, taking ground on that religious system, of which we are now in possession, we continue to act on the early received and uniformly continued sense of mankind" (364). Notice that the Church Establishment is a natural grounding which is also described as an artificial system. It is also difficult not to notice the stress on continuity of transmission in the passage above. Consecration of the state is a means of accomplishing this transmission, a way to "preserve the structure [the august fabric of states] from profanation and ruin."

Further in the same paragraph Burke equates "profane and ruinous" events with those preoccupied with "the paltry pelf of the moment." The idea of immediate gratification sickens Burke, who would domesticate all wild impulses in the name of reason, order, and above all, longevity.[13] Rather than discuss consecration in theological terms, Burke insists that religion is a means to worldly glory. He writes:

> This consecration is made, that all who administer in the government of men . . . should have high and worthy notions of their function and destination; that their hope should be full of immortality; that they should not look to the paltry pelf of the moment, nor to the temporary and transient praise of the vulgar, but to a solid, permanent existence, in the permanent part of their nature, and to a permanent fame and glory, in the example they leave as a rich inheritance to the world. (364)

Burke does use expressions like "the permanent part of their nature," which seem to indicate the possibility of constructing ties to the operations designed by what Hobbes calls the "Almighty Artificer." But his political strategy against the malice of time does not ever rely on the establishment of such a linkage. Instead his maneuver resembles those many theorists, like Machiavelli and Hobbes, who write, respectively, on "ecclesiastical principalities" and "free gifts from God" without becoming dependent, at least in their political thinking, upon heavenly sources of political order. It is more satisfactory to suggest that Burke's suggestion of natural ties to the divine is part of a strategy to develop fear as a source of the sublime.[14]

This is why Burke continues this passage with the claim that such "sublime principles" (364) as those institutionalized by the British Church Establishment are the means to its continuity, not ends in themselves. In Burke's words, the principles ought to be "infused" into religious establishments "provided that may continually revive and enforce them." The end of such an infusion of sublime principles is "to build up that wonderful *structure*, Man" (emphasis added, 364). Here Burke promises that if man is constructed "as he ought to be made," he will hold a superior place in creation.[15] This promise seems to itself be a statement of prejudice, which is perhaps Burke's point.

Burke next uses sublime principles to consecrate political institutions. It is necessary, we learn, "to operate with a wholesome awe" upon ordinary people. Just as it is important for exalted persons who lord their superiority over others to be as perfect as possible, so it is important for free citizens to exercise their power in a disciplined way. That is, all persons stand in need of the prejudice that they must account for their conduct in that trust to the one great Master, Author, and Founder of society. Collective bodies have an even greater need for religious prejudice because they would otherwise know no bounds. "Where popular authority is absolute and unrestrained, the people have an infinitely greater . . . confidence in their own power." The problem with this confidence is that it frees civic bodies to do whatever they please. What is wrong with that? Boundlessness frees bodies to act fearlessly and, therefore, shamelessly. To Burke, acting fearlessly is dangerous, courts extravagance, and unleashes the "lust of selfish will." Fearless republicans, who might go so far as to purge their ranks of aristocratic elements, are sorely in need of religious prejudice.

Burke extends this theme to say that religion is the only means available for ridding people of the lust of selfish will. That is to say, popular power can be trusted only when it is attended by religious prejudice. Burke writes:

> When the people have emptied themselves of all the lust of selfish will, which without religion it is utterly impossible they ever should,—when they are conscious that they exercise . . . the power which to be legitimate must be according to that eternal, immutable law, in which will and reason are the same, they will be more careful how they place power in base and incapable hands. (366)

In fact, this passage—which illustrates Burke's prejudice at the edge of the sublime—suggests that purely democratic power can never be legitimate because will and reason are never the same on earth. What Burke fears most is the lawless domination of a fearless sovereign people; such domination cannot stand the test of time. To maintain continuity of the sovereign body across time, the people must be emptied of much of their individual will.

Burke next considers the consequences of a lusty politics of selfish will, of a sovereign power unbounded by outside forces. He assumes that the extent to which one deviates from the high-road is the extent to which one walks the low-road of "proud and lawless domination." But this passage emphasizes the chaos Burke associates with the low-road. First, to ignore the consecration of the state is to ignore past and future generations; those prideful selfish people who do so destroy "the whole original fabric of their society" (367). Here we encounter vintage Burke: "By this unprincipled facility of changing the state as often, and as much, and in as many ways, as there are floating fancies or fashions, the whole chain and continuity of the commonwealth would be broken. No one generation could link with the other. Men would become little better than the flies of a summer" (367). Second, and more specific, the science of jurisprudence, "the collected reason of ages" would no longer be studied by these arrogant self-sufficient creatures who know no wisdom greater than their own. Third, no laws "establishing invariable grounds of hope and [positive] fear" would restrict these slaves to their lust. Fourth, there would be no "solid ground" in property; inheritance would become an impossibility. Habits would remain wild; honor would become unknown. "No part of life would retain its acquisitions." This road leads to certain disintegration for Burke: "The commonwealth itself would, in a few generations, crumble away, be disconnected into the dust and powder of individuality, and at length dispersed to all the winds of heaven" (368). And it is in these senses that the "evils of inconstancy and versatility" are "ten thousand times worse than those of obstinacy and the blindest prejudice." In other words, Burke needs the darkness of the low-road, as "other," to defend the virtue of purblind prejudice.

The Entrenchment of the Distinctions

It is now possible to read the paragraph often cited as evidence of Burke's adherence to natural law as an illustration of the prejudice Burke has been defending in a rather rhetorical fashion.[16] The passage below is a black-and-white contrast of reason and order on one hand, and madness and confusion on the other. "Society is a contract" consecrated by God. To disobey this is to disobey what Burke now freely calls "nature," and this is to be "cast forth, and exiled, from this world of reason, and order, and peace, and virtue, and fruitful penitence, into the antagonistic world of madness, discord, vice, confusion, and unavailing sorrow" (369). This masterful illustration of the prejudice Burke defends earlier as a means for regime stability continues as he summarizes his position and claims to speak for others. Burke extends the sublime in these paragraphs as far as is within his reach.

No longer is the state a set of artificial institutions established by man alone. Now consecrated, the state is part-and-parcel of God's order. Religious prejudice has become entrenched. Burke and those for whom he would speak "conceive that He who gave our nature to be perfected by our virtue, willed also the necessary means of its perfection.—He willed therefore the state—He willed its connexion with the source and original archetype of all perfection" (370). It is difficult not to notice the circularity required by this reversal. We have been reading that the high road to nature is a means of stabilizing the state. On the strength of such consecration Burke now proclaims the state as a means to walking the high road of nature. In other words, we forget that the established church is a prejudice. Burke embraces this circularity by relying on a union, or "double yoke," defended in *Vindication*. If church and state are united, then which is the end and which is the means become disguised, if not unimportant.

Burke makes this move immediately after summarizing how his plan fits into the order of the universe (370–71). Without his plan the order of the universe is unavailable to man. Speaking for all Englishmen from "very early times to the moment," Burke describes the Church Establishment "as the foundation of their whole Constitution, with which, and with every part of which, it holds an indissoluble union." He continues: "Church and state are ideas inseparable in their minds, and scarcely is the one ever mentioned without mentioning the other" (371). The theoretical high/low distinction is now completely entrenched. It is clear to Burke that the French are heading down the low road of unavailing sorrow, while the British are marching forth on the high road of universal order and regime stability.

Reading Burke as a latter-day Thomist begs the question of prejudice; such a reading relies on a teleological ordering of the world which is itself prejudice. Only on the strength of such a prejudice can one say that the political and natural worlds Burke has been working so hard to unite with prejudice have been united all along, even if only in potential. On the strength of this prejudice, negative fear is like fear of sin and positive fear is like fear of God. Burke's use of words invites connections between the bestial, the bodily, and the sinful. But he also speaks of the madness and chaos of boundless, or extravagant, speculation. Here we encounter the problem of the third face of the power of fear. If wildness is boundless, it cannot be fitted to the high-road/low-road tension which organizes Burke's thinking on traditionalism. In other words, how can the total derangement Burke summons forth to plead for blind prejudice be placed in a tension with any other element? Is it not really the "other" of orderly tensions and their continua in general? Burke attempts to stretch the fabric of prejudice across time to solve the problem of the gulf between political and natural systems. But if there is such a gulf, prejudice cannot be expected to work as a fabric; and if there is no gulf, Burke has no reason to rely on prejudice. Burke must establish the gulf between politics and nature if he is to advocate prejudice as an element of statecraft, but the presence of such a gulf makes the continuous prejudice he would advocate impossible. Burke's principle of prejudice would replace the inconstancy, uncertainty, and bewilderment of a lower order of life with the permanence, nobility, and security of a higher order of life. But if there is really a gulf between nature's order and political order such that nature cannot guide and prejudice must step in, then human beings cannot reasonably rely on the principles of symmetry and polarity Burke is so eager to provide. If there is sufficient order in the world to speak of the symmetry of high and low natures, then prejudice is not necessary for cohesion; faith and reason should suffice. If there is insufficient order in the world to speak of symmetry, then prejudice cannot possibly supply the cohesion Burke promises. While Burke must suppose bewildering disorder as a condition for prejudice, prejudice cannot acknowledge this need if it is to constitute a whole fabric.

(Re)writing the Agenda of Avoidance

It is, of course, quite possible to read Burke's *Reflections* and to avoid the problem of the power of fear. Such a reading permits Burke to play the role of the defender of collective integrity against the reduction of civilization to the powder and dust of individuality. This is precisely the role he struggles to play. But this polarity is possible only because elements which are neither individual nor collective have been banished. Interestingly, Burke comes rather close to confessing the simple terror of primordial chaos. Nevertheless, *Reflections* draws attention away from the terror of formlessness by posing a struggle between individual and collective integrity. It is reassuring to reduce political considerations to such struggles, but such reductions can only be diversionary. We have watched how Burke draws the sublime integration of positive fear together in a relation with the negative fear of disintegration. This maneuver domesticates the terror of boundlessness. What are the implications of placing an element like terror, which can admit no tension, in a tension?

The major implication of traditionalism and its critics is, from my perspective, the agenda of avoidance. Avoid the question of formless chaos and accident by stressing the importance of maintaining integrity against the flow of time. Whether one sides with Burke and the national state or with their "opponents," this mission of avoidance is widespread in political theory. The juxtaposition of positive and negative fear leads Burke to a claim that pits traditionalism against celebrated aspects of individualism. Burke, in this individual/collective debate, follows an agenda written by his fear of boundless speculation, or what he calls "speculative extravagance." This fear, hidden by approaching boundlessness as the opposite of knowing bounds, keeps Burke from confessing the intimate "relation" between madness and reason and order.

In other words, Burke's political theory carries a double prejudice. First, there is the very noticeable prejudice we have been studying, "which renders a man's virtue his habit": the lighter side of inconstancy. Politics needs prejudice, according to Burke, because of the lack of principles of constancy. To stray from the high ways of prejudice is to walk the low roads of animalistic uncertainty. But one can also detect a less noticeable prejudice, one which Burke cannot stress without undermining his position. Burke presupposes that the relation between his thinking and the forms it operates in terms of, the order it provides, is fixed. The best example of this is the relation of his thinking about traditionalism to such forms as the line of time or the national state. If chaos is viewed as a perpetual state of flux, if all questions of form are permitted to remain questions, and, accordingly, if the relation between political thinking and its forms is never presumed to be fixed, then one is less inclined to fight flux with reasonable, orderly strategies. If everything is boundless without limit, it is difficult to detect an enemy. Treating chaos as the timebound flow of particulars gives theorists sufficient resources to fuel a plea for continuity across time.

I can now restate the dilemma reached in the last section as one which is not Burke's alone. His defense of purblind prejudice requires a Heraclitean view of flux, but the possibility of prejudice working to maximize continuity over time requires the more reassuring version of chaos. Ignoring this problem—blurring the distinction between the first and third faces of the power of fear—Burke pretends that theories can supply the fabric of continuity (which may either be torn or torn off), and that humans are not necessarily always already naked, shivering animals. Burke's hidden prejudice holds that there is enough order in the world to make the prejudice of his statecraft possible.[17]

To illustrate this, let us consider two ways of reading the following anonymous editorial (which most readers attribute to Burke):

> Not contented with shewing, what is but too evident, the narrowness and imbecillity of the human understanding, they [the skeptics] have denied that it is at all calculated for the discovery and comprehension of truth; or, what amounts to the same, that no fixed order existed in the world, so correspondent to our ideas, as to afford the least ground for certainty in anything. . . . It is evident that, if such an opinion should prevail, the pursuit of knowledge, both in the design and the end, must be the greatest folly. . . . It is evident too, that morality must share the fate of knowledge, and every duty of life becomes precarious, if it be impossible for us to know that we are bound to any duties, or that the relations which gave rise to them have any real existence.[18]

On the surface this passage is likely to remind readers of Burke's more familiar references to eternal order in the *Reflections*. But to examine this passage closely is to notice that Burke could just as plausibly be saying that we humans had better pray that such reassuring devices as the correspondence theory of truth are never exposed as shams. This reading of

Burke's references to natural law can be explained away as lame attempts to keep the message of modernism secret; this is the least obvious but most compelling of the many ways these references can be interpreted as the "kind of hat-doffing to the Deity that one can expect of politicians" (Wilkins, 1967:11).[19]

I prefer the latter interpretation because it accommodates Burke's skepticism about a universal kingdom and helps make sense of his obsession with keeping the fabric of society intact and free from corruption. One can argue that Burke is indeed hat-doffing when he mentions natural law; that he swears publicly by natural law because of a deeply rooted fear originating in his lack of faith in natural law. And rather than confess his deepest fears—of going mad on the brink of being most rational—he endures and would have us endure a forced maintenance of either individual or collective continuity across time.

Read in this fashion, Burke's work anticipates the coming of an age described by Mill as "destitute of faith, but terrified at skepticism." His preoccupation with fear reminds me of Mrs. Hobbes's twins. Burke feels, I believe, that madness, not liberty, awaits those who are sufficiently brave or foolish to overturn the bedrock assumptions required by worldmaking. To avoid spreading the temptation to become overzealous in the exercise of speculative human rationality, Burke relies on natural law as a prejudice, reassuring his audiences—including his critics —that their worlds are not lacking solid foundations, even if they have not discovered them yet. Because these foundations already exist as prejudices, they do not require discovery. Such reliance is well-suited to the politics of crisis.

At the end of his critique of Foucault (1961) Derrida suggests that in time of crisis it is perhaps more sane to confess the terror of insanity than to continue to insist on reason and order. According to Derrida, the worlds of reason and order never succeed, at least in principle, in driving away chaos, flux, or accident. Burke seems prepared to go to any lengths—prejudice, obsession, state authority—to avoid giving in to flux. We are living the political crises brought on by a forced reconciliation between nature and artifice.

Another strategy is to cut through the evasive tactics we have been investigating and suggest instead that chaos and accident are not best approached as earlier "metamorphoses" that human beings passed out of when the earth was poised in air. Instead, these aspects of life are elements always already implicated in political writing. Facing up to monstrous fears can give theorists permission to deviate from the agenda of avoidance.

III Extravagance

The next three chapters are designed to supplement the forces of reassurance, not to replace them. In fact, a major problem with the avant-garde criticism of Lincolnian and Burkean reassurance is that it becomes so frustrated with sober reasonable life that it, almost literally, celebrates death. Community and postmodernity are viewed as incompatible mostly because of the difficulty of reconciling such solitary desperation with mutual service.

Attempting to put these misapprehensions to rest, I show how the forces of extravagance are already available, already a constitutive element of discourse. First, I address the technical aspects of Derridian writing. Then I practice a well-known deconstruction of Foucault. Finally, I distinguish Bataille's eruptive attempt to break out of the prisonhouse of language from the force and irruption of Derridian gift-giving.

7 Announcing Derridian Confession: Spacing, Deferral, Writing

The concepts of present, past, and future, everything in the concepts of time and history which implies evidence of them—the metaphysical concept of time in general—cannot adequately describe the structure of the trace.—Derrida (1974:67)

Jacobson (1978) presents historical political theory as the vocation of giants who snatch human subjects from the edge of the abyss of chronic nonmeaning and provide them with sufficient order for security; one feature of his remarkable text is that it shows that political theory can no longer provide this service (even though there is some solace in being told by a text that there is no solace). The boundaries established by the classical theorists described by Jacobson are like any boundaries in the sense that they permit an inside and an outside.[1]

If this commonplace is applied to the most general levels of meaning, we notice that the meaning most human subjects rely on is made possible by pushing nonmeaning out to the silent fringe and forgetting about it. Within artificially concocted areas of meaning, subjects reassure one another—that is, distinctions are drawn, balances are attempted, and hegemony is gained and lost in a series of power plays like those described by Foucault.[2] But this inside/outside couple draws attention away from the extent to which political discourse is always already riddled with nonmeaning.

Aristide Zolberg (1972) relates those moments when all possibility without bounds is given up at once (in extravagant "moments of madness") to the possibility of social change. Such moments are, no doubt, best described in hyperbole, because meaning and nonmeaning, time and timelessness, subjectivity and objectivity, etc., have not been distinguished. In other words, this primordial chaos is not reasonable and orderly. One cannot describe it as a universal unity; nor can one rely on the language of particulars to describe it. All combinations of universals and particulars are similarly unsuited to giving a voice to its untamed wildness. As we shall see, to speak well and to be understood it is necessary to act reasonably normal. Primordial chaos must be explored subversively, through hyperbole, as a supplement to the totalities governed by distinctions between universals and particulars.

As we saw in chapter 3, it is terrifying to turn one's gaze toward the silent monstrosity of excess. Jacobson plays the competent statesman in time of crisis when he grants political theorists the power to draw boundaries between what can and cannot be said. But the solace he provides is attended by subjugation. The mad, chaotic aspects of life are exiled in the individuating and totalizing pressures of subject-centered discourse. Foucault tells good stories about dominated people lost in brutish imitation. This chapter announces a confession that the solace promised by competent statesmen in time of crisis is inextricably related to madness, a confession that reason is always already unreasonable.

Using the language of "outcomes," Foucault documents the suffocating aspects of domestic life as events in time. His texts show that domesticity is a function of the play of domination, of one side gaining power over the other. But Foucault locates the dualities he studies within eras, or epistemes, whose boundaries in time do not receive an equally critical review. As a result, his texts suggest that the human subject is an artifact, developed over time, which must be smashed if history is ever to escape the domination of "simultaneous individuation and totalization." The fact, however, that time is not placed on his agenda of critical inquiry suggests that Foucault is, at bottom, also reassuring us. This reassurance of time's continuity, though, perpetuates the prejudice that time is a force to be guarded against, or to be defeated by individual, collective, or mixed strategies, all of which Foucault would dismantle. In this sense Foucauldian reassurance is a cruel manipulation of the insecurity found in Burkean texts. Yes, Foucault seems to be saying, time's flow threatens the human subject, but one can either be dominated by strategies of continuity or dismantle oneself by resisting these strategies. The chapters in this section struggle to avoid the reassurance of linear time and its bleak implications.

An inquiry into the passage of time which is less matter-of-fact than Foucault's might show that the problem of time is subject to the same boundary formulation as other problems. If so, then the problem of subjugation examined in Part I could be reexamined. No longer would it suffice to ask how self-images are transmitted across time; we would also have to ask how it makes sense to speak of the forms of time. Is the timeless/timebound distinction presupposed by Pocock, Foucault, and scores of less playful, less critical writers, possible only because of a meaning/nonmeaning distinction drawn in an act of force so subtle that its solace is immune from criticism? To prefigure in hyperbole: is history in any sense always already over?[3] If it is only by neutralizing nonmeaning, or placing it in a straitjacket, that one can provide sufficient meaning to make all of the usual distinctions that now fight for hegemony in political writing on community, then all meaning is contingent upon breaking the silence of nonmeaning and therefore provisional. And because silence is never broken completely, nonmeaning is never exiled to an outside. Exploring such a possibility, I begin the radical play mentioned in chapter 3. Radical play allows theorists to challenge the double bind brought on by the stalemate between communitarian and liberal texts.

One way to announce the uncertain doubleness of Derrida's work is to understand that what he calls "différance" is a principle of extravagance, not mere negativity. This radical principle addresses the foundational questions of metaphysics without restricting itself to the purity of metaphysical terms. Derridian différance indicates both the difference between any graphic or phonic entities separated by spaces and the deferral of any consideration of the origin of meaning (transcendental signified) associated with signs. Différance, then, gives the same promise of intelligibility that it necessarily postpones. That is to say, this doubleness allows for giving in to the madness of flux in principle while permitting de facto intelligibility. Less critical work is concerned only with what Derrida insists upon calling de facto intelligibility. Most of the secure doubleness, the play of domination, takes place in this reassuring world. Derrida's uncertain doubleness would, in a dangerous, bewildering way, supplement this more familiar territory.

Very few readers can be expected to dispute the simple point of Derridian différance, but even fewer know how to act (especially politically) upon accepting it. Yes, some might agree, the principle of difference can be applied to meaning in general —we can only mean to the extent we sequester nonmeaning —but because nonmeaning is bewildering and unnamable, it is difficult to see how it can be included in discourse. Is it not better, these readers might suggest, to relegate such considerations to an untouchable zone outside of space and time, and to get on with the lives of reason and order its abandonment make possible? The alternative to such thinking, or such a plea for normalcy, is to confess that a border between reasonable order and epistemological insanity is impossible. The two are related in the way Saussure describes the relation of sounds to the thoughts they signify: namely, as two sides of a sheet of paper, both of which one must necessarily cut when using scissors.[4]

Before embarking on a detailed treatment of how différance addresses the problem of the line of time, I wish to introduce my method of reading various strands of the Derridian project.

After showing what is at stake, or how Derrida's work is at once too simple to misconstrue and too radical to comprehend easily (Staten, 1984), we should be in a position to sense elements of its economy.

My plan is to distinguish the bewildering principle of différance from the more domesticated Saussurean principle of difference. I follow Saussurean difference to the point at which it cannot name everything that Derridian différance indicates. After showing why I even bother with Saussure, I contrast Saussure and Derrida on the idea of spacing, show how Derrida critically examines the movement of temporalization, and introduce Derrida's extravagant usage of *writing*.

The Way to Formation of Form and Imprinting

One cannot discuss difference without relating thought to word by using the concept "sign"; relating sign to structure as if they were part (speech/act) and whole (rules of language); and supplementing considerations of sign and structure with silent, formless monstrosity (flux). As strange as the last of these three interests may sound, it is the key to overcoming the preoccupation with part/whole relations which results in such predicaments as the dilemma of modern liberalism. In presenting these three theoretical areas of inquiry—technically speaking, signs as the relation of signifier and signified; the relation of la parole and la langue; and the deconstruction of the sign—I present "différance" as a twin consideration which is radically playful. This involves, first, the formation of the forms theorists would impose and, second, the imprinting of these forms prior to their signification.

Saussure (1966) introduces the sign in terms of two primordial characteristics.[5] First, signs are arbitrary; second, images used to signify concepts, are auditory and unfold solely in time. I wish to explore this bonded simultaneity of thought and sound in greater detail in order to introduce the importance of the principle of *difference* to traditionalism's problem of continuity.

According to Saussure, the sign has two aspects, or faces: the signifier, which transmits a message, and the "other," or the signified, which is the message. As indicated by the primordial characteristics listed above, while all signification is in principle arbitrary, systems of meaning are established all the time. One learns how to use a sign only by sensing its difference from all other signs. Because the meanings of signs are arbitrary, they can change over time, according to Saussure. All signs enjoy synchronic life within systems (systematic relations between speech-events [la parole] and structures of rules [la langue]), but these systems are themselves diachronic. Saussure's model allows for permanence and change in any given community of speakers, as it engages in discourse across time. Consider the diagram introduced early in his major text:

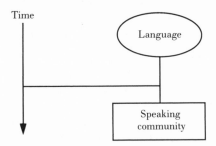

Figure 1. The Relation of Sign and Structure

The twofold nature of the sign, while wholly conventional, takes root in a community of speakers, to the point of being treated by them as a natural form. At this point one can study the relation of sign and structure.

At last, readers can see why I must mention Saussure at this juncture. The Pocock model, in all of its remarkable complexity and political sophistication, is constructed entirely of relations between what Saussure might call the signifier and the signified, within possibly overlapping structures. In Pocock's model, competing codes (signifiers) are used to transmit overlapping messages (signifieds) to a community of speakers across time. It is difficult not to observe the resemblances shared by these structural models. Both theorists stress the importance of both the synchronic and the diachronic aspects of language. Reading Lincoln and Burke has allowed us to see how practical statesmen have fought for communion by creating and/ or transmitting various "signifieds" across time. These middle chapters show how the significance of collective efforts to maintain continuity is so often authoritarian. Citizens are asked to be religious about political attachments, and to endorse the blindest prejudice in the name of sovereignty. Contemporary readers might justly feel that if this is community it is not worth the price. Indeed, this is one reason for distinguishing a communal pursuit of shared oneness and common values from the politics of community. Perhaps the possibility of radically free play might unlock the double bind of modern liberalism. Indeed, we have seen in chapter 3 the possibility of an infinite play of signifiers in the absence of a transcendental signified. While it is easy to admit the absence of a so-called external world, it is difficult to admit the absence of oneself. To do so results in the death of the subject. This is bewildering beyond discourse and must not be confused with Derridian extravagance. Derridian extravagance adds uneasiness to reassurance; but you can rest assured it does not wipe it out. Extravagant theorists think that Pocock's model contains an excess that its binary oppositions lead us not to see.

There is, of course, an obvious difference between the Pocock model and Saussure's. We have seen that Pocock introduces literacy on the eve of the greatest complexity in the development of his model, and he spends most of his time discussing reading and writing. Saussure, on the other hand, writes about speaking and listening. Saussure is concerned with signifiers as sounds and signifieds as thought images. The resemblance Pocock and Saussure share leads us to inquire about the relation between speech and writing.

Usually we consider writing as a signifier of the signifier of a signified. One uses graphic symbols to write down what is otherwise carried by phonic symbols. Writing serves the spoken word. Pocock's presentation, as it passes quickly from oral to written traditions, shares this understanding of writing. Saussure sees it this way too. Saussure (1966:23) writes:

> Language and writing are two distinct systems of signs; the second exists for the sole purpose of representing the first. The linguistic object is not both the written and the spoken forms of words; the spoken forms alone constitute the object. But the spoken word is so intimately bound by its written image that the latter manages to usurp the main role. People

attach even more importance to the written image of a vocal sign than to the sign itself. A similar mistake would be in thinking that more can be learned about someone by looking at his photograph than by viewing him directly.

Notice that Saussure pushes writing out of his system as if it were the conventional "other" in a nature/convention dichotomy. Writing sits on the sidelines and, in a capacity of secondary importance, represents the natural speech-acts which occur within linguistic structures built throughout history. If the questions of the formation of form and primordial imprinting are not addressed, the priority of "natural" speech-acts over "conventional" writing might stand uncontested. But raising these questions results in a plea for the priority of writing over speech. One can argue that, in general, the imprinting of available forms makes the use of phonic and graphic signs possible. This is part of Derrida's project. I will show how this project is related to Saussurean difference. The question "How is meaning produced within a natural zone?" becomes "How is a natural zone produced?"

Spacing and Difference

Imagine sitting at a desk, eating spicy jelly beans. The red ones are cinnamon, the black licorice, and so on. Suppose that midway through the jar you empty the contents on the desk and sort the jelly beans by color. Imagine, at this point, giving in to brutish inclinations and devouring all of the red ones. You might say during this indulgence, "My favorites all taste the same." But how is it that you can say this? Could you as easily say that the candy factory which produced the jelly beans achieved quality control?

Common sense, or conventional wisdom, suggests that the candy factory has a formula which each red bean carries, allowing it to be identical with all the other red ones. But there is nothing sacrosanct about the relation of such a formula and the color of the bean. Each color could in principle stand for any flavor; the one you prefer—suppose it is cinnamon—could just as easily be yellow or white as red. Indeed this could happen either by mistake or by design or for some other reason. You can say with assurance, however, that all the red jelly beans on the desk are the same in that they taste different from the other beans. To say "cinnamon" is to distinguish a flavor from all the others. The same flavor, then, is the same flavor only in relation to all of the others.

Such a discussion carries the prerequisite that there be spaces between the individual jelly beans. If one empties the contents of a jar of jelly beans into a melting pot instead of on a desktop, one is unable to apply the principle of difference. Difference requires a spacing of the elements (whether they be sounds, graphic markings, jelly beans, or whatever) to be distinguished. Spacing indicates that elements must stand apart; it also indicates the process of separating elements (for example, unsticking jelly beans on a muggy day).

Saussure uses a similar procedure when describing the system of phonic signs. Just as variously colored jelly beans are associated with various flavors, so various sounds are associated with various thoughts. And just as I cannot ever count on a flavor being inherent in a color, Saussure says that we should never presuppose that any given thought is inherent in any particular sound. Any association between sound and concept is in principle arbitrary.[6] One can only say that two sounds (for example, "yum, yum") are the same in that they both carry the thought of a pleasing taste, only if both signs are other than non-"yum" sounds. The principle of difference gives distinctions a fundamental significance. A is either X or not-X; to accept A as X is to reject it as not-X. A red jelly bean is either spicy or it is not; to accept a red jelly bean as cinnamon is to reject it as not-cinnamon.

Saussurean difference is, of course, indebted to the Aristotelian principle of noncontradiction: A is either B or opposed to B. The habit of not being self-contradictory is often presented as, or assumed to be, an effective check against madness, which one might juxtapose with reason and order. Structure, sign and history, properly arranged, can create the impression that life is—at least in potential—a series of logic problems. So while signs are in themselves arbitrary, they acquire meaning in time by their use within structural orders, by virtue of the play of differences.

Derrida does not dispute either of the primordial characteristics Saussure attributes to the sign. The idea of spacing and the attendant notion of différance are also important to Derrida. But Derrida insists upon asking how the principle of difference can do its work, and how spacing is possible. This inquiry leads him to notice that if temporal movement were not already in place, spacing would be impossible. There would be no spaces between entities if all were experienced at once, in a *nunc stans*. When Saussure claims that, within structures, the articulation of signs among themselves creates meaning for communities of speakers over time, he is presupposing a form of temporal movement which Derrida wishes to examine critically. Derrida is not content to ask questions of the relation of sign, structure and history; he attempts to get down to the foundations of the worlds other theorists seek to encounter; unlike Husserl he is looking for cracks, not purity. Thus he is concerned with the formation of form and with how such a propensity is written into the worlds eventually organized by sign and structure across time.

It is easy to grant Saussure the notion that signs are arbitrary, that the sound "yum" could in some other system indicate a concept other than pleasant taste. But, for his scheme to work, it is not possible for everything in principle to be arbitrary. Is it? If everything were arbitrary, how could we place faith in such a truthmaking principle as the principle of noncontradiction? A time-honored way of digging down to a solid ground which is not arbitrary is to establish the principle of noncontradiction— not to mention the subject—outside of the play of differences studied by Saussure. This allows us to treat the principle of noncontradiction as a principle of principles, a pure form, outside of speaking subjects and phenomenal jelly beans. Such a principle is form-giving because it allows meaning to get started; such a principle might reasonably be called the origin of reason and order. But we shall also read it as a reminder of how origins are, in principle, impossible.

The Significance of Deferral

The impulse to assign a resting place that allows everything to get started and allows the subject a way of not being fully implicated in discourse, is an impulse for reassurance that all meaning is not arbitrary. We have studied some of the political implications of this impulse, many of which are commonly confused with community. Many authors still cling to the hope that in time the fullness of meaning will emerge; that the problems facing Western civilization will be solved by reasonable and orderly minds put to the task of assembling the remaining pieces of the human puzzle; that madness, chaos, and bewilderment, like a frontier will eventually be settled. I struggle to curb such impulses.

To do this requires applying the principle of noncontradiction in the least reasonable ways possible. Sooner or later this involves applying the principle to itself. That A is either X or not-X is the same principle when used to sort jelly beans as it is when used to distinguish the sound "yum" from the sound "gross" if and only if the principle of noncontradiction is different from the unprincipled madness of self-contradiction or willful ignorance. One employs the principle of noncontradiction every day again and again, but it would be impossible, in principle, to call it the same principle if there were not, lurking in the silent margins and spaces, "moments" of madness.

If the origin of all reason and order requires an "other" of chronic bewilderment, then the possibility of purity in expression is out of the question. All meaning must necessarily carry trace elements of madness. Because I am speaking in such general terms, no form in political theory can be exempt. Spacing is necessary for meaning, and, if there are spaces, there is always already room for monstrosity. The sleep of reason produces monsters and we are never continuously awake, even for a short amount of time.

This wild extension of the principle of difference leads to a disturbing conclusion about the relation of signs and meaning. It is flatly impossible to treat phonic or graphic signifiers as vehicles in the expression of pure thoughts—or transcendental signifieds—which stand clear of the process of signification. Indication and expression are equivalent because signs can only defer the representation of reality, which is therefore necessarily attended by spacing. But to see how difference does its work, we must think about more than spacing. Yes, spaces are required and, yes, any consideration of life without spacing (such as an origin) is necessarily postponed; but this necessary deferral presupposes the form of a line of time. To be consistent, we would have to argue that the units of time are themselves knowable only by virtue of their being the other of flux. And Derrida (1976:62) is prepared to be consistent: "Without a retention in the minimal unit of temporal experience, without a trace retaining the other as other in the same, no difference would do its work and no meaning would appear." So there must be traces of flux or movement other than the linear movement of time if the common line of time is to make any sense at all. The necessity of deferring true representation not only threatens Husserlian expression, it also colors any metaphysical project of how being is possible. Derrida continues asking the foundational questions of metaphysics, but in a double way. In his formulation the rocky ground of reason and order is necessarily tainted by trace elements of accident and confusion.

We have seen that Derrida's radical extension of spacing—to the point of an insistence upon maintaining the difference between orderly principles and meaninglessness—leads him to claim that signs can only stand temporarily, as markers, for the relation of thinking and form. In other words, the use of signs only defers consideration of a fixed relation between signifier and signified. Because the relation between message and code is never fixed, signs necessarily carry trace elements of the meaninglessness which, following the principle of difference, makes principled life possible. This is not to say that messages cannot be transferred across time. Rather, it is to insist that texts do more than this. Pocock can agree that texts can be read in as many ways as there are readers, but Derrida's point is that texts carry trace elements of a silent world of flux which can never in principle be overcome by any reading.

Derrida is more concerned, then, with incompleteness than multiplicity. Signs are traces which necessarily fall short of performing the functions described by Saussure. They always come too soon. Flux is silent motion; signs are movements which stand in for meaning, allowing a sense of synchronicity, but all the while carrying traces which are neither synchronic nor diachronic. Derridian différance is movement which permits the spacing required by difference while necessarily deferring fixed relations between signifier and signified. We must now consider how the spacing and deferral involved in the formation of form are imprinted.[7]

Writing and Confession

Perhaps the best way to describe this venture is to distinguish two tensions which are easily mistaken for each other: presence versus nonpresence and presence versus absence. The business of distinguishing meaning in the play of differences by applying the principle of noncontradiction is signified by the present/absent tension. But the sameness of the principle of noncontradiction is made possible by its other: silent nonpresence. So while presence is always *now*, it is never unadulterated—there is always already an element of nonpresence. This primordial play, or give, in the structure of any experience makes binary relations (absent/present) possible. That is, the formation of form is necessarily prior to the imposition of form on worlds which theorists seek to encounter.

The principle of difference requires that reason have an other, even if it is unnamable. Derrida claims that something must mediate the unnamable and the namable. He seeks to exaggerate a movement which plays the role of a zero-point, or origin of sorts, but does so in such a way as to rule out unity or attunement. This is why he speaks of an originary movement. Silence is broken by writing but its madness lingers like an open wound. The use of signs postpones drawing attention to this unhappy arrangement. One can use signs in a de facto way to make sense of a world which, in principle, can never be made sense of.

When sitting in front of any text, or encountering any text-analogue it is possible to decipher the structure which organizes the motion of the thoughts transmitted, but it is also possible to notice peculiarities which cannot be addressed within the structure. Any work can be supplemented by deconstructive inquiry. But because there can be no unity for it to grow into, such critical work may actually be subversive, may actually supplant the order of the day. Just as one might make friends with a security guard in an effort to supplement her discipline with humanity and only make her more vulnerable to the tendency to let things slide, so Derrida would supplement the provision of order with exaggerations of monstrosity which only work to supplant orderly lives. It appears that monstrosity, or flux, is always kept out for a reason.

Derrida's depiction of a general writing, which at once breaks and hinges ("la brisure") structure, sign, and history with unnamable monstrosity, allows us to supplement structural models such as those worked out by Pocock, Saussure, and others. Derrida insists that one remain loyal to sign and structure while working out an extravagant perspective. To approach meaning through différance rather than mere difference is to view all signs provisionally, as traces. Tracing is Derrida's way of reminding readers that the flux has never been defeated (though it has been neutralized, sequestered, straitjacketed) by reason and order. That there is play in the very structure which makes form (including temporalization) possible opens a doubleness of great significance, and might even open new territory for political thinking.

It is as if Derrida would add an element of extrachronicity to the usual structural considerations of diachronicity and synchronicity. There is always already an excess of possibility overflowing the boundaries of reasonable and orderly discourse. We could depict this supplementary version in the following way.

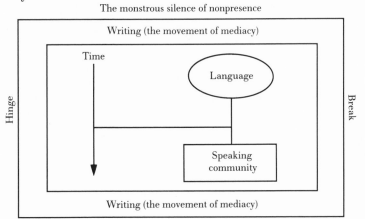

The monstrous silence of nonpresence

Figure 2. Writing, Sign, and Structure

Part/whole polarities can now be viewed as only some of the considerations facing political thinking. One cannot articulate the other of absent/present polarities without exaggerating, but such exaggeration might lead theorists to work differently.

Derrida's insistence that writing in general is prior to tensions between speech and conventional writing is his way of calling attention to these foundational questions. He is not claiming that words must be written down before they can be pronounced; rather, he is claiming that flux must be mediated by formation of form (imprinted in subjects' various perspectives) before questions of binary opposition can be raised. For example, he would include in writing in general such basic signifiers as genetic codes. Writing, therefore, permeates every significant consideration.[8] Derrida uses *writing* to name a procedure that resembles the imprinting of a format on a diskette, an imprinting which enables the disk to receive binary codes. Michael Ryan (1982:28) describes Derridian writing this way: "Writing in the general sense is the word Derrida uses to name this movement of mediacy, which makes possible the supposedly underived immediacy of speech and presence." Derrida uses the notion of writing in general, then, to expand the considerations of sign, structure and history.[9]

But if writing makes meaning possible, if the codes one embodies make it possible to create codes to transmit messages, then it is rather shortsighted to restrict thinking to the relation of sign and structure. One is driven to face the unnamable and yet one cannot take a stand there. Flux is in this sense the death of reason and also its most profound resource.[10] We are forced to confess that one makes sense only by provisionally postponing flux. My task—after practicing this confession by repeating Derrida's confession—is to show how its political implications are compatible with community as mutual service.

Retracing My Steps

All signs, graphic or phonic, are arbitrary; they act only as markers. Because signs do not carry their sense, they must be shown to differ from each other if they are to mean anything.

Differences among signs, then, are a necessary part of their meaning. In any situation in which differences between signs are eliminated, there is no basis for meaning. To attempt to dig deeply into the foundations of thinking, to access what Husserl might call "pure" ideality or a principle of principles, is not to earn exemption from the rule. Regardless of the endeavor, the same is the same only in that it is affected by the other. Thus the Aristotelian principle of noncontradiction can be applied again and again in the same way—as I have applied it in the pages of this book—only if it is affected by an other. This other is so deeply repressed that many radical critics forget that this is what it is. In other words, the origin of meaning can have no meaning unless it also carries trace elements of nonmeaning. While Derrida has been influenced by the Husserlian project of locating a pure origin of thought, he confesses outright that purity is not possible.[11] Purely and simply put, there is always a trace of monstrosity. This includes the subject at the center of Western political thought. Derrida considers this trace in a highly general way, as a motion which must be neutralized if only for a moment so as to make reason and order possible. The play of this primordial flux comes "before" first; it makes it possible for the metaphysician to speak, if mistakenly, of origins; it is originary. Because such movement is anterior, in principle, to all form, including linear time, it is always already at hand in margins and spaces. Because it cannot be obliterated without violating the principle of difference, the pure meaning of any sign, including one's self-image, is continually deferred. The movement trace is a name for the principle of différance. Writing involves multiple overlapping layers of signs, all of which defer the transfer of pure meaning. The "thing itself" (including *man*) is a sign, a trace, difference. This means that it is always possible, after all, to speak of an excess to the binary oppositions of metaphysics. Difference can never be reduced to opposition. Those who deconstruct texts show the problems these excesses pose for unity. Indeed if there is always an excess lurking in the spaces and margins of a text, unity is impossible. Gaining even the will to confess without reassurance that one makes sense only at the brink of madness, to admit that nothing "adds up" and never did, to say that the sleep of reason has always already infiltrated reason and order, is an important part of developing extravagance. In short, there is primordial play in the world, which makes the binary tensions used so often in political theory possible. To confess this doubleness—extravagance and reassurance—is to realize that the relation between thinking and form is never fixed. Regardless of the form, writing is also excess.

If the relation between thinking and form is not fixed, then political theorists must take their constructs less seriously. The constructs studied in Part II are citizen, state, and time. Now we can suggest that the citizen is always already attended by moments which lie at odds with identity, that state sovereignty tends to blur at given moments, and that time's line is not continuous. What is required to mobilize the space—or maintain the silence—that is necessary to make sense in the world? A will to confess that individual and collective lives as we know them are in principle incomplete; that these lives require a supplement; and that, if such considerations were not themselves always already postponed, such a supplement would completely undermine all that they stand for.

I have been offering glimpses of the strange doubleness (of extravagant monstrosity and reassuring binary thinking) throughout my book. The claim needs to be repeated in greater detail to underscore a basic problem: if using language is necessarily reasonable and orderly, why must one not be silent about excess? Derrida attempts to answer this by distinguishing between the de facto use of signs and the de jure impossibility of overcoming flux. To use a sign is always already to carry a trace.

8 Practicing Derridian Confession: Supplementing Foucault

This interminable unhappiness of the disciple is a result of what he does not know—or still hides from himself—that, like real life, the master is perhaps always absent.—Derrida (1967/1978:52/32)

Without dreaming of doing justice to the mind-boggling projects of Derrida, I shall zero in on one of his efforts to criticize theorists who rely on linear time. The name Derrida does not often inspire confidence in political theory. All too often it spells the death of our vocation, the trivialization of politics, the silence of monstrosity.[1] Nevertheless Derridian texts accuse others of naively carrying signs of conventional polarities, and of ignoring the radical play which makes a status quo possible from time to time. For example, in the essay I shall read and practice, Derrida accuses Foucault of being naive about the flow of time, or temporalization. That is, he accuses Foucault of relying on the very foundations of political theory he is trying to undermine. There is, of course, a sense in which such reliance is inevitable. One cannot stop making sense on the way to opening different perspectives in political discourse. But Derrida works to supplement ("supplementer")[2] conventional polarities: enhancing the way in which these forms presently govern political thinking while supplanting their totalizing or hierarchizing influences.[3] This effort to add to polarities, thereby replacing their sovereignty with merely provisional, de facto sense, can be shown to differ from mere reliance on the legitimate rule of polar opposites. Without going so far as to call Foucault "naive," I wish to show that Derridian extravagance is more critical than the force of reassurance and to suggest that this difference may be politically significant.

The passages I shall now read can be introduced as a comparison of how Derrida and Foucault read Descartes's *First Meditation*.[4] Descartes speculates about people whose "judgement is so troubled and clouded by the vapours of black bile . . . that they constantly assure [us] that they are Kings when they are very poor, or that they are clothed in gold and purple when they are really naked, or who imagine themselves to be pitchers, or to have a body of glass" (406). For Descartes these are examples of how extravagance can lead one astray: "But they are mad, and I would not be less extravagant, if I were to follow their examples" (406). The issue is the purity of the Cogito. Foucault insists upon tracing back in time to "the Decision," the moment when reason interned madness so as to permit that most subjective of subjectivities, the Cogito, to be reasonable and orderly. Derrida is less inclined to genealogy because he can exaggerate ways in which pure subjectivity is impossible. Rather than look for a "decision" against madness, he prefers to write in terms of a "dissension," making madness out to be an open wound which can never heal.[5] That is to say, madness is never exiled totally, and is always already wrapped up in human possibility, including the inaugural moment of the Cogito. Thus he explains the passage in question as an attempt by Descartes to reassure the timid nonphilosopher of the purity of the Cogito.

I shall now look at aspects of their conflict by reading Derrida's critique.[6] I am not concerned with Foucault's reaction[7] because I wish only to use Derrida's critique of linear time, regardless of how wrong he might be about Foucault, in my investigation of the problem of community.[8]

Derrida's reading of Foucault contains at least five general movements, or sections: a strategic introduction (51-55/31–33); some questions for the margins of his reading (55-70/33–45); commentary on Foucault's reading of the Descartes (1967:177–82/404–18) text (71–80/45–51); a stunning critique of Foucault's uncritical acceptance of temporalization (80–95/51-61); and a suggestive conclusion (95–97/61–63).[9] I shall retrace several steps in each movement, reserving the closest reading for the fourth movement.

Derrida's Strategic Introduction

In the first part of the first movement, and calling Foucault his teacher, Derrida prepares to teach him a lesson. Of course, in order to be a subversive disciple one needs an opening, a cover, a section of a text that can repay close reading. Derrida will show Foucault how to read Descartes in a way that criticizes Foucault's entire book. Accordingly, he makes this incision:

> In this book of 673 pages, Michel Foucault devotes three pages (54–57) . . . to a certain passage from the First Meditation, wherein madness, extravagance, dementia, insanity seem, I emphasize *seem* to have been . . . dismissed as soon as they were summoned in the presence of the tribunal by Descartes, in the presence of the extreme instance of a Cogito which, essentially, would not *know how* to be mad. (52/32)[10]

Aside from setting the stage for a distinction between Foucault's reading, which is caught up in mere appearance, and his own, these words indicate that a battle will occur about which side of the reason/madness distinction to place "extravagance" on. Foucault sees it interned with "madness" and "dementia," but Derrida has special plans for this bewildering notion. Derrida filters the Foucault project through the passage he has selected by raising a twin series of questions.[11]

The first series asks if Foucault has interpreted Descartes in the way Derrida does. Raising this question involves placing the sign (the passage from Descartes mentioned above) in a plausible relation with the structure (for Derrida this means Western metaphysics; for Foucault, the "classical age"). As one might expect, the answer will be no. The second series asks what one can learn about Foucault's presuppositions from his naive reading of Descartes. Again, predictably, Foucault will be eventually pronounced naive in general.

The second series of questions is most useful here because it produces the Derridian critique of Foucault's critical project. Derrida accuses Foucault of failing to criticize the façade of totality created by part/whole (polarity-driven) thinking. In other words, Derrida claims that what signs indicate is never exhausted by their historical context; whenever form is imposed it must differ from the bewilderment of flux, but form can only defer the reawakening of the looming monstrosity of flux.

If the essay we are reading were conventional, we would work through the first series on the way to the second. Derrida, as if to challenge the serenity of a series, scratches markings in the margins while asking the predictable interpretive questions of the first series. These markers return later as the remarks of the fourth section, in which he addresses the second series of questions. As if to illustrate the case for the de facto use of polarities while impugning their de jure authority, Derrida inscribes, among other things, three polar distinctions in the margins of this essay. Before attempting to show where Derrida is headed, I wish to read the marginalia and to notice how these distinctions organize the more serious critique of Foucault in section four.

Some Marginal Questions

The first polarity is a tension between archaeology and genealogy. Derrida describes Foucault's attraction to an archaeology of silence—in which madness is the subject and therefore "speaks itself" in the way an unearthed vase carries its stories

—as the project of "greatest merit" (56/33). The obvious difficulty is that one cannot escape the dominion of the language
of reason. Nevertheless, one can attempt to uncover the roots
of rationality and determine at what point in time it became
impossible for madness to speak. This is Foucault's "more effectively ambitious" (60/36) project: namely, to study the twin
existence of madness and reason, to write a genealogy of rationality.

Within the domain of a genealogical project, Derrida
scratches out another polarity, still within the margins of preparing to ask the first series of questions. Foucault's tracing of
the ancestry of rational language can be read to contain a distinction between *logos* and *pathos*. Logos names the reasonable
and orderly way words combine to make sense. Pathos—"in its
best sense"—names the extravagant, overflowing sensibility of
what Aristotle calls "an admixture . . . of strange words and
metaphors, . . . of the various modified forms of words . . ."[12]
Derrida says that, even though it has been directly neutralized
by logos, the "silence of madness" is indirectly present in the
pathos of Foucault's book. That is, even though it is impossible to allow madness to speak itself, the admixture of forms of
words in the text can indirectly present silent monstrosity even
if the pathetic Foucault does not read the text in the same way,
even if he is not always in touch with his writing.[13] In other
words, the reader (cum disciple) can subvert the authority of
the text by rereading its writing.[14] The genealogical extreme of
the first tension, then, can be read to divide against itself; its
reasonable tracing back in time is always necessarily attended
by signs of the violence incurred by silencing madness. But because it cannot speak itself, the silence of madness can only be
indicated or glimpsed in exaggerations of the shortcomings of
logos. That is to say, the pathos of a text must be exaggerated,
in acts Derrida describes as hubris, if its extravagance is to be
presented.[15] Hubris draws pathos out of logos.

Finally, while the silence of madness has always already been
available as exaggeration in language, there are two opposite
ways to appreciate this. The naive way is to view hubris, like
pathos, as a mere opposite of logos; the other, more critical
approach is to view hubris as the "other" of all oppositions in

general. It will take Derrida some time to spin this suggestion into a remark, but hubris is eventually developed into the will to exaggerate in a most unreasonable manner.[16]

These three distinctions indicate the stages from naive genealogy and its traditions, disruptions, and outcomes (des événements), to the hyperbole of madness and, finally, to the interminable possibility of critical hyperbole. Derrida is already anticipating the fourth movement, during which he will show Foucault to be anchored to the first stage, the phase of reassurance. But to practice the genre of commentary we must turn, or return, to the first series of questions.

Derrida on Foucault on Descartes

With the margins so inscribed, Derrida begins his commentary. This movement divides easily into three parts: Derrida reading Descartes over Foucault's shoulder; Derrida reading Descartes; and Derrida playing Foucault responding to what Derrida notices when reading Descartes. Derrida begins his first series of questions: how well does this writer read Descartes? In the *First Meditation*, as we have already seen, Descartes is searching for certainty. One way to conduct this search is to remove all obstacles to doubt. A troublesome obstacle is that sensations are both a foundation of certainty and a source of deception. Descartes cautions: "All that up to the present time I have accepted as most true and certain I have learned either from the senses or through the senses; but it is sometimes proved to me that these senses are deceptive, and it is wiser not to trust entirely to anything by which we have once been deceived" (71/45). His search for certainty, then, must exclude all data of sensory origin as a foundation for knowledge. Exceptions could be made, of course, if a distinction could be drawn between sensory data which can and cannot be doubted. This is a crucial distinction which Derrida finds that Descartes does not make. In the course of entertaining such a distinction, however, Derrida reads Descartes *feigning* the plausibility of data of sensory origin which cannot be doubted. The question then becomes whether Foucault will fall for the pretended reassurance of Descartes. This is the Cartesian passage in question:

> How could I deny that these hands and this body are mine, were it not perhaps that I compare myself to certain persons devoid of sense, whose judgement is so troubled and clouded by the vapours of black bile . . . that they constantly assure [us] that they are Kings when they are very poor, or that they are clothed in gold and purple when they are really naked, or who imagine themselves to be pitchers, or to have a body of glass." (Descartes, 1967:406; Derrida:72/45–46)[17]

At this point Derrida interjects that the next line by Descartes is the "most significant" (72/46) in Foucault's eyes: "But they are mad, and I would not be less extravagant, if I were to follow their examples." Clearly, Derrida is about to accuse Foucault of falling for the feigned distinction. Derrida has not yet, however, left his perch on Foucault's shoulder.

Rejecting the distinction between madness and reason in this last sentence, but retaining the knowledge of what is reasonable by using the absence of the reasonable as a comparison, Derrida continues reading Foucault reading Descartes generalize about how to live in the absence of certainty. The text is now concerned with dreams and sleep. Generalizing dreams to the point of hyperbole, Descartes engages in a sort of thought-experiment to spin truths of nonsensory origin. These truths are true "whether I am awake or asleep." They can capitulate only when faced by an "assault of the Evil Genius."[18] For Descartes, the madness example, which Foucault finds most significant, is just a preliminary move on the way to the question of extending hubris to the demonic hyperbole of the Evil Genius.

But, of course, Foucault does not see this. Foucault does not read Descartes's treatment of dreams as a hyperbolic extension of philosophic skepticism. Instead, Foucault takes seriously the earlier feigned distinction, rejected by Derrida, between objects of sensory origin which can be doubted and those which cannot be accepted unless one is mad. Thus Foucault reads Descartes interning madness in the name of reason and order. Foucault writes on Descartes: "let us assume that we are asleep

—truth will not entirely slip out into the night. For madness it is otherwise." This is the moment of the "Decision" for Foucault.

Having read Descartes over Foucault's shoulder, and having presented what appears to Foucault to be on the page, Derrida notices two things. First, Descartes does not manage to avoid sensory error or dreams within the structure of truth; the hypothesis of dreams is only the hyperbolic exaggeration of the hypothesis that senses can sometimes fail. Madness is just one example of many possible examples of obstacles to certainty. Derrida argues this in some detail. For example: "All significations or ideas of sensory origin are excluded from the realm of truth, for the same reason as madness is excluded from it" (77/50). This leads straightaway to the second point.

According to Derrida's reading, Descartes never excludes madness in the "Decision" Foucault attributes to him. To make his point Derrida needs to distinguish between the totalizing paralysis of an epistemological extravagance and mere madness as a partial debilitation. Derrida wonders aloud (while perhaps glancing at the margins he filled in the second movement) if, when Foucault sees the text ruling against madness, Descartes is not merely attempting to soothe the nonphilosophical reader, who is not sufficiently audacious to contemplate the subversion of a complete (if only hyperbolic) break with reason and order. As we come to the end of the first series of questions, Derrida allows Foucault a hypothetical response.

First, Foucault might, on second reading, say "Yes, perhaps madness is only one of many cases of sensory error. But the fact remains that, if one is to have clear and distinct ideas, madness must be exiled, forced into the shadows. Madness is the other of the Cogito." We shall see that Derrida admits as much, and applauds Foucault's recovery of negativity, but pronounces Foucault naive for never seeing past the de facto situation.

Second, Foucault might even say upon second reading, "Yes, your hypothesis of extravagance is right (I'll take leave of my preoccupation with negativity), but Descartes in the extravagance of the inaugural moment ("originalité") of the Cogito is forced to neutralize madness by viewing it as an epistemological deficiency. And this is just one step away from regarding it as a moral lapse, which would guarantee its banishment."

Derrida is quite willing, within bounds, to concede these

points to Foucault. In one sentence he calls these "two truths" (81/52); in the next sentence they become "vulnerable" (81/52). The difference between these two sentences is a distinction Derrida has been alluding to for some time now: naive versus critical. At a naive level Foucault speaks the truth, reads Descartes well; at the critical level he does not. This distinction announces the beginning of the fourth movement, the critique of linear time.

Derrida's rejoinder to Foucault's so-called truths ushers in the second series of questions. The distinctions of the second movement can organize a presentation of this movement: the naive level can be divided between nonhyperbolic and hyperbolic levels, and then can itself be separated from the level of critical hyperbole. Just as we moved from genealogy through pathos and beyond hubris in the second movement, we shall here move from nonhyperbole to naive hyperbole to critical hyperbole. Before this can happen, however, Derrida must be more explicit about the naive/critical distinction. He elaborates this distinction immediately, in a discussion of Foucault's first truth. Then in discussing the second truth, Derrida operates on all three levels of inquiry.

Derrida's Critique of Foucault on Temporalization

Immediately after saying that Foucault would be perfectly right about his two truths if all discussion were restricted to the naive stage (l'étape naïve), Derrida begins to distinguish such a stage from the critical stage, one which takes metaphysics more seriously (if only to escape its preoccupation with original unity). The first step is to offer a distinction between the hyperbolic moment within natural doubt ("le moment hyperbolique à l'intérieur du doute naturel") and the absolutely hyperbolic moment ("le moment hyperbolique absolu") (81/52).

Derrida needs this distinction to present properly the role of the fiction of the Evil Genius in the *First Meditation*. Only such a presentation can convey how totally Derrida treats the possibility of total madness ("d'une folie totale") (81/52). Consider the possibility of total derangement, that is to say, of a madness which is no longer *only* a disorder of the body, of the object, of the body-object outside the boundaries of the *res cogitans*, that policed and reassuring city of subjective thinking, but of a madness which will enable subversion to enter *pure* thinking, its *purely* intelligible objects, the field of clear and distinct ideas, the domain of mathematical truths, [all of] which are in the process now of escaping natural doubt. (81–82/53)[19]

This passage illustrates the distinction between the hyperbolic moment within natural doubt (there is no Trojan horse about which reason in general is not right) and the moment of absolute hyperbole, wherein madness penetrates all territory within which one might attempt to escape doubt.[20] To appreciate the possibility of total derangement more fully, Derrida invites readers to cross over to the critical stage. It would appear that Foucault has decided to stay behind.

Derrida writes that absolute derangement is so extravagant that it refuses to spare the expense "épargner" of either naive or critical inquiry.[21] Moreover, Derrida insists that Descartes refuses thrift up to a point. While watching Derrida support his reading of Descartes, it is important to keep in mind that absolute derangement is an extravagant fiction, not a de facto possibility.

First, Derrida reads Descartes who, no longer worrying about reassuring the nonphilosopher, describes the hypothetical Evil Genius on a flight of power and deception—"I shall consider myself as having no hands, no eyes, no flesh, no blood, as not having any senses, but believing falsely to have all these" —and comments that this kind of discourse indicates, contrary to Foucault's reading, that Descartes has not dismissed the height of extravagance (82/53). Second, Derrida reads Descartes on what kinds of data (only sensory?) are engaged in the process of escaping doubt. "How do I know that even mathematical truths," asks the Evil Genius, "are not caused by a deceiving God?" So, according to Derrida, Descartes agrees that neither questions of the body nor questions of the mind can cover themselves on this new stage of critical doubt. What was set aside in earlier, reassuring discussions with the timid nonphilosopher as extravagance is now "credited" or welcomed within the most essential interior of thinking, the Cogito.[22] But, before asking at what point Descartes becomes economical and puts doubt in its place, one must ask how it is possible to be so extravagant.

On the way to addressing how the subversive Evil Genius can be at once found out and effective, Derrida uses familiar, time-honored, legal terminology to discuss the two stages of doubt. The naive, reassuring stage of doubt is called de facto ("du fait"); the critical, subversive stage of doubt is called de jure ("du droit"). These descriptions allow Derrida to say that while nothing in principle ("en droit") can oppose the subversion of extravagant criticism, there is no factual reason to be unsettled by this. But it is one thing to be reassured about de facto order and quite another to escape, once and for all, the extravagance of total derangement. Derrida allows the former while ruling out the possibility of the latter.

Derrida can now confront the impossibility he has posited. He acknowledges that even though in principle one can never evade total madness, that is what must be done if language itself is to be intelligible: "namely, if discourse and philosophical communication (that is, language itself) are to have an intelligible meaning, that is, give form ("conformer") to their essence and vocation of discourse, they must in fact and simultaneously in principle escape ("échapper") from madness. They must carry normality within themselves" (83/53).[23] This is the problem: it is impossible for language to do what it must do. In principle, discourse can never banish the monstrosity of extravagant criticism.[24]

So armed, Derrida can now use what he calls Foucault's (1961) most profound sentence—"Madness is the absence of a work"—against Foucault.[25]

The sentence, of course, can be read at the naive stage of Foucault (1961), which allows only the polarity-driven thinking of absence and presence in a play of dominations. If the idea of pretending that discourse has escaped total derangement, and that reason has succeeded in banishing madness, is in operation—as it is at the naive level—then discourse carries normality within itself and the work ("d'oeuvre") can be defined as the polar opposite of madness ("la folie"). Derrida has set up the limitations of this stage so superbly in the marginal markings that there is little need to consider his remarks closely here. But the same sentence can now be read at the critical stage Derrida has read(ied) in Descartes. This stage manages to avoid all reassurance. I must spend some time here because this second reading of "Madness is the absence of a work," in its dizzying generality, is a main reason for reading Derrida in political theory.

We now see more completely why Derrida has used the word *dissension* to mark in the margins what Foucault calls "the Decision": "And if madness in general . . . on the other side of all . . . structure, is the absence of a work, then madness is . . . the silence . . . in a caesura and a wound which are in the process of opening up life as historicity in general" (84/54).[26] Madness in general is on the "other side" of history; and yet madness is somehow located in the "opening up" of "historicity in general." What might these words indicate within the order and reason of language? [27]

The key to getting these words to work together is, of course, to recall that discourse must and cannot escape total derangement. The critical stage corresponds to the general principle; the naive stage corresponds to the particular de facto situation. But readers must not confuse these words with the assertion of a universal/particular polarity.[28] When Derrida mentions historicity in general he is not using historicity in Pocock's sense of a society having a history. Derrida is, after all, working on the stage of hyperbole, of hubris. He is indicating something like the opening up of the possibility of a continuum of lapsing time (linear time) along which society might sense its history.[29] Madness must be silenced in order to open up the possibility of having the instants in time presupposed by Pocock and Foucault. The elapsing time continuum requires an inaugural moment which silences madness; but this silence can never in principle be enforced like a decision. Perpetual dissension is most indecisive and ambiguous; it lives on like an open wound.[30]

The inauguration of historicity in general, then, is the hyperbolic, impossible, and extravagant idea of being neither in time nor timeless. In this sense it "comes before first"[31] and denies any original unity or lack of dissension. Just as an open wound is both a source and a limit of pain, madness is a limit and resource of meaning in general.[32] The nonmeaning of total derangement is a permanent menace ("menace permanente"). Foucault is right to see the unreason of madness (silence) as making reason (the work) possible, but he wrongly operates at the naive level of natural doubt. This level presupposes continuous temporalization and is governed by binary oppositions. The best Derrida can say about Foucault's book is that it encourages the recuperation of negativity at the naive level of inquiry (85/55).

This ends Derrida's response to Foucault's first "truth," that one cannot be mad and have clear and distinct ideas. Derrida's position is that to have clear and distinct ideas requires exiling madness at the highest level of generality, and that it is impossible in principle to do this. Foucault holds, says Derrida, to the reassuring de facto security reserved by Descartes for nonphilosophers. Now Derrida turns to Foucault's second "truth": that madness is, for Descartes, at least a deficiency in an epistemological sense if it must be silenced at the inaugural moment of the Cogito. Derrida's response can be read as a plea for extravagance as an excess to be celebrated, not a deficiency to be covered up. Descartes, as we shall see, leaves shortly before the celebration can begin. Foucault never responds to the invitation to celebrate, and continues fighting the flux that Derrida would give in to.

By now the forces of negativity have been recovered sufficiently to allow the question of whether extravagance is a deficiency or something else. The best way to approach this response is to read it as a grand finale, during which the distinctions of the second movement join in a remarkable chorus. In fact, the three levels of the second movement—nonhyperbolic naïveté, hyperbolic naïveté, and critical hyperbole—can organize my presentation.

In response to the second so-called truth of Foucault, Derrida announces immediately (85/55) that, as was the first, this "truth" is valid only during the naive stage of inquiry. But this time Derrida goes further to claim that the hypothesis of extravagance ("l'hypothèse de l'extravagance") is a threat to all knowledge, whatever the stage. He does this by subdividing the naive stage into two phases, hyperbolic and nonhyperbolic, and then showing that Descartes only "seems" to exclude extravagance during the nonhyperbolic phase of the naive stage.[33] Madness is, then, not a deficiency of reason; it is not any singular state at all. Madness, whatever it names, is only one way of exercising the Cogito, one of many ways of thinking. Whether or not I am mad, I can think and exist as a person.[34] This having been said, Derrida is no longer interested in the illusionary moment of the internment by logos of madness.

At the hyperbolic phase of the naive stage one encounters the inaugural moment of the Cogito: pure thinking. Derrida describes this moment of pure subjectivity as a kind of "zero point at which determined meaning and nonmeaning come together in their common origin."[35] This is why it is decidedly wrong to view madness as a deficiency in knowledge; there is no prior whole knowledge (or unity interior to logos) for madness to have fallen away from. Derrida describes this zero-point, or inaugural moment, this juxtapositioning of sense and nonsense:

> It is the point of unopened certainty where the possibility of Foucauldian reading is embedded, as well as the reading of the totality, or rather of all determined forms of exchange between reason and madness.[36] It is the point[37] where the project of thinking the totality in the process of escaping it is embedded. In the process of escaping it, that is, exceeding the totality, that which is possible—within existence—only in the direction of infinity or nothingness. . . . (86–87/56)[38]

To escape the totality is impossible because this requires moving in the direction of nothingness or infinity. Even if one is sufficiently audacious to speculate about moving in that direction (the direction of critical hyperbole) from point zero, instead of moving toward the future in the direction of reassurance, one is still thinking. Extravagance and normalcy, bravado and boredom, are all wrapped together in the zero-point—or Cogito—at the hyperbolic phase of the first stage. Moreover, it is impossible to distinguish these ways of thinking from one another in this primordial moment.

The demonic hyperbole of the Evil Genius is a generalization of all the reasonable and deranged symbols of the Cogito and for this reason is taken most seriously at the next level of inquiry, after Descartes pretends to overcome it and loses his nerve. Because the zero point must allow both meaning and nonmeaning to the point of denying their distinction, Derrida claims that nothing could be less reassuring than pure subjectivity in its inaugural moment (87/56). Efforts by theorists like Foucault to reduce this bewildering moment to a determined historical structure, a classic decision, risk missing the point that in principle madness, and all of the other extravagant symbols of the Cogito, are never escaped. As we shall see from the critical stage, THEY HAVE ALWAYS ALREADY BEGUN and thus are interminable; they are moments unmarked by temporalization.[39]

We are now in a position to bring temporalization out of the background, where it has been camouflaged by its very self-evidence. Derrida explains how the flow of time reassures naive readers: he shows how the Cartesian Cogito can stand as a source of terror and a source of certainty.

Derrida is quite open about this complexity. He has already insisted that madness is one case of the inaugural moment of the Cogito, which is therefore not reassuring. We have also read that the Cogito cannot be reduced to an historically determined polarity. But Derrida never claims that history is irrelevant.[40] Saying that the hyperbolic project cannot be reduced to the totality of historical totalities is not to deny the relevance of totality. Without it one cannot speak of an absolute excess. There exist totalities of facts—for example, those accumulated by social science and studied indirectly through "laws" of chance and accident[41]—that can be studied "objectively," but in principle there is always an excess which cannot. Derrida writes: "I know very well that this hyperbolic point which must be, like all of pure madness in general, silent, is not alone there, in the movement which one calls the Cartesian *Cogito*" (89/58).[42]

The other element in the movement called the Cartesian Cogito is, of course, the one which provides the certainty one normally associates with the name Descartes. Derrida explains this de facto reassurance (which makes logos possible) by using the language of time. He explains that as soon as Descartes reaches the point of hyperbole (the zero-point of the Cogito wherein he must move toward nothingness or infinity to escape totality) he finds it necessary to reassure himself. At this point—the zero-point—Descartes imposes a timeless/timebound distinction. God occupies the throne of the timeless and logos is sent down the line of timebound particularity (linear time). In the beginning was the word, so to speak.

Descartes's lapse into reassurance just when the Cogito is getting interesting—that is, defying all polar distinctions—indicates why his hyperbolic project is, after all, naive: the Evil Genius is forced to obey God and his logos. The possibility within the Cogito, then, of both heading toward the economical reassurance of immanence and the continuity of time (on both hands), and (on neither hand) of floundering without polar symmetry as if the earth were not poised in air, is the instant Descartes brings an end to his hyperbolic project. Derrida puts it this way:

> As soon as he has overtaken this point [the hyperbolic point], Descartes seeks to reassure himself, to affirm the Cogito itself in God, to identify the act of Cogito with the act of reasonable reason [logos]. And he does this as soon as he proffers and reflects the Cogito. That is, as soon as he has to place the Cogito in the flow of time ("temporaliser"), the Cogito which finds its price ("valoir") only in the instant of intuition, of the thought attentive to itself, in this point, or this point of the instant. (89/58)[43]

To comprehend this complex passage it is best to imagine a continuum that ranges from the earliest instant in time to the eternal, but not infinite, future. Imagine an elapsing time continuum. Its left most point is the point of unopened certainty. But to escape the totality of this form, one must abandon the continuum altogether and struggle to give in to the irrational. Genealogy stays to the right and studies events in time, only pretending that madness has been interned. Hyperbolic naive thinkers speculate about the inaugural moment of silencing madness, which is more of an enemy than a deficiency. The hypercritical Derrida is sufficiently audacious to confess that by temporalizing the Cogito, Descartes is also naive; the natural stage of doubt never succeeds in banishing pure madness in general.

It is, of course, impossible to move to the dizzying critical stage where discontinuity is finally appreciated. If it were possible, I could go there and bring back Derrida's truth, perhaps assessing its political implications. Instead, the third stage is like the radical extension of a perspective which one can, moving beyond acts of hubris, only will to adopt. The will to speak demonic hyperbole, to play the Evil Genius, is an affirmative way of confessing that reasonable and orderly discourse only postpones the conclusion that our worlds cannot be made sense of. Critical inquiry keeps this confession alive while madness is necessarily deferred. Indeed, one can only make sense in the provisional or de facto way allowed by Derrida by differing from the madness which resides in all discourse.

The will to adopt such a perspective gives a radically different flavor to the notion of play. Instead of speaking only of the play of words on a page, which may permit delightful and irritating reversals of meaning, Derrida is speaking of a more radical play: namely, play in the world. The total madness which refuses exile makes the more obvious word play on a page possible.[44] There is always an excess in any structure, in any sensemaking operation, and at any point in time.

Derrida is writing here about multiple statements of excess. It may appear that he is gearing up for a paradigm shift over time, resembling Kuhn or Pocock. But this is not at all what is going on; Derrida remains consistent with his occasional disillusionment with temporalization. Even though he speaks of the forgetting (a crisis in the sense that one forgets an enemy one has not yet escaped) and the reawakening of madness happening again and again, Derrida in not describing a "series" of extravagant reawakenings. He is quite explicit about this:

> From the first breath, speech submits to this temporal rhythm of crisis and reawakening, opens its speaking space [breaks silence] only by locking up madness. Furthermore, this rhythm is not an alternation which would besides move through time. [Ce rythme n'est d'ailleurs pas une alternance qui serait de surcoît temporelle.] It is the movement of temporalization itself, within that which unites it with the movement of logos. (94/60–61)[45]

We have already seen how Descartes is forced to temporalize the Cogito in order to reassure himself at the height of hyperbole. Derrida insists that this is not a "one time" philosophical act which might stand as an origin in time, even though in a sense it is an origin of time. Because it is impossible in principle to escape madness, madness lives in the margins and spaces of all writing.[46] It constitutes a crisis which has always already begun and is thereby interminable.[47] So ends the fourth movement.

The Final Movement

Derrida draws his essay to a close by moving ahead three hundred pages in Foucault's text, to a passage in which Descartes's name appears once more. Derrida's reaction to this passage is the fifth movement, or conclusion, of his essay. The passage in question reads like this: "In the moment during which doubt ran afoul of its major peril, Descartes realized that he could not be mad—except to recognize for a longtime more, and to the point of the Evil Genius, that all the powers of irrationality were keeping watch over his thought" (95/61).[48] Derrida says, in summary, that he is trying in this essay to keep from extinguishing the "black and hardly natural light" of irrationality, unreasonableness "déraison" that causes Descartes and Foucault so much remorse. This is an important task for Derrida because, from his extravagant perspective, madness plays a constitutive role in the possibility of reason and order. Unlike Foucault, who explains the rift between reason and its other as a moment in history, Derrida recognizes the production and sorting out of reason and madness from undifferentiated raw material in the Cogito as a matter of economy. Derrida explains that in an effort to economize ("s'economiser") or save themselves, thrifty philosophers sequester madness, doing violence to it in the name of logos. Derrida shows how one can be more extravagant: one can learn how philosophy is an exaggeration made possible by, first, the difference between the totality of form (being and nonbeing) and its excess (all of the flux left out by Parmenides' distinction) and, second, the fact that the question of excess is never annihilated, only deferred. Derrida coins *différance* (differ + defer) to name this double play.[49] He would, then, supplement the thrifty economizing position by adding the différance of absolute excess.[50] Accordingly, madness is a bit more apparent, near; one might speak of its murmurings while maintaining its silence. This supplants the sovereignty of totalizing, hierarchizing forms.

In conclusion, if read from an extravagant perspective, philosophy is a gigantic confession: as Derrida's reading of Descartes illustrates, one can confess that truths are gleaned precisely because they draw close enough to total derangement for readers to sense the difference. Because the inaugural moment of truth is also the inaugural moment of time, the screaming, murmuring silence of madness is always already a crisis for thinking.

Derrida's most subversive reversal in this essay is perhaps its most subtle. The social sciences are quite accustomed to using the de facto/de jure distinction. Even the least philosophically inclined use these terms to contrast the world of order as it might be if people were perfectly reasonable creatures, and the world of imperfections, the de facto world, in which reasonable principles are violated in the name of practicality. Derrida has just accomplished a total reversal of that usage. In his essay reason and order are accepted as de facto structures which take their life from being different than the chaos of a world which is radically irrational in principle. For political theory the implications of this reversal are so overwhelming that they cannot all be said. A politics of community which cannot confess such a reversal will, no doubt, continue fighting the flux, maintaining patterns of subjectivity across time. This fight involves protecting citizens from the worst of life even as it denies them its joys. Community as confession, however, might face the crisis of reason, take time out to give in to flux, and glimpse the monstrosity of possibility.

Toward Maintaining Silence

The will to maintain and pass along what one has accumulated —whether private property, identity, or national boundaries— presupposes the continuity of time. Putting lives on the line for the sovereignty of the nation-state, killing others for the sovereignty of property, turning away from others in need because of the hold of the sovereignty of identity; all of these strategies presuppose the possibility of having histories, even discontinuous histories that cannot be squared with one another. The point, however, is that these histories, discontinuous or continuous, all presuppose the continuity of time (or the elapsing time continuum). When discontinuity in history becomes the accepted fact conflicts are inevitable. Chapter 2 has shown some of the impact of this conflict in political theory. Those with liberal aspirations are attracted to the notion of a sovereign nation perpetuating itself across time; those with communal sensitivity are damned if they will turn their backs on all liberal aspirations. And those who either ignore this by denouncing metaphysics (from within) its grasp, or embracing any of its principles, such as the historical dialectic, continue to rely on the continuity of time.

Derrida shows how insane the principle of sovereignty can be, because it guards the traces of violence which make unflinching stands possible. By mobilizing the silences (margins, spaces, blanks, blinks of the eye, hesitations, being at a loss for words) he confesses that the traces always already exceed or overflow all time (including the timebound and its other, eternity). Derrida admits in writing that sovereignty is merely a deferral of the distance between determined historical structures and their absolute excess, which in fact must be silenced in the name of constructing worlds of reason and order.

Because remunity is based on self/other reciprocity and communion is based on part/whole congruity, one might conclude that they have no place in a politics of Derridian extravagance. But this ignores the point that silence must be maintained even though binary language is used. We have seen that most studies fall somewhere along the continuum formed by the remunity/communion couple. A politics of Derridian extravagance begins with these couples, but rearranges the fields they pretend to cover by revealing a close-up in which the presence of the subject is, in principle, always already deferred.

Reversing the relation of de facto and de jure legitimacy of reason, Derrida opens the infinite play of signification. In principle, there is no limit to the substitution of signs (whether man, conscience, soul, etc.). But such signs do provide provisional order. A challenge for political theory is to avoid being reassured by what are, after all, only arbitrary signs. A politics of Derridian extravagance necessarily begins with the de facto presence of the subject in discourse, but this politics grows by maintaining silence, not by transgressing the limits of discourse. For if play is infinite, such limits make no sense.

9 Redrawing the Lignes de Bataille

And I forgot the element of chance introduced by circumstances, calm or haste, sun or cold, dawn or dusk, the taste of strawberries or abandonment, the half-understood message, the front page of newspapers, the voice on the telephone, the most anodyne conversation, the most anonymous man or woman, everything that speaks, makes noise, passes by, touches us lightly, meets us head on.—Jacques Sojcher (in Certeau, 1984:xvi)

All that you can call gift . . . is forbidden by the dual opposition. . . . The gift must be given by chance.—Jacques Derrida (1987:198)

The last chapter shows how madness is both the death and the resource of writing. Drawing up close to death can release a nearly inexhaustible pathos that brings joy to life. After a good performance of music or dance we might say, "She was really into it," or "She really let herself go during the second movement," indicating that passion is tied to the death of the subject. To give ourselves to a practice with such intensity that our subjectivity becomes a function of the practice (instead of the other way around), is to give a gift. During gift-giving something mysterious takes over; the practice seems to determine the identities of the giver and the receiver. The gift charts its own destination. To concentrate solely on gift-giving is, of course, impossible; but it is all too possible to stunt the growth of gifted children, to brutalize gifted people who live on the wrong side of the balance of power, or to fight the flux of indeterminate subjectivity in the name of reason and order.

One cannot constantly live at the intensity of gift-giving without burning out. The gift is accidental, cannot be calculated, comes and goes, multiplies differences. Drawing up close to the death of the subject permits, within reason, an escape from patterns of subjectivity; such escape is possible because reason and order are always already pervaded by the irrationality of flux. Energy is expended with no end in sight.

Unfortunately, there are more solitary ways to fight against patterned subjectivity: such as dismantling the modern subject as if it were a fragile artifact and dancing on the shattered fragments. Energy is expended destructively with no end in sight. Gift-giving is, from this perspective, a form of humiliating other people. This chapter is an effort to contrast Derridian extravagance with the more transgressive battle called "joy before death." Bataille travels out to the limits of reason and annihilates the self; but perhaps there are many small deaths available to those who redraw the battlelines, regroup their energies, and concentrate on the silent spaces, the blinks of the eye, that give "one" room to breathe in the practice of everyday life.

The language of MacIntyre's (1988:369) contempt for the "presupposition of Derrida's choice between remaining 'within' . . . the already constructed social and intellectual edifice . . . to deconstruct it from within, or brutally placing oneself outside in a condition of rupture and discontinuity" is problematic for at least two reasons. First, Derrida (1967/1978:427–28/293) states explicitly that there is no reason to choose between the reassurance of the traditions he deconstructs and the extravagance of his radical interpretive tactics. But MacIntyre knows this. Second, and more serious, is the inside/outside opposition in MacIntyre's indictment.

The habit of thinking in terms of opposites is so deeply entrenched in contemporary political theory that one might safely bet—though the odds may be getting worse—that theorists who do not spend time writing within the limits of reason and order spend time transgressing these limits, moving back and forth at the edge of discourse.[1] Thinking in terms of inside/outside couples tends to draw attention away from what Certeau (1984) calls the "practice of everyday life."[2] On the one hand, inside the limits of discourse everyday life is portrayed as if governed, though perhaps incompletely or badly, by reason and order; chance happenings and accident are viewed as exceptions to reason's rule. Beyond the borders of discourse, on the other hand, life is bewildering, chaotic, irrational, and nomadic.[3] Because deconstruction celebrates accident and chance, challenging the limits of reason, it is assumed to be hell-bent on transgression. Georges Bataille does not encourage us to think differently.[4] Indeed, as we shall see, Bataille is in the direct line of fire when MacIntyre takes aim at Derrida.

But Derrida is elsewhere: his work does not offer choices between remaining within the continuity of a tradition (MacIntyre's edifice) or risking the discontinuity of epistemological insanity. These two aspects of life are as closely related for Derrida as the two sides of a sheet of paper: one does not choose which side to cut into. MacIntyre's thinking about the true and the pure contains misleading rhetorical strategies which imply that rupture lies outside literary and philosophical foundations.

I want to be able to say that Georges Bataille does not have to transgress reason's allegedly outer limits to locate the conditions of rupture and discontinuity he calls "joy before death." I want also to say that such transgression risks lending legitimacy to the totality one would flee. This risk includes confirming the illusion that the Law, or discourse, or man, is doing a good job providing order and covering up what is bewildering about existence. As luck would have it, Derrida has already made these points, which follow from his reversal of the relation of rationality and irrationality.[5] If reason and order are only provisionally in charge, as Derrida holds, then there is no reason to speak of outer limits that must somehow be transgressed to grant sovereignty to silent irrationality. If the "black and hardly natural light" (Derrida, 1978:61) of accident and flux cannot be extinguished, its forces are always already available.

I first introduce Bataille's "outside" approach to joy before death. Next, to focus on its political implications, I read his essay on expenditure. Then, I wish to mention a Derridian way of drawing up close to death without abiding the supervision of inside/outside couples. Finally, I comment on what stands in the way of freeing expenditure from the "choice" between destroying its infinite possibilities or letting it destroy fellow beings.

Bataille's Celebration of Joy Before Death

Martin Jay (1984:510) opens his necessarily unsympathetic reading of Foucault and, especially, of Derrida with a version of this quote from Georges Bataille (1988/1954:36/48): "Like a herd chased by an infinite shepherd, the bleating flock which we are would flee, would flee without end the horror of a reduction of Being to totality." Standing alone, these lines signal an end to dialectical thinking, announce a rejection of Hegelian metaphysics, and suggest a dangerous supplement to the time-honored *aufhebung* that affirms, negates, and transcends both sides of opposition in one synthetic moment. This might exempt Bataille from MacIntyre's attack. But a few of the lines above this striking metaphor sound like what MacIntyre leads us to expect from Bataille: "I destroy myself in the infinite possibility of my fellow beings: it annihilates the sense of self. If I attain, an instant, the extreme limit of the 'possible,' shortly thereafter, I will flee, I will be elsewhere" (36/48). Where will this avant-garde ancestor of Kristeva, Foucault, and Derrida be? Bataille's self-annihilation appears to play into the hands of postmodernism's critics, but a closer look at Bataille's debt to Western metaphysics might surprise such critics as Jay and MacIntyre.

Perhaps the annihilation of self these critics so carefully condemn is the very future they are progressing toward. Both Jay and MacIntyre are revising older traditions to ward off self-annihilation, but neither is even cautiously optimistic. Perhaps there is something about the way their totalizing projects work that sets up and encourages an opposition to savagery and destruction. Could not Bataille's "solitary erection" of brutality be the only option available to beings who are forced to fit the patterned self-images of their age? Is death all there is left to celebrate in these worlds of brutality or boredom that reduce difference to opposition?[6] As the battalions around the world increase and compete with each other in a self-destructive, gross-feeding consumption, a turn toward postmodernism sans Bataille might avoid precisely that which reassuring theorists now fear it represents.

When Bataille writes, "I destroy myself in the infinite possibility of my fellow beings," he is struggling with a question of subjectivity raised by Foucault. Recall that in addition to the more familiar questions of state domination addressed by contract theorists and of exploitation addressed by civic humanists, Foucault (1983:212) would advertise a struggle "against that which ties the individual to himself and submits him to others in this way." Foucault refuses the sense of self produced by the simultaneous individuation and totalization of modern power structures, and affirms a self more concerned with empowerment than domination.[7] Bataille is less willing than Foucault to compromise with life and thus he vigorously pursues the death of the subject. Bataille's celebration of joy before death takes place during moments of transgressing the bounds of discourse. Such moments neutralize meaning and free the self from the confines of subjectivity. But the infinity of being, because it is experienced outside significative discourse, cannot make sense of the principle of difference. The major question is how to neutralize the oppositions that disfigure being—how to curb what Connolly calls the "designer's urge"—without eliminating the possibility of all meaning whatsoever, without sacrificing difference.

We all know the problem with a gender-blind, color-blind, difference-blind neutralization of opposition: everything quiets down and nothing structural ever changes. Bataille's journey to the fringe of reason and order, an interior journey, seeks to escape the "noises of struggle"; this alone should raise suspicions about the political implications of the so-called joy before death. His essay on the practice of joy before death (1970/1985: 552–58/235–39) begins in exasperation with reasonable, orderly modernity. But one can hear in this exasperation a tone of the totality he was so desperate to flee.

Bataille (1970/1985:532/235) draws readers in as he paints a picture of a man on a "beautiful spring morning" during which one is likely to be "carried away" by "enchantment or simple joy." Then—all of a sudden—everything becomes too quiet. The romantic moment is not so simple, after all: "At that moment, something cruelly rises up in him that is comparable to a bird of prey that tears open the throat of a smaller bird in an apparently peaceful and clear blue sky." [8] Bataille finds "violence . . . acting on . . . his being with a rigor that frightens him." He questions how to recognize this propensity for violence while at the same time not succumbing to the sense of vertigo it causes so completely as to invite violent death. Bataille comes up with advice that heats the blood of vertiginous readers while making the blood of their critics run cold. "He alone is happy who, having experienced vertigo to the point of trembling in his bones, to the point of being incapable of measuring the extent of his fall, suddenly to turn his agony into a joy capable of freezing and transfiguring those who meet it" (553/236). Do not miss the tarnished mean between the agony of complete chaos and the crippling repression that comes from denying the cruelty of one's propensity for violence. Bataille moves back and forth—in and out—at the limit of reason and order, now transgressing, now toeing the line. [9] What kind of transfiguration does Bataille associate with living transgressions? Is he as Nietzschean as he sounds?

Borrowing the religious mystical expression of joy before death (as opposed to the "simple joy" of a spring morning), Bataille reinterprets this phrase in the context of the death of God. [10] This leads him to invert the sanctity of spiritual contemplation and to celebrate instead the ecstasy of appetitive delight: "Prudery may be healthy for backward souls, but those who would be afraid of nude girls or whisky would have little to do with joy before death" (554/236). Bataille's celebration calls for man to stop "behaving like a cripple, glorifying necessary work and letting himself be emasculated by the fear of tomorrow" (554/236). Living life without measure, as if in a mystical trance, Bataille's transgressions would lead us into "an apotheosis of flesh and alcohol" (554/236).

Bataille seeks peace from opposition by living beyond fields of dialectics, and in so doing discovers the excesses of everyday life that are not productive and do not conserve life. But his interpretation of excess is governed by an inside/outside polarity to such an extent that his loss is, in the end, totality's gain. Struggling to flee totality, Bataille establishes its presence. He continues by chanting toward the peace that accompanies close brushes with death:

> I abandon myself to peace, to the point of annihilation.
> The noises of struggle are lost in death, as rivers are lost in the sea, as stars burst in the night.
> The strength of combat is fulfilled in the silence of all action.
> I enter into peace as I enter into a dark unknown.
> I myself become his dark unknown.
>
> I AM joy before death.
> Joy before death carries me.
> Joy before death hurls me down.
> Joy before death annihilates me. (555/237)

However else this passage—which is designed to glorify the infinite possibility of his fellow beings—might be read, it resounds with the noises of male dominance under reconstruction. Bataille's peace certainly does not pass Dworkin's (1987: 190) understanding: "Some classy men say that sex is connected to the *awareness* of death . . . that man fucks with the certain, tragic knowledge of death . . . They mean penile sex." Dworkin would remind all readers that Bataille's (1986) work on eroticism illustrates how "The poor little penis kills before it dies" (Dworkin, 1987:190).[11]

One might expect, then, that Bataille's sense of the "infinite possibility of my fellow beings" may be less radical than his avant-garde reputation. This carries heavy implications for all that lies behind the lines as well. That is, Bataille's efforts to neutralize the tensions of totality may work, in a complicated way, to conserve the male privilege or at the very best confer this time-honored privilege on certain women.

Because I am interested in the political implications of Bataille's eruptive visions of excess, I want to read his famous essay on expenditure. This essay is a detailed study of joy before death in the everyday world of production and consumption. Bataille, of course, is interested in highlighting the nonproductive side of consumption, the side some college freshmen explore outside of economics class. In this sense his essay may resemble a deconstruction of expenditure. But I want to take a closer look.

Reading Bataille on Expenditure

Bataille shows the way to the nonproductive corners of life by inverting the relation between our so-called dark sides and the sides that are easier to discuss. The extent to which his pursuit of a vertiginous sovereignty (that obliterates all opposition, outside of meaning) continues to rely on oppositions is the extent to which Bataille does not illustrate how deconstruction happens.[12] Bataille cannot seem to preclude the establishment of new syntheses.

Bataille's (1970/1985:302–20/116–29) essay on expenditure is designed to show that "in the practice of life, it [humanity] acts in a way that allows for the satisfaction of disarmingly savage needs, and it seems able to subsist only at the limit of horror" (304/117). To discuss life near the edge, Bataille needs to resist the "principle that all particular [individual] effort, in order to be valid, must be reducible to the fundamental necessities of production and conservation" (303/117). Bataille's interest in "nonproductive expenditure" takes him beyond necessary, mundane, consumption to consider activities which have no end beyond themselves. Examples include mourning, sexual activity deflected from genital finality, and games. In all of these activities, according to Bataille, "the loss must be as great as possible for the activity to take on its true meaning" (305/118). It would appear that Bataille has located an excess which lies outside the economical relation of production and conservation, a hidden layer of life which has lost out to the hegemony of reason. One might expect him to reverse this power relation and to show how insubordinate expenditure can be. In fact he does attempt to show that rather than consume to live the human subject lives to consume; that is, human beings perform functions of survival (production and conservation) in order to threaten survival in acts of unproductive expenditure. As relevant as this view may be to late-twentieth-century Western life, such relevance discourages the idea of community. If Bataille is right about an insubordinate need to self-destruct, and if his work speaks for contemporary nihilism, then there is nothing affirmative to say about community. Rather, one should prepare for the "orgiastic" frenzy of practicing joy before death.

The essay on expenditure is a model of symmetry. Its seven sections build a case across time, from tribal days to the here-and-now, achieving a crescendo in the fourth section on the capitalist stage wherein he claims that "All that was generous, orgiastic, and excessive has disappeared" (313/124). This is the moment of hegemony, when the primitive need to expend freely is turned back against the human subject, making it petty, jealous, cowardly, and a seeker of glory. And then the remaining sections decline (as if) to say what comes next. In these sections Bataille discusses revolutionary politics and Christianity in terms of the insubordinate need of classes of people to be destructive. A class victory in the streets would, of course, reverse the hegemonic relation. Thus for Bataille, like Foucault, "history advances from domination to domination."[13] Bataille wishes to draw attention to the losing side at this point in time, anticipating the moment when the "beautiful phrases" of the bourgeoisie "will be drowned out by death screams in riots" (318/128). Predictably, Christianity is presented as an attempt to gloss over this savage, insubordinate truth.

Bataille opens the last section sounding very much like Derrida: "human life cannot in any way be limited to the closed systems which are assigned to it in reasonable conceptions" (318/128). But when Bataille elaborates, he relies upon just the sort of reasonable conceptions he would supplant. Of course, anyone who is not silent must do this. At issue is whether his reliance treats irrationality as an insubordinate exile or as an inseparable, if irreconcilable, part of making sense. Bataille writes: "life starts with the 'déficit' of these systems." The presence of *déficit* suggests that the forces of "déraisin" are exiled in Bataille's writing. Using this word to name a principle of downfall, or loss ("la perte") commits Bataille to an opposition as reasonable and orderly as the one he eschews. His text is unable—despite its plea for insubordination—to subvert or supplement the authority of this opposition. Deficit (from the latin *de* + *facio*) is the mere dismantlement of what was constructed. Bataille's efforts to neutralize oppositions seem only to inaugurate new oppositions.

This last section, after such an incisive opening, collapses into a summation of the essay that makes extravagant gift-giving seem as destructive as possible. Bataille reminds us that human beings, rather than living for productive values, such as balancing their accounts, live for unproductive values, such as the glory in deficit spending. What glory can be found there? The excitement of degrading oneself makes glory complete because it gives vent to the insubordinate desire to expend freely with no end in mind, a desire hidden within us all. Bataille achieves this reversal by pointing out that social existence has been dominated all along by glory. This urge (that so many struggle to keep under control) to live outside the bounds of reason and order, is actually insubordinate. It continually declares itself sovereign, like an exiled monarch. Instead of living to achieve goals, we assure our subsistence in order to acquiesce to the insubordinate function of free expenditure. And the greater the deficit the more intense the pleasure.

So the pleasure of gift-giving lies in the glorification of loss, waste, and excrement.[14] The glory in giving extravagant gifts lies in the pleasure of giving in to the insubordinate urge to ruin life, to use it up, to burn it out. This is best accomplished by humiliating those folks called "less fortunate" because they have less money to burn. Gift-giving is a form of domination at the limit of savagery.

The problem with presenting the excesses ignored by reason and order as a deficit, or loss, is that it inaugurates a new hierarchy: loss/gain. This, coupled with the implicit elapsing time continuum in Bataille's essay, leads his work straight to a nihilism which cannot be anything but solitary and mad, unless it lingers in apathy on the fringe of reassurance. Bataille, despite his avant-garde reputation, does not think play radically. For if the play of absence and presence—in this case irrational loss/rational gain—is to be thought radically, play must be imagined to neutralize opposition without destroying the infinite possibilities of difference. Bataille is forced to substitute new oppositions for old along the line of time. His extravagant expenditure is a form of deficit spending, an alternative to gainfully balancing the books.

Georges Bataille is taken seriously by the likes of Foucault and Derrida because he seeks to neutralize the tensions that govern the practice of everyday life. But critics determined to —or "by" as the accidental substitute saying goes—work for radical change cannot afford to be neutral about neutralization. Derrida (1987:199) writes "There is a certain neutralization which can reconstruct the phallocentric privilege. But there is another neutralization which can simply neutralize the . . . opposition, and not [racial or] sexual [or cultural, etc.] difference, liberating the field . . . for a very different sexuality [ethnicity, culture, etc], a more multiple one." I wish next to read Bataille over Derrida's shoulder to show what is involved in liberating fields from oppositions.

Reading Bataille Over Derrida's Shoulder

Derrida (1967/1978) opens his deconstruction of Bataille by commenting that those who are the most blasé about rejecting metaphysical (in general and Hegelian in particular) systems are often those who are most caught up in its fields of opposition. To reject Hegel lightly is to remain Hegelian. Bataille is saluted for not rejecting Hegel too lightly. To deliver a radical critique of Western metaphysics, Derrida tells us, requires the following: "To bear the self-evidence of Hegel, today, would mean this: one must, in every sense, go through the 'slumber of reason,' the slumber that engenders monsters and then puts them to sleep; this slumber must be effectively traversed so that awakening will not be a ruse of dream. That is to say, again, a ruse of reason" (252/370). Effectively traversing the sleep of reason, according to Derrida, must not, as we shall see, be equated with escaping the world of significative discourse because the sleep of reason is not just another way of talking about putting reason to sleep; nonmeaning must never be confused with the polar opposite of meaning. "The slumber of reason . . . is . . . the slumber in the form of reason." ("Le sommeil de la raison, ce n'est peut-être pas la raison endormie mais le sommeil dans la forme de la raison, la vigilance du logos hegelien" (252/370).) The two ways of reading this warning—despite Derrida's salute to Bataille—introduce how Bataille and Derrida differ on the monstrosity produced by the sleep of reason.

The first is the more obvious. Reason has a vigilant border patrol. It sleeps with one eye open. So even its slumber is vigilant. The sleep of reason is just another form of reason, another form of the vigilant Hegelian logos looking over that in which it has an interest.[15]

But these words permit a more subversive reading in which reason's form can be said never to be fully awake. In this reading the sleep of reason is the barely natural drowsiness of sense, the periodic hibernation of reason.[16] Thus, in contrast with sleep as a form of reason lies sleep in the vigilance of reason's form, or reason caught off guard.

Derrida reserves the second reading as ammunition for when he forces Bataille to testify against himself at the end of his reading. He uses the first right away, revealing that his salute is a warning shot. Bataille's vision of excess sells irrationality short, and pretends that he is escaping to a sovereign, silent, monstrosity of joy before death ("sommeil éternale"). But such a silent monstrosity outside of discourse is never an option for Derrida: one is either naive about having to escape totality or critical of either/or thinking (while using it).[17]

Derrida reads Bataille, then, in ways that celebrate the degree to which his predecessor sought out monstrosity by attempting to escape metaphysics. But Derrida whenever possible echoes his reminder that "there is no sense in doing without the concepts of metaphysics in order to shake metaphysics" (Derrida, 1978:280). The problem is learning to effectively traverse metaphysics.[18]

As Derrida begins to explore Bataille's debt to Hegel, or to philosophy, he mentions how Bataille uses a notion of transgression to separate the world of discursive difference (which Hegel, we are told, conceived more profoundly than anyone else) from the sovereign, silent world of slumbering reason, which Bataille conceives as an external zone.

> Since it excludes articulated language, sovereign silence is therefore, in a certain fashion, foreign to difference as the source of signification. It seems to erase discontinuity, and this is how we must, in effect, understand the necessity of the continuum which Bataille unceasingly invokes . . . the continuum is the privileged experience of a sovereign operation transgressing the limit of discursive difference. (Derrida, 1967/1978:386/263)

Notice how Derrida is positioning Bataille and Hegel on either side of the limit of discourse. Bataille attempts to find an area outside the play of difference; Hegel attempts to cover all the ground within.[19] Bataille is portrayed to resemble the graduate student who avoids a thesis topic because of "the definitive book" already in the library. Not writing the thesis magnifies the book's image of covering the subject totally. Bataille's strategy of writing in a way that "*exceeds* the *logos* (of meaning, lordship, presence etc.)" (Derrida, 1967/1978:392/267) implies that he could not locate excess within the prisonhouse of discursive difference. Bataille has the right idea about looking for sovereignty that is not reason, but "there is no Trojan horse about which reason is not right" (Derrida: 1967/1978:58/36). Bataille's will to transgress leads him into a kind of death of the subject that is governed by that light sleeper, reason.[20]

Derrida (1967/1978:393/268) deliberately points out Bataille's totalitarian flight from totality. Derrida states that "the transgression of meaning is not an access to . . . the possibility of maintaining nonmeaning." The idea of indeterminate identity—so important, as we shall see, to anonymous gift-giving —and the idea of maintaining the sovereign silence Bataille seeks both require one to "inscribe rupture in the text": "to place . . . discursive knowledge . . . in relation to an . . . absolute unknowledge from whose nonbasis is launched chance" (394/268). This relation of knowledge and unknowledge is maintained only by admitting that reason and order never succeed in eliminating all traces of the violence of breaking silence. Accident and chance are a constituent element of everyday life; there is nothing reason can do to change this situation. Bataille neglects the accidental slips and chaotic pockets of silence in discourse when he breaks the rules, as if he could exhaust all meaning. Derrida is concerned that such anarchy makes it impossible to say anything at all because all difference would be destroyed or neutralized. In a world where everything is neutralized, the status quo wins.[21]

But the disagreement between Bataille and Derrida is not only about how much Bataille misses by positing the neutrality, or oblivion, of silent monstrosity outside of discourse. Derrida also wants to show how much Bataille conserves. He does this by reversing Bataille's rejection of Hegel. So, we are told, Bataille's transgressions of the rules of discourse not only would erase all difference in their search for the other of meaning, they also, in a sense, confirm the Hegelian system they oppose. Derrida (1967/1978:403/274) writes this: "But this transgression of discourse . . . must, in some fashion, and like every transgression, conserve or confirm that which it exceeds." The difference between Derrida and Bataille on irrationality is perhaps best illustrated near the end of Derrida's reading. By implication, Derrida paints a self-portrait of one who would read Hegel while listening for the "infinite murmur of a blank speech erasing the traces of classical discourse" (403/274) within discourse. This erasure opens the possibility of a working relationship between de facto rationality and de jure irrationality.[22] But as Derrida effectively traverses texts within the rules of discourse, he paints Bataille as one who annihilates himself to glory in the loss, just as in the essay on expenditure. Here is Derrida's portrait of Bataille:

> The destruction of discourse . . . multiplies words, precipitates them one against the other, engulfs them too, in an endless and baseless substitution whose only rule is the sovereign affirmation of the play outside meaning . . . a kind of potlatch of signs that burns, consumes, and wastes words in the drunken affirmation of death: a sacrifice and a challenge. (403/274)

Derrida condemns this kind of human sacrifice and will not accept the challenge to come up with an even more destructive scheme. The endless substitution of signs does not bother Derrida.[23] And elsewhere Derrida goes so far as to imagine passing beyond the use of such signs as "man" and "humanism" to defer presence. But this "beyond" still lies within discourse, follows the rules of discourse, and discovers play within meaning, stretching the name-ing operations perhaps, or inscribing rupture, but never consuming words or burning signs in the glory of joy before death. Discourse is already infinite and thus Derrida cannot abide a presentation of Bataille's desperate efforts to escape its outer limits as a choice. Bataille's efforts to break out from the rules of discourse instead of working with force and irruption from within give them a de jure legitimacy Derrida is seeking to subvert. But Derrida's subversion begins with a confession that reason stands in an irreconcilable but unavoidable relation with the sovereign forces of monstrosity. The point is not to pretend to choose between reason and its monstrosity, because reason always carries traces of monstrosity. The point that Bataille misses is to maintain a silence within discourse that neutralizes such oppositions as man/woman, individualism/collectivism, and inside/outside while taking chances and celebrating difference in the infinite play of signification.

So in the end we see that Bataille is not really so dangerous (to white Western males) after all. His daring work is captured by reason. He dreams a way out of the oppositions that make Western metaphysicians sure they are right, but awakens only to the ruse of reason. Deconstruction, whatever else happens whenever it happens, leaves new hierarchies, syntheses, and totalities undetermined. Bataille becomes, in spite of himself, an agent of the most recent *aufhebung*, struggling to negate Hegel while affirming his system and passing on to the next phallocentric totality. But Derrida reminds us: "The Hegelian *aufhebung* is produced entirely from within discourse." Bataille does not see the "nonbasis of play upon which (the) history (of meaning) is launched" (406/276) because he looks for room to maneuver outside discourse. But play, if it is thought radically, lies in the accident and flux of everyday practice. To avoid establishing new hierarchies or syntheses in the name of celebrating the "infinite possibility of being," one might give Derridian extravagance a chance.

Wendell Berry (1987) and Georges Bataille (1988) illustrate the charming couple that those who embody a Derridian politics should be marching against. Berry is a solid citizen of God's universe; Bataille is a soil'd denizen of Nietzsche's multiverse. Berry illustrates the enemy in Bataille's interior war. Bataille illustrates Berry's recurring nightmare of the sleep of reason. Derrida, on neither hand, points out that pretending to exceed reason by transgressing its limits serves to conserve and confirm its image of totality: it is perhaps more radical—however conservative it may appear at first—to draw attention to the impossibility of being totally controlled by reason and order.[24]

I should like to illustrate in the clearest way possible how a politics of Derridian extravagance can adopt neither an inside strategy nor an outside strategy. I shall start with a down-to-earth comparison of an affirmative and a negative view of community and then speculate about what difference Derrida might make.

In a letter to Wes Jackson, Wendell Berry (1987:4) criticizes science's confusion of mystery and randomness. Science, we are told, is dishonest to call random what it cannot explain. "To call the unknown 'random' is to plant the flag by which to colonize and exploit the known." Berry allows the wildness of the unknown by acknowledging its mystery, but only to a point. He writes: "To call the unknown by its right name, 'mystery,' is to suggest that we had better respect the possibility of a larger, unseen pattern that can be damaged or destroyed and, with it, the smaller patterns." In this way, Berry plants his flag next to all that God knows. Everything is potentially knowable, if now unseen, or seen through a glass darkly.[25] His work makes room neither for the necessity of accident and flux nor for the notion that mystery is always already wrapped up in what he calls patterning. Connolly (1987/1988), whose unflagging efforts to show the dangers of patterning are well known, would describe Berry's as the voice of "attunement" crying out against the voices of scientistic rationality. And because community is so often "central" to theories of attunement (for example, Charles Taylor), we might expect to find that reassuring word in Wendell Berry's down-to-earth writing.[26]

Berry (1987:189) reports that a farmer he knows, David Kline, was once asked what community "meant to him." Kline's response leads Berry to pose community as an early modern form of the insurance industry: "He said that when he and his son were plowing in the spring he could look around him and see seventeen teams at work on the neighboring farms. He knew those teams and the men driving them, and he knew that if he were hurt or sick, these men and those teams would be at work on his farm." Berry rightly refuses to distinguish between economics and community. Communities practice the conservation and production that economists study. "The community accomplishes the productive work that is necessary to any economy; the economy supports and preserves the land and the people. The economy cannot prey on the community . . . it is the community" (189).

These reflections help explain how Berry can be so affirmative. But before reducing community life to production and conservation, one ought to consider other desires people have that do not fit within the confines of such an economical matrix. Bataille may not be highly subversive to Western metaphysics, but he can certainly cure its romanticism.

Georges Bataille is not a name we ordinarily associate with the farming of the earth, except perhaps metaphorically, but his work reminds us of how much one can crave annihilation. Recall that his list of so-called expenditures includes "luxury, mourning, war, cults" and so on. If I may imagine a "Georges Kline" for a moment, his response to Berry's question, "What does community mean to you," might sound rather Bataillean; that is, familiar:

> He said that when he and his son plowed in the Spring they would take their best stud out, to a place where their seventeen neighbors could see it, and give it to the poor, sick neighbor and his daughters next door. He knew those teams and the men driving them. He knew how much they would like to see him hurt or sick, his son too young to take over yet, so that they could emasculate both of them with such a gift, as if to sneer at their fear of tomorrow, temporarily forgetting their own, in the infinite possibility of humiliating one's fellow beings.

Berry's manifest teleology (faith in a larger, unknown pattern) would lead him to domesticate Bataille's savagery, but he could not deny its presence. Berry celebrates God's order; Bataille celebrates the death of God. Berry's use of community is quite consistent with the communion of Charles Taylor. We know our horses, neighbors, family, and lives as a *We* as well as an *I*. I plow your land in your time of need because We share a common oneness; working your farm is much like working my own. Bataille would be quick to condemn this reassuring life-style of charity and life insurance. Bataille, foreshadowing Foucault (1983:215) sees much of the gift-giving of community as an exercise of power, asking: How can I gain sufficient resources to maximize the power of my ability to humiliate you? This is the spirit of reciprocity taken to the limit of the other not being able to repay. Whereas David Kline, in his least communal moments, might use the remunerative cliché, "I owe you one," Bataille has the ancient potlatch in mind. Humiliation and domination pollute the atmosphere of community Berry tries to conserve.

Radical political theory cannot seem to find its way out of thinking up politics that are either too good to be true or too true to be any good. Few, especially those who celebrate difference, can buy the idea of people all being the same. And watered-down reciprocal exchange seems to sell most people short. Must a politics of mutual service and defense be presented along such a boring continuum? Can expenditure survive community and vice versa?

It may sound strange to mention Derrida when talking about people serving and defending each other, but it should not. Deconstruction must be politicized to avoid being encouraged by it to unravel all political accomplishments, avoid political conflict, and trivialize the more important power struggles in academia. But Derrida (1987) writes about free gifts in ways that are consistent with both his theoretical maneuvers and community life in its everyday sense (local community, municipal building, munificent person). His notion of the force and irruption of the free gift is at odds with both Berry's romanticism and Bataille's nihilism. Perhaps more concentration on tactics at the level of the municipality (where common ground is usually taken literally instead of metaphorically) in addition to but alongside strategies on the high frontier of the individual/collective tension is the most radical politics of community available.

An important beginning is to notice that, when writing, cutting into a page breaks the silence of infinite possibility. Many people think it the other way: that spilling ink on a page makes sense. One can make sense only by denying infinite possibility. But one can never make sense without spaces and margins; and these blank zones can be mobilized to maintain the silence that is not broken. So while silence is broken by discourse, it is always already ripe for maintenance.

One need only notice this to make sense of the following progression, which might draw this chapter closer to maintaining its silences.[27] First, until being subjugated to patterns (man/woman, plant/animal, old/new) our infinite differences are arbitrary, subject only to accident and chance. Second, patterns must be oppositions to be reasonable and orderly; that is, by definition patterns are fields of opposition. Third, significative discourse—the use of arbitrary signs to make sense—relies on fields of opposition. Fourth, because discourse breaks silence, silence is a resource one can also maintain. Fifth, the free gift, because it is accidental and in a certain way anonymous—that is, free gifts are practiced prior to the determination of a giving subject and a receiving subject; indeed they determine who and what those subjects are—maintains the sovereignty of accidental silence. In other words, the practice of free gift-giving determines the patterning of subjectivity. Sixth, this practice is heterogeneous to both conservative and subversive political programs because it is not a program at all: it is a maintenance of silence, not the "parson's pattern," and carries no guarantees (See Derrida, 1987:201). Free gift-giving stands beside the reassuring forces of shared oneness and reciprocity in an accidental, silent, extravagant way that strikes with force and irruption until silence is again broken by discourse.

And, if I may imagine a "Jacques Kline," this is what Berry might hear from him about community:

> He said that when he and his twelve-year-old were plowing in the Spring they could look around them and see seventeen teams at work on the neighboring farms. An un-

expected thunderstorm darkened the sky and his neighbors were leaving the field. Common sense was telling them how unreliable horses can be in thunderstorms. But he sensed that his kid, who was perfecting a new plowing technique designed to increase the yield while causing the horses less anxiety, wanted to finish the field. They seemed to lose themselves in their work, trying feverishly to beat the storm, pushing the pace to the limit of losing all coordination. The new practice of plowing determined them to be a team of adult experience, 4-H husbandry, animal strength, and hardened steel edges. He knew the other teams and the men driving them and was excited by the prospects that their children were as gifted, in their own ways, as was his daughter in innovative husbandry. He was surprised not to have lost the day to the storm. She had lost all track of time.

Perhaps "I can annihilate myself in the infinite possibility of my fellow beings" without violence or brutality if being is conceived as never having been reduced to totality. Perhaps the cage that Bataille is rubbing his paws against contains doors to an infinite number of chambers. Perhaps the mutual service of community is possible without the unity of sharing anything in common.

Reason and Order at Bay

There can be no escape from reason and order but neither can discourse escape the dark and barely natural light of irrationality. And this latter point, which is so easily overlooked due to the silence of the irrational and the noise of reconstruction, must not be passed over lightly. If reason and order are held at bay, one can sense that doors are nearby. These doors can never be said to be openings in the so-called walls of rationality because rationality is inseparable from accident and chance. Doors are nearby in the sense that one can find openings in the walls of subjectivity protected by reassuring political theorists who only examine the first two questions of Foucault (1983): fighting mass exploitation by discovering shared oneness and countering state domination by appealing to the self-interest of citizens. Passing through these doors gives us room to raise Foucault's (1983) third question, on subjugation. But it will take political ploys, beyond wordplay, to draw out the possibilities of a new age of excentric subjectivity.

Supplement

This study has passed through several stages. Part I examined the question of subjugation: how to live life more fully without abandoning all reason and order. Part II explored the forces of reassurance that hold up the provisional reason and order modernity cannot abandon. Part III stressed the importance of neutralizing binary opposition and giving oneself away to the practice of giving gifts, during which the gift determines the identity of the giver and the receiver. In such situations no side can direct the behavior of the other because opposition is neutralized; power is set aside because patterned subjectivity has been deferred.

We can now reread the editorial in the Christian magazine, discussed in chapter 1, and make room for the obvious facts —that indigent folks have infinite resources and middle-class folks have crying needs of their own—without merely reversing the balance of power. Gift-giving, by definition, determines in what senses mutual service is mutual. Middle-class folks cannot be role models for the poor and the poor folks who are building sweat equity cannot be expected to feel thankful for the goodness of the somewhat alien Christians visiting their neighborhood from outside. The practice of gift-giving neutralizes the opposition between the caring "in crowd" and the people in need "out there." Such language of domination is silenced or, rather, silence is not broken in this way. Instead, gifted people with multiple differences and infinite resources do what they can to raise shelters; the raising of the shelters takes charge of the substitution of signs and determines who is what, when, and how. Binary opposition is effaced. One speaks instead of multiple differences between signifiers which are themselves arbitrary.

There are far too many houses, protein levels, children, and so on, to raise in this world for us to conceive of difference as an individual affair, such as doing whatever we like with "our" lives. Living life to the fullest on our own terms is a weak substitute for the joy of being determined by the practice of community: joy before life. This is because difference can be celebrated most effectively while being given over to the infinite play of substitutions. Our being determined to be strong, weak, male, female, animal, or human by the practice of gift-giving is not at all like our being systematically individuated and totalized by the Law. Gift-giving accidentally irrupts, takes extravagant people by surprise, and leaves us more free from patterns of subjectivity—man, America, etc.—than we were to begin with. We can then think extravagantly about municipal services, that orderly field that would otherwise balance habitual charity with Thoreauvian self-reliance.

10 Taking Time Out for Community

We need to recur to examples of associations where human beings have found a basis for cooperating and nurturing power without being tempted to surrender their active roles for some impersonal process that promises relief from involvements and greater efficiency; where intelligence, skill, and inventiveness have a dignified place but are not reified into omniscience which demands power to match its hubris; and where taking care of people and things, rather than using them up, is the basic stance toward the world.—Sheldon Wolin (1983:21)

The forces of reassurance have managed in modern times to eclipse the forces of extravagance. But Goya's enlightened reassurance about the monstrosity produced by reason's slumber can be read differently at the close of the twentieth century. We are living the human monstrosities of waking reason. I have tried to show how the strict dichotomy between reason and its slumber cannot be maintained because of the slumber inherent in reason's form. This permits us to think simultaneously about extravagance and reassurance while permitting their differences. Such an economy opens up extravagant readings of municipal life.

The practical implications of a politics of extravagance cannot be justified in discourse without jeopardizing the elements of accident and chance which must be maintained in such a silent politics. But we can articulate ways to maintain silence in discourse. And when we do, the justifications of current practices look rather mean in comparison. First, I illustrate, in terms of everyday life, the relation between giving gifts freely and community life. Second, I place accidental community in a relation with reassuring community; this is the relation of chaos to reason. Third, I explore the political implications of supplementing what others take to be a part/whole totality. Finally, I mention some impediments to community and suggest how more deconstructive readings might contribute to their downfall.

Gift-Giving and Community

Aside from the presence of *munus* in *community*, what is the importance of the gift to community, in practical terms? Derrida calls marriage a gift in the sense that practicing it gives spouses their identity as spouses; only after marriage (formal or otherwise) can spouses speak the language of transgression. Similarly, municipalities can be said to be founded on accidental gifts.

The decision to incorporate as a town, or some other body, gives identity to subjects. This free gift phase is one step removed from what Foucault calls the "Decision." That is, prior to the subjects' individuation by the State, subjects allow the state to become whole by allowing themselves to be founded, or by allowing their identities to be determined by the practice of politics. What is gift-giving in the first generation degenerates into reciprocity and communion afterward. If the first generation is like marriage, the second is like an arranged marriage, which can never be a gift. Lincoln shows the difficulties of managing community in the absence of the pathos that attends accidental service-delivery.

To deliver with municipal services in ways that eclipse extravagance is rather like other reasonable and orderly ways of living, some of which are criticized in the pages above. Admitting extravagance to the world of municipal services fully implicates every "one" in the process. Being fully implicated is never reassuring. The many decisions one makes in a day begin to be crowded by immediate needs and emergencies. We cannot—at least if we are middle-class folks—"decide" whether to feed our own hungry children; but the children of strangers are not as immediate because we are not implicated in their hunger. Similarly, middle-class folks cannot "decide" whether to call the plumber when their sewage backs up; but sewage working its way into a stranger's water supply does not seem to be the same because we are not implicated in its stench. Because extravagance considers all differences arbitrary and multiple, every life is fully implicated in discourse and the comfortable distances that permit rational decisions are erased. This is not to say that one begins to share the hunger or the stench in a communal oneness, substituting "We" for "I" while reaching for a checkbook. Rather, the practice of giving allows the gift to determine "I" and "We" and cannot be controlled by a check-writing-centered subject. In a politics of extravagance all lives hinge on how silence is broken and maintained.

To live extravagantly is to give gifts freely, to cultivate one's gifts in all directions. The word *extravagance* signifies the madness of losing oneself in the practice of everyday life. The life of nothing but sliding signifiers in the absence of a transcendental signified is totally deranged; but this does not rule out drawing up close to the death of the subject in heated moments of absorption in what one is doing. Reassuring political theories do not connect this pathos with politics; these are private rather than public moments, they might say. The personal is not the political. And they might remind an extravagant theorist of the importance of being responsible, accountable, and dependable, as they extol the virtues of, or at least try to embrace, the modern subject. But this reasonable, orderly method of political theory makes the subject less responsible for any practice not forbidden by law. For example, pleonexia is usually not a sign of irresponsibility. In this formula, then, reassuring theorists are worried about the transgression of reason's rules. But we have seen that Derridian extravagance is not transgressive; rather, the extravagant theorist makes do, draws the battlelines to permit an exploration of the irrationality of reason and order. The practice of gift-giving exposes weaknesses in reason's laws and, therefore, one need not transgress. The difference between the mass murderer losing herself in the annihilation of fellow beings and the concert pianist letting the music take over is, for the purposes of this example, the difference between transgressing the law and supplementing its binary oppositions by cultivating one's gifts. As we saw in the last chapter, solitary transgression is quite likely to reinforce existing law: high crime-rates usually justify the presence of the police. Widespread transgression is much more effective at changing existing laws, but law in general wins in these situations as well. Law simply changes the side it protects.

The mutual service and defense of community can benefit immeasurably from gift-giving, this "accident" that determines its own destination and the identities of givers and receivers, while implicating everybody. Rather than demanding obedience to laws which also individuate the obedient, the practice of community keeps the state in shock with irruptions that unravel patterned subjectivity.

Gift-giving is communitarian in the sense that it is never solitary: one becomes fully implicated in the play of differences between arbitrary signifiers that are arranged and rearranged to make sense. Because this sense of community without unity is accidental and free, a politics of extravagance is necessarily incomplete. Its relation to a more reassuring politics is rather like the relation of silence and sound. But this does not lead extravagant theorists toward quietism. Once silence becomes noticeable—what was that? a murmuring?—things and people are never quite the same. Uneasiness resounds, tempers flare, and conflicts surface in what would otherwise be safe play.

Reassurance and extravagance are not only as different as the distinction between safe and radical play, but they also defer any consideration of dialectical affirmation, negation, and synthesis. Their clash is always deferred because the radical side effaces all opposition. The practice of gift-giving, which happens when the subject is fully implicated in the substitution of signifiers, is a politics of Derridian extravagance. I have been rehearsing such a politics throughout this book. Accidental community without unity is not designed to replace the other, more reassuring, usages of communion and remunity; it is designed, however, to thwart their claim to govern political theory.

But aside from the différance of the differences between extravagance and reassurance, everyone seems to agree that bodies of individuals—communities—need some mutual service and defense. This suffices, I suppose, to remind us of the literal common ground beneath all possible theorists of community, from the least to the most extravagant: all of the bodies on the planet need food and shelter to be strong. While the reassuring service delivery the government provides is totally irreconcilable with the accidental, irruptive service-delivery of free gifts, all interpretation concerns how well these bodies, and the planet for that matter, are doing.

If the body is the common ground shared by reassuring and extravagant service delivery, we must keep it in focus throughout a discussion of the accidental or chaotic aspects of life. The body is imprinted by both the enlightened rational contributions to order and the dark, barely natural light of irrationality; we have no choice in this matter. But we struggle to choose reason and order. The practice of living as subjects, as subjugated parts that are forced into wholes, has been such a preoccupation that, while we notice the extent to which we are not reasonable persons, this is not treated as a sign of the extent to which everyday life is constituted by accident and chance. A politics of community must practice gift-giving to keep the entanglement of reason and déraison from being lived as disentangled. Mutual services can be delivered unoppressively as gifts, in ways that are not dependable or reliable. Because such practices are heterogeneous with both subversive and conservative programs, they are easily seen as apolitical. This is, as we shall see, a most convenient depiction for those who would choose not to be implicated fully in the play of the world.

Any household can illustrate how the practice of everyday life is both dependent on reassuring services and open to extravagant services. In the household reassurance is granted a hegemonic position. Waste is to be collected and pushed out as quickly as possible. Few care where it goes and would rather not talk about their excrement. Spouses are rights-bearing individuals, with whom one makes compromises, deals, and promises that invert and revert balances of power unless domination sets in and violence, or other abuse, deprives one side of its power. (Notice how neutral language can disguise violence toward women in the household.) Tools are as disposable as garbage. When a screwdriver becomes ineffective from too much chiseling or paint stirring it is replaced; the one caked with toxic paint is pitched who knows where.

Extravagant approaches to people and things require gift-giving. Giving freely does not imply serving another person as their butler, maid, or slave. And driving the garbage to the recycling plant is not necessarily a free gift either. Free gifts can never be calculated; they happen prior to the determination of patterned subjectivity. Couples who lose themselves in lovemaking may, if they are lucky, let whatever their bodies are doing determine the giver and receiver, the identities of the subjects, the destination of the gift. The free gift celebrates multiple differences by neutralizing the man/woman opposition.

One might even think about the practice of waste disposal in terms of gift-giving. The banker walking to work who, on a whim or a dare, boards a garbage truck making its rounds and puts in a full day from curb to landfill, is apt to think differently about the waste basket in the kitchen. During the day the bank uniform begins to get in the way of garbage-collecting. Muscles unused for years are used. Cultural, social, racial, and sexual differences seem to multiply in ways unnoticed in her bank. The banker might buy different products and use them differently: live differently. What starts by accident carries implications for all daily routine.

All of these are efforts to support and defend each other in ways that take time out of our lives. Life becomes more complicated. The past/future of the tyrannical elapsing time continuum, that source of resentment, is an opposition, like the man/woman opposition perhaps, that is neutralized each time any gift is given. When the ninety year old who lives alone and never has visitors celebrates multiple differences with the family next door in a spontaneous afternoon of singing, age is only one difference among many. Time's "it was" is not so terrible in the silent spaces and margins of extravagant living, where the gift determines the subject instead of the other way around. The silent spaces of rational service-delivery emphasize what happens to make life reasonable. To live more fully is not to live more efficiently or easily. But joy before life demands drawing closer to what cannot be said. The point is that this need not be discovered in phallocentric solitary confinement. We are neither all the same nor all alone, nor restricted to their balance. The modern subject can always give more; its reasonable ways are provisional and always brutally unfair to someone or other. In this sense irrationality is less mad than reason and order.

Community and Social Change

While those who pretend to choose between extravagant and reassuring politics are misguided, one should note that this kind of pretending can be approached from either perspective. That is, when one ignores the gift-giving sense of community one chooses reassurance over extravagance. They do not balance because they do not stand in a binary relation. And because binary situations lose their force when supplemented, I cannot pretend that community without unity fits neatly into politics as usual. Moreover, to say that gifts cannot be calculated and are by definition accidental is not to say that the politics of reassurance cannot be arranged to improve the odds of our practicing free gift-giving at all.

The struggle between remunity and communion might begin to seem less important than the vague murmuring of monstrosity in the offing. Just what these voices are saying must await their inclusion in discourse, at which time we can assess the changes. But it is clear that the politics of reassuring service delivery must change if it is to stand alongside a politics of extravagance. For example, services—such as health care, education, or transportation—would have to be improved, because it makes little sense to expect people to cultivate gift-giving while denying their basic needs. Connolly's (1988) expansion of social democracy in the direction of radical liberalism makes many of the changes that could make community without unity possible. For example, income differentials would have to be narrowed dramatically to avoid choosing, in reasonable and orderly ways, which bodies are allowed to be strong. The resources of the world can feed, clothe, and shelter every body standing on its common ground, but resources are easily depleted by the greed and thoughtless abuse of the modern subject.

We cannot speak of a program of radical play because radical play maintains silence. And yet after the practice of gift-giving determines the subjectivity of those involved, articulation is possible. Speakers may be quite vocal as they perform their functions; but the presence of their form is deferred. For example, at the construction site one (sufficiently gifted) speaks as a carpenter, not as a poor person, or as an investment broker.

The usual social democratic program might sound less boring, or threatening, if supplemented by a politics of extravagance. Without community, the ambiguous subject is free to use up all the people and things this side of the law. Social democracy threatens to take away the rights-bearer's toys. With community the ambiguous subject is free to cultivate gifts in all directions by annihilating the self in the infinite possibility of fellow beings. Community without unity is a way to convince recalcitrant liberals to associate social democracy with joy before life. Many of their toys begin to be embarrassing. Communion, however, leads people to associate social democracy with having to be just like, or even to be, people they have never met. This threatens liberals and many others because of the explicit threat to difference. And yet the same liberals are uncomfortable with their watery reciprocity. Community without unity provides a way out of this dead end.

Impediments to a Politics of Derridian Extravagance

While it might promise to strengthen the case for social democracy, a politics of extravagance faces the overwhelming impediments of language, reason, and knowledge itself. Political theory needs to be more determined to point out how its discourse perpetuates the fields of opposition that stand in the way of community. Advocates of social democracy who decry sexism, racism, and cultural imperialism can perhaps be shown to rely exclusively on binary oppositions. If so, these oppositions would have to be neutralized to permit extravagance, to maintain silence. This is to suggest that the most supportive advocates of social democracy are ripe for deconstruction. Madness is not only the limit, but is also the resource of writing, a resource that communitarians cannot tap so long as their friends are standing pat, and thinking exclusively in the terms of the enemy. Because it might tap the silent resource of madness, there is no end to what community without unity might be.

Notes

1 Mutual Service and the Language of Domination

1 This may not always be noticed by either side. I wish to consider the possibility of calling attention to hidden injuries.
2 See Yancey (1986:64).
3 See Hyde (1979:99).
4 See Augustine (1958:321).
5 See Flores (1984:9) for someone else who uses *deconstruction* in this way. Or consult Wood et al. (1988) for a note by Derrida (1–5) on deconstruction.
6 It would be insane to pretend to live outside of such reasonable and orderly forms as timeless-timebound polarities. Only an unsequestered mad person would draw an inside/outside distinction between reason and madness and go over to the silence of the out side. But to speak of exceeding the totality of reason and order in full confession of its madness—the kind of extravagance re-

hearsed by my perspective—may actually make more sense than to pretend full presence of mind. It may not be necessary to push out all of the mysteries (or missing data) which, in principle, elude the categories of any continuum. The play of the world, that heap of random sweepings, does not from an extravagant perspective depend upon a pure subject of consciousness which it is one's duty to keep pure across time. There is both more and less at stake.

2   Reciprocity, Commonality, Mutual Service

1 The *Oxford English Dictionary* distinguishes between the body of individuals and a quality, or state, of being.

2 This distinction is effaced by the easy translation of *communis* as commonality.

3 Compare Connolly (1981:187).

4 See Rawls (1985) for a response to Sandel (1982).

5 Indeed, this is why a critique of Rawls from the altruistic point of view is not very much of a critique. See Barry (1973).

6 Macpherson (1973:135) writes about the public nature of the environmental concern.

7 *Munus* (or *muner*, gift, from *munerare*, *muneat*, meaning both to give and to discharge the duties of an office [Shipley, 1945]) conveys the idea of mutual service, or giving, when it is combined with the prefix *com* (*con* if not used before *b*, *m*, or *p*). This prefix can be used in a variety of ways—to express collation or simultaneity, joint action, partnership, enclosure, intensity of action, or completeness. See *The Oxford Latin Dictionary* for a more complete listing of usages.

8 That "I" would rather not use the word *subject* to signify persons (and other forms of subjectivity) is perhaps a sign of my Anglo-American orientation to political theory. But I must do so because certain communitarians, such as Charles Taylor and Michael Sandel, speak of subjectivity which extends beyond the finite body and of intersubjectivity which is richer than the relations between otherwise unencumbered persons.

9 Descombes (1981:76).

10 Balancing individual and collective extremes, like all ambivalence, only legitimizes the distinction involved, precludes the alternative of laughing at the distinction, ties knots in the double bind. The grammar of the word *community*, as I have shown, permits usage which signifies serving (each other in lives of common involvement), but how the seven words in parentheses are used presents a problem. If "each other" is viewed from an individualist

perspective and "common involvement" is viewed from a collectivist perspective, this usage is apt to be confused with mere forms of balancing unity and diversity. Studying notions of subjectivity helps to illustrate how this confusion dominates thinking about community.

11 It is perhaps significant that the simplistic tension between altruism and egoism was introduced to the English language in a translation of the positivist author, Auguste Comte (1953).

12 Berger is sometimes cited as a member of the interpretive school. See Sandel (1985).

13 One might hypothesize that realizing the need for communion but being unable to lay a foundation for it leads liberal theorists to pretend they neglect metaphysics, while buying into the metaphysics of presence.

14 This is why we are only partly constituted.

15 It would be convenient to distinguish three uses of *share*: altruism (sharing), common meaning (sharing sharing), and extravagant free gifts (sharing in the absence of the reassurance and unity of sharing sharing).

16 The connection between mainstream social science and Western liberalism cannot be defended here, but should not be surprising, even to non-Marxists.

17 See Arendt (1961:264): "the truth is the ground on which we stand and the horizon that stretches above us."

18 For a reasonable discussion of such circularity without a cleverness that passeth all understanding, see Geertz (1983:55–70).

19 As we shall soon see, other interpretive theorists see the subject itself as an artifact.

20 This is obviously a form of communion. For a commonsense treatment of commonality without communion, see Geertz (1983:36-54).

3 Opening Up the Dialogue Between Remunity and Communion

1 "The instability of the limits set: the frontier yields to something foreign. On the margins of the page, the mark of an 'apparition' disturbs the order that a capitalizing and methodical labor had constructed. It elicits 'fluttering thoughts,' 'whimsies,' and 'terror' in Robinson Crusoe. The conquering bourgeois is transformed into a man 'beside himself,' made wild himself by this (wild) clue that reveals nothing. He is almost driven out of his mind. He dreams and has nightmares. He loses his confidence in a world

governed by the Great Clockmaker. His arguments abandon him" (Certeau, 1984:154).

2 See also Certeau (1986).

3 Written 14 January 1976 and never published in French.

4 Foucault (1980:94) writes: "In the end, we are judged, condemned, classified, determined in our undertakings, destined to a certain mode of living or dying, as a function of the true discourses which are the bearers of the specific effects of power."

5 A good example of an accident that determines people prior to their subjugation to the law is the Declaration of Independence, that text which Lincoln in chapter 5 will treat as an axiom and Derrida in chapter 9 will treat as a free gift.

6 Foucault (1980:96) is quick to point out that by domination he does not "have in mind that solid and global kind of domination that one person exercises over another, but the manifold forms of domination that can be exercised within society." See also Foucault (1988:3): "When an individual or a social group manages to block a field of relations of power, to render them impassive and invariable and to prevent all reversibility of movement—by means of instruments which can be economic as well as political or military—we are facing what can be called a state of domination."

7 "The problem for me is how to avoid this question . . . regarding sovereignty and the obedience of individual subjects in order that I may substitute the problem of domination and subjugation" (Foucault, 1980:96).

8 "I hardly ever use the word "power" and if I do sometimes, it is always a short cut to the expression I always use: the relationships of power. . . . power is always present" (Foucault, 1988:11).

9 Later, in chapter 9, we will see Bataille's treatment of the "potlatch" (as a form of humiliating or holding power over another) draw these two threads together. Chapter 10 attempts to conceive of gifts more freely.

10 These three categories are borrowed from Connolly (1987) (though I use *rationalist* in a Thomist rather than a modern designative sense).

11 At least MacIntyre practices his search for the golden mean openly.

12 MacIntyre (1982:190) explains that although his "account of the virtues is teleological, it does not require any allegiance to Aristotle's metaphysical biology." All other quotations from MacIntyre (1981) and the same in MacIntyre (1984).

13 Taylor (1985) cites suffrage for women as a sign of progress.

14 I do not share Connolly's implied equation of deconstruction and dismantlement.

15 To say that there is no real person at the center of the tensions that structure the world is not to practice a disappearing act. Of course our bodies exist, but does this mean that we as modern subjects are always present and accounted for? Of course not. We use phrases such as "he is not all there today," and "she carried an absent expression" without worrying that we signify bodily disappearance. But such excentricity does implicate all the bodies in the world in the infinite play of signification. This is a way of insisting that the play of difference is the basis of existence instead of pretending not to notice the play in the structure of binary oppositions.

16 This plagiarism is a rather cheap maneuver—and I shall play by the rules from this line forth if only to avoid the pretense of a confessional—but I wanted to introduce Derrida in a way that convinces those who do not read his books of his relevance to my topic. All passages listed below can be found in Derrida (1978).

"But metaphor is never innocent. It orients research and fixes results" (17).

"a reassuring certitude, which itself is beyond the reach of play" (279).

"And on the basis of this certitude anxiety can be mastered, for anxiety is invariably the result of a certain mode of being implicated in the game" (279).

"Successively, and in a regulated fashion, the center receives different forms or names" (279).

"there is too much, more than one can say" (289).

"the moment when language invaded the universal problematic, when in a manner of speaking, everything became discourse" (280).

"explicitly and systematically posing the problem of the status of a discourse which borrows from a heritage the resources necessary for the deconstruction of that heritage itself" (282).

"For there is a *sure* play: that which is limited to the *substitution* of *given* and *existing, present* pieces" (292).

"Play is always play of absence and presence, but if it is to be thought radically, play must be conceived of before the alternative of presence and absence" (292).

"there is something missing from it [the field]" (289).

"a center which arrests and grounds the play of signification" (289).

"And the absence of such a transcendental signified extends the domain and the play of signification infinitely" (280).

"no longer turned toward the origin, affirms play and tries to pass beyond man and humanism, the name of man being the name of that being who, throughout the history of metaphysics . . . has dreamed of full presence, the reassuring foundations, the origin and the end of play" (292).

"There is no sense in doing without the concepts of metaphysics [God, man, consciousness] in order to shake metaphysics" (280).

"The quality and fecundity of a discourse are perhaps measured by the critical rigor with which this relation to the history of metaphysics and to inherited concepts is thought" (282).

"that the passage beyond philosophy does not consist in turning the page of philosophy (which usually amounts to philosophizing badly), but in continuing to read philosophers *in a certain way*" (288).

"these two interpretations of interpretation are absolutely irreconcilable even if we live them simultaneously. . . . I do not believe that today there is any question of choosing" (293).

"away when faced by the as yet unnamable which is proclaiming itself and which can do so, as is necessary whenever a birth is in the offing, only under the species of the nonspecies, in the formless, mute, infant, and terrifying form of monstrosity" (293).

4   Pocock, Foucault, Forces of Reassurance

1 For a compelling case for distinguishing de facto sense-making and de jure epistemological insanity, see Jacques Derrida (1978: 53ff).

2 Norman Jacobson (1978:3).

3 The continuum can bring reason and order to any cluttered territory. Consider, for example, Alexander's disciplinary housecleaning in sociology, or Barber's conceptual house-cleaning in political theory. See Jeffrey Alexander (1982:40); Benjamin Barber (1984: 219).

4 *Series* is related to *serere*, *sertum* (to join or bind together).

5 I wish to mention Plato (1973) and Husserl (1970).

6 Aristotle (1985).

7 Heraclitus (1979).

8 The issue here is not whether it is reassuring to use tensed language or to speak of inheriting resemblances to one's ancestors. The issue is how totally a text relies on temporal unity or any other imposed form. The assumption of temporal unity can be called reassuring only if it forces everything under the sun to contract, to rotate, on its terms. One need not inhabit a wholly tensed universe to make oneself understood with tensed language. Derrida is right to suggest that slippage, or play, in the structure of our world(s) makes it possible to think in binary terms. In other words, the orderly world of the either/or distinction is made possible only by denying chaos. Those reassured by underlying unity forget what makes the field of opposition possible. Amidst ensuing struggles for or against the hegemony politics creates the illusion that thinking creatively in binary terms makes play in the structure of the world possible. But this relation is backwards.

9 Divorced particulars can only provide theories of time similar to Rousseau's native Caribbean; divorced universals, like Platonic Forms, are immutable and need not worry about time. Gunnell claims that Aristotle leads most readers to view time as an "infinitely divisible continuum" (See Gunnell 1968:234). Time is a river within which one can splash about. Perhaps the way Western readers use tensed language makes it too easy for them to imagine the river (past, present, future), but what is the analogue for the water splashed about? Augustine's silence speaks for most of us as we continue to assume linear temporality. We unconsciously unite universals and particulars to make the idea of an elapsing time continuum possible.

10 While time-as-a-continuum requires immanence, immanence does not assure historical continuity. Pocock shows the possibility of denying continuity to history without denying continuity to elapsed time. For example, disagreements over the content or worth of a heritage can arise from within a perspective that is indisputably inherited.

11 Most people realize that a continuum signifies dimensions such as the line used by social science to capture the range of a frequency distribution. But many miss the point that this requires establishing a relation between particular parts and a namable whole. To constitute a continuum all points must, by definition, share something in common. For example, income distribution in any particular country might range from no income (a point on the continuum far to the left of the mean income) to a very high income (a point on the continuum far to the right of the

mean income); it is difficult to imagine an income not falling at or in between either extreme because all points have income in common. Any group of people managing to survive in ways not measured by the given definition of income cannot be included in the distribution, even at the negative extreme.

12 Pocock's (1973:237) plan is "to elaborate and extend the model of a tradition . . . and attempt in doing so to discern the directions which conceptualisation of a tradition may be expected to take, and something of the alternatives, choices and strategies which may confront minds engaged in such conceptualisation."

13 For more on "matrices" and "paralanguage," read Pocock (1981: 50ff) and Pocock (1985:30ff).

14 As if to remind readers that one cannot stop the river of time for purposes of analysis, Pocock (1973:239) adds: "We study the form which its [a society's] self-awareness has *for the present* assumed" (emphasis added).

15 This statement is consistent with Pocock's (1973:40) announced intention to establish a politics of time as a subdepartment of a politics of language. At issue is whether he must necessarily fail in this endeavor because of uncritical presuppositions about time.

16 The importance of this point cannot be underestimated. If it is possible to show this, then present historians should be able to excavate and locate the matrix which limits possibilities, and offer definitive statements (or at least hypotheses) concerning the intended meaning of an author's text. See Pocock's "Political Ideas As Historical Events: Political Philosophers As Historical Actors," in Melvin Richter (1980:153–55).

17 Recall that Pocock's paralinguistic treatment of their modes of reception treats inheritance as the sole mode of reception.

18 It is interesting that Pocock illustrates being outside of time with a dream metaphor. See the Derrida-Foucault-Descartes trio in chapter 8.

19 You may recall that immanence is a presupposition of a time series. All elements must possess a certain universality to exist as a "series." This is only the first imposition of a polarity in this text. After it restricts possibilities to being either more or less secular, the elapsing time continuum can emerge as societies "move away from imagining society in terms of the sacred." This will be developed as the model grows.

20 Please note the signification of sacredness here, although the purely rational founder is, according to Pocock, always miraculous and therefore is also included here.

21 Pocock (1973) offers three cases of radical strategies to return to the past, all within the context of traditional society: (1) the search for an origin so old that it can be seen as a more legitimate foundation than the presumptive tradition of the conservative (245–48); (2) the plea to replace current usage of society's origin with a more correct, renewed understanding of that origin (249–50); and (3) the attempt to invent origins (250–51). To Pocock all three strategies tend to be "self-abolishing." Assuming "the reality and ubiquity of tradition," any attempt to ground authority outside of tradition is an attempt to establish it nowhere, so to speak. Thus Pocock quickly grows impatient with these three radical attempts to "abridge tradition." He calls them ideological postures but cautions against typecasting all critics of tradition as ideologues (252). Pocock prepares instead to extend his model to the second stage.

22 And this, of course, must include the sharing of how to use *sharing*. See Charles Taylor, "Interpretation and the Sciences of Man," in Paul Rabinow et al. (1979:27–72, especially 52ff.). Pocock says: "At this point literacy emerges as the force modifying the character of tradition" (254). Historical thought will eventually emerge from this development.

23 See also Pocock (1980:147–48). Please note that to say that words can short-circuit the processes of transmission is to presuppose the existence of an original circuit.

24 See also J. Gunnell (1981:30–32).

25 He domesticates history with a troublesome wife metaphor.

26 See Smith (1985).

27 Compare A. Gramsci (1959:118–25, especially 124).

28 The play in the structures modifies these rules.

29 For an example of such experimentation, see the last section of this chapter and the Derridian usage of "always already."

30 See Derrida (1978:31–63).

31 See J. Derrida (1981:330ff.).

32 This critique is important because it illustrates "différance," the "supplement" to elapsing time. To be prepared for this idea, however, one must distinguish linear time (what I call "elapsing time") and linear history. This chapter attempts to draw such a distinction. Readers should know that Derrida finds that Foucault accepts uncritically the totality of linear time, stressing the madness of discontinuity (and its other, continuity) while failing to imagine the extravagance of exceeding totality. According to the more extravagant Derrida, there is always "an excess which overflows the totality of that which can be thought." Hence the charge that

Foucault remains yarded by the reassurance of temporalization despite his claim of unfolding discontinuities in history.

33 Foucault's essay has seven sections: (1) a distinction between genealogy and the search for timeless origins; (2) a distinction between timebound origins and timeless origins (this is Pocock's distinction between sacred and secular time); (3) an analysis of the movement from present to past in the search for timebound origins; (4) an analysis of the serial movement from present to future after the discovery of timebound origins; (5) a distinction between anti-traditional voices (3 and 4) of genealogy, and the traditional voices of linear history; (6) an application of genealogy; and (7) a conclusion. I shall read sections 3 and 4 most closely because they show how completely Foucault is yarded by the immanence of elapsing time despite his flirtation with discontinuity.

All page numbers in this section refer to Foucault (1971:145–72). My translations rely heavily on Foucault (1977:139–64). The numbers to the left of the slash mark refer to the French version; the numbers to the right of the slash refer to the English.

34 Recall that *series* is related to *continuum* in both English and French. For more on series and discontinuity, see Michel Foucault, "The Discourse on Language," in Foucault (1972b).

35 Given this distinction, it is easy to see why Foucault regards Derrida as a metaphysician; if one has to be high or low, Derrida is high: he is exercised by coming before time. But to do so is to precede (borrowing temporal language) such distinctions as timebound/timeless presupposed by Foucault.

36 Or, "in the direction of the Gods." Note that to be before time is to move in the direction, or to the side, of the gods.

37 Note that lowliness does not indicate being meek for Foucault. Rather, unearthing lowly, timebound origins permits him to undo the reassuring continuities established by pretentious metaphysicians on the haughty side of the haut-bas polarity.

38 This would eliminate the interpretation I am advancing; his text would no longer be reassuring.

39 For example, Foucault might have described history the way Proust describes war; "une état du perpétual devenir."

40 Foucault also offers "la souche," or the stump (as of a family tree), or "stock" in the sense of family lineage. Note the resemblance of lineage and linearity. Foucault translates "la provenance" as "descent," also implying a move back in elapsed time.

41 "[The work of a genealogist is a question of] repérer tous les marques subtiles, singulières, sous-individuelles qui peuvent s'entre-croiser enlui [individuals, sentiments, ideas] et former un réseau

difficile à démêler" (151/145). Compare this to the "code breaking" Pocock describes in J. G. A. Pocock (1979:165).

42 "Une telle origine permet de débrouiller, pour les mettre à part,
tous les marques différent" (151/145).

43 The idea of distinguishing between the form of history in general
and the form of history (high continuity versus low discontinuity)
is nowhere in sight in this text. After the flow of time is presupposed, as with Pocock, the only questions worth asking concern
what has been lost and what has been remembered: memory and
its other, counter-memory.

44 I wish to summon Derrida, not Darwin.

45 But it is still a heritage, you see, because genealogy cannot be
critical of elapsing time without putting itself out of business. But,
of course, genealogy is unaware of the reassurance it emits.

46 This comes perilously close to the notion of "descriffer" condemned by Derrida.

47 If NOW is like a dam on the river of time, section 3 is like swimming
upstream in search of the source, or feeding stream; section 4 is
like the gushing forth of water the dam cannot retain.

48 These systems are described as "series" above.

49 "Plaçant le présent à l'origine, la métaphysique fait croire au tra-
vail obscur d'une destination qui chercherait à se faire jour dès le
premier moment. La généalogie, elle, rétablit les divers systèmes
d'asservissement: non point la puissance anticipatrice d'un sens,
mais le jeu hasardeux des dominations" (155/148).

50 Derrida can be shown to reverse this relation; that is, to argue
that play makes hegemony possible and not the other way around.
More important, however, is his emphasis on diversity and hazard.

51 The word *rétablir* also connotes health; soon Foucault will mention
"youthful strength."

52 "C'est celle que répètent indéfiniment les dominateurs et les do-
minés" (156/150).

53 "L'humanité ne progresse pas lentement de combat en combat
jusqu'à une réciprocité universelle, où les règles se substitueront,
pour toujours, à la guerre; elle installe chacune de ces violences
dans un système derègles, et *va* ainsi de domination en domination
(157/151, emphasis added).

54 "Si interpréter, c'était mettre lentement en lumière une signification enfouie dans l'origine seule la métaphysique pourrait interpréter, le devenir de l'humanité. Mais si interpréter, c'est s'empa-
rer, par violence ou subreption, d'un système de règles qui n'a pas
en soi de signification essentielle, et lui imposer une direction, le
ployer à une volonté nouvelle, le faire entrer dans un autre jeu et le

soumettre à des règles secondes, alors le devenir de l'humanite est une série d'interprétations. Et la généalogie doit en être l'histoire" (158/151–52).

55 Derrida (1978:292–93) makes this point at the end of the essay introduced in chapter 3.

56 Flux can name arbitrary matter so universal as to defy immanence and transcendence.

57 This postmodern idea dates back at least to Bataille. For a discussion in terms of contemporary life, see Kroker et al. (1986).

58 Jacques Derrida (1978:60).

59 Heidegger describes this as a "note from the posthumously published writings surrounding *Zarathustra*." See Heidegger (1984, II:215).

5 The Problem of Time in Lincolnian Political Religion

1 This does not of course rule out studying the debates. Nor does it pronounce the project of studying the relation of multiple authors uninteresting; but it is not my project.

2 For an appreciation, unencumbered by natural law assumptions, of Lincoln on justice, see Schaar (1983:107–29).

3 One can observe Lincoln refusing to "flinch" by reading his famous speech at Cooper Union.

4 "Between public measures regarded as antagonistic, there is often less real difference in its bearing on the public weal, than there is between the dispute being *kept up*, or being *settled* either way" (II: 89).

5 "The wisdom of his course . . . is doubted and denied by a large portion of his countrymen; and of such it is not now proper to speak particularly" (II:126–27).

6 See III:550.

7 See MacIntyre (1981) for a distinction between living and dead traditions, but keep Pocock in mind.

8 See III:374–76. This letter was widely circulated by the Republican press.

9 For capacity, forecast, and coolness, see III:376.

10 Elsewhere Lincoln (IV:168–69) writes: "All this is not the result of accident. It has a philosophic cause. Without the *Constitution* and the *Union*, we could not have attained the result; but even these, are not the primary cause of our great prosperity. There is something back of these, entwining itself more closely about the human heart. That something, is the principle of "Liberty to all"

—the principle that clears the *path* for all—gives *hope* to all—and, by consequence, *enterprize*, and *industry* to all.

"The *expression* of that principle, in our Declaration of Independence, was most happy, and fortunate."

11 This in itself is evidence of the presupposition of linear time.
12 This is an apt metaphor for the neutralization of nonmeaning required by all meaning.
13 Again, I am foreshadowing that madness is the absence of a work.
14 Lincoln is, however, addressing the Washington Society.

6   The Power of Fear in Burkean Traditionalism

1 References to volume one of this collection will be cited in this section by page number only.
2 The principal question of this chapter is how the ground one is hurled upon might be said to originate.
3 We shall see that his notion of prejudice is designed to bridge this gap without relying on speculation.
4 For Kramnick's interpretation, see Kramnick (1977:79).
5 See Wilkins (1967).
6 The idea of an ever-present gash, or open wound, could be said to lie at the heart of postmodern criticism if such a perspective did not also tear asunder center/periphery and heart/head metaphors.
7 In *Inquiry* Burke distinguishes between the simply terrible and the awe-filled before setting out to construct a continuum which ranges from ordinary astonishment to the sublime.
8 Just as it does not make sense to speak of the range of a continuum before all points on it share some quality in common, so it does not make sense to say that primordial chaos is in any sense the opposite of the reason and order of a civilized sense of continua and polarities.
9 Note how convenient it is to insert a time dimension here, allowing the house to be on the brink of ruin. But we have seen this linear notion of time is itself a form of order which makes prejudice unnecessary.
10 See Smith (1985) on Burke's reading of the Glorious Revolution.
11 Thus it might be said that to deviate from this holistic vision is a crime against nature, whatever that might be.
12 Here we should begin to wonder what has happened to the claim that boundlessness is the result of jeopardizing prejudice. The continuum is a rather severe form of boundary maintenance.
13 Like Machiavelli, he places regime stability in an opposition with selfish lust.

14 This, of course, is what I wish to call positive fear.

15 One cannot help but contrast the bold Hobbes outdoing God (Jacobson, 1978) with the timid Burke trying to aid God.

16 See White (1984) for a rich discussion of Burke's rhetorical strategy.

17 It should now be clear that these two prejudices are not compatible. If we live in a world in which it is possible to enjoy a fixed relation between thinking and forms supplied by political theories, then prejudice is not necessary; there is no problem for it to solve and one might as well allow people to shift for themselves. And if we live in a world in which it is impossible to say that theories and their forms enjoy a fixed relation, then prejudice is impossible because it is a form of fixed order which can never allow itself to be subject to multiple interpretations from other perspectives. Thus Burke needs a notion of woefully unthinkable chaos to warrant the happy prejudice which such chaos renders impossible. His theory works magically with all readers who share the deeper prejudice. Yet to allow Burke to speak for us on this matter of the deeper prejudice is to accept continuity across time. One might advance more individualistic strategies, but this would only illustrate the double bind of modern liberalism. Even competing theorists can fall under the dominion of the third face of the power of fear.

18 This anonymous editorial has been credited to Burke by Thomas Copeland and is cited in Canavan (1960: 19–20).

19 This is, of course, not Wilkins's position.

7 Announcing Derridian Confession:
   Spacing, Deferral, Writing

1 Thus the only way to know which side one is on is to know that one is not on the other side. For example, a clearing is marked by the absence of trees, a region of statistical significance is marked by the absence of the effects of random error.

2 This is why I agree with Derrida (1978) that Foucault is a master of "negativity" (55). My task is to inquire into the foundations of this positive-negative tension.

3 See Descombes (1981) for a discussion of this expression.

4 All too often we might instead view the relation of order and chaos as if chaos existed in the tails of a normal curve and order hovered within two or three standard deviations of the mean.

5 It is possible to use the word *primordial* to name deeply rooted characteristics which work in ways that resemble what Collingwood calls "absolute presuppositions." Such radical characteris-

tics are primordial, then, in the sense that they are presupposed by less fundamental characteristics. To criticize a text, or text-analogue, at its root (perish the metaphor), then, is to seek out the assumptions of the argument, without demanding necessarily to locate an origin (such as Husserl's "ideality").

6 This is not to say that systems of relations do not exist.

7 Derrida (1974) names the relation (of forming form and imprinting it) a "unity" of a double passage (62).

8 Derrida (1974:9) writes:

> And thus we say "writing" for all that gives rise to an inscription in general, whether it is literal or not and even if what it distributes in space is alien to the order of the voice: cinematography, choreography, of course, but also, pictorial, musical, sculptural "writing." One might also speak of athletic writing, and with even greater certainty of military, or political writing in view of the techniques that govern those domains today. All this to describe not only the system of notation secondarily connected with these activities but the essence of the content of these activities themselves. It is also in this sense that the contemporary biologist speaks of writing and program in relation to the most elementary processes of information with the living cell. And, finally, whether it has essential limits or not, the entire field covered by the cybernetic program will be the field of writing.

9 Read about this in Derrida (1978:278–93, especially 292–93).

10 Read Derrida (1974:73) to see how I borrow this expression and what I leave behind.

11 See the connection between the trace and original sin in Derrida (1974:15–16).

8   Practicing Derridian Confession: Supplementing Foucault

1 For example, "The main question about Derrida remains the one Foucault raises, namely, whether Derrida's method of textual analysis is too restricted in scope, and too evasive about the question of truth and social context." (David Hoy, 1985:62).

2 *Supplementer* can indicate both "to replace" and "to add."

3 Many texts associated with Derrida's name give permission to question obstacles in the vocation of political thinking. This could lead to the removal of time-honored impediments. In general, reading Derrida can encourage us to question the totality with which any assumptions are permitted to govern the foundations of political thought. Certain assumptions questioned by Derrida

even enjoy sovereignty in contemporary circles; for example, the use of the continuum to organize thoughts. Derridian criticism supplements conventional wisdom in two ways: it adds to it (in the way the crossword puzzle can be said to supplement a Sunday newspaper) and it replaces it (in the way a hostile regime might supplant the powers-that-be). My task is to consider the political implications of such supplementary writing, to determine if politics in general is necessarily replaced in the play against totality. For a defense of totality, see Martin Jay (1984).

4 René Descartes, (1967, II:404–13). All page numbers not followed by a slash note this volume.

5 The idea of a wounded discourse is borrowed from Georges Bataille. We will watch Derrida work with Bataille in chapter 9. For a discussion of how Derrida doubles/mutilates Bataille there, see Allan Stoekl (1985:104–23).

6 Jacques Derrida (1967:51–97); for an English translation, see Derrida (1978:31–63).

7 Michel Foucault (1979:9–28).

8 Felman would, in a seemingly "neutral" way which is theoretically significant, defend Foucault. She uses the very distinctions Derrida would supplement, in an attempt to find Derrida's reading of Foucault wanting. See Shoshana Felman (1985).

9 My translations of Derrida borrow ruthlessly from the excellent Bass translation. All page numbers to the left of the slash refer to my translations of Derrida's original work. Page numbers to the right of the slash refer to the Bass translation of it.

10 "Dans ce livre de 673 pages, Michel Foucault consacre trois pages (54–57) . . . à un certain passage de la première des *Meditations* de Descartes, où la folie, l'extravagance, la démence, l'insanité semblent, je dis bien *semblent* . . . révoquées aussitôt que convoquées par Descartes devant le tribunal, devant la dernière instance d'un Cogito qui, par essence, ne *saurait* être fou."

11 This twin series resembles the two interpretations of interpretation found at the end of Derrida's famous essay on structuralism and the human sciences. See Derrida (1967:409–28).

12 See Aristotle (1984:2337). This is from his *Rhetoric* (1460b 11–13). Perhaps *différance* is an example of such reformulation.

13 Pocock (1973:255) would agree on this point, at this level. For a theoretical essay which gives permission to read authorial "intention" this widely, see Stanley Cavell (1969:213–37).

14 To be subversive this rereading must be conducted from a critical perspective, such as the extravagant perspective illustrated by Derrida's essay on Foucault.

15 To be consistent Derrida must counter Foucault's claim that at one
   point in time the Greek logos had no contrary; such an origin is
   (in principle) impossible from an extravagant perspective.
16 Derrida calls this "to will to say demonic hyperbole" ("vouloir-
   dire-l'hyperbole-démonique" [95/62]).
17 René Descartes (1967:406).
18 The "Malin Génie" names the attempt to cast all certainty into
   profound doubt.
19 "Affolement total, c'est-à-dire d'une folie qui ne sera plus seulement un désordre du corps, de l'objet, du corps-objet hors des
   frontières de la *res cogitans*, hors de la cité policée et rassurée de
   la subjectivité pensante, mais d'une folie qui introduira la subversion dans la pensée pure, dans ses objets purement intelligibles,
   dans le champ des idées claires et distinctes, dans le domaine des
   véritiés mathématiques qui échappaient au doute naturel."
20 Derrida does not take seriously Foucault's plan ("projeter") to
   refuse the language of reason, and yet he is exercised by its impossibility. There is no other language than the language of order and
   reason. To speak, one must find a voice in a language which admits
   only voices of order and reason. Therefore even an archaeology of
   silence is a work the definition of which is the absence of silence.
   To write such an archaeology would require "total disengagement
   from the totality of the historical language" (58/35), and this is
   possible in only two ways, both of which rule out writing: either
   keep quiet or face exile along with the insane. In other words, it is
   impossible to write an archaeology of silence without first crossing
   over to the side of order and reason. Derrida rides this passage
   into the margins: "Il n'y a pas de cheval de Troie donc n'ait raison
   la Raison (en général)" (58/36). Here one would expect a sentence
   like, "There is no Trojan horse about which Reason (in general) is
   not right"; in fact, the order and reason of language demand this.
   But note how close Derrida is to saying the opposite. The second
   ne is perilously close to being pleonastic. That is to say, the sentence itself may be a Trojan horse which we are forced to pretend
   is not a Trojan horse if we are to make sense of the paragraph.
     This deadly serious play—beneath the merely amusing play be-
   tween "avoir raison" and "Raison (en général)"—sets the stage
   for Derrida's call for subversion. The attack on order and reason
   must take place within order and reason. Thus the plan to ignore
   rational language is ruled out—and with it must go the project (of
   greatest merit) of allowing madness to speak itself—but this rules
   in the twin existence of madness and reason. Such a ruling leads
   to the more effectively ambitious project of locating the roots of

reason's dominion over madness. Thus the genealogical project of discovering origins is the only possible project (given the binary choice). But to sense its possibility requires a new distinction: hyperbole versus reason.

21 "Cette fois la folie, l'extravagance n'épargne plus rien, ni la perception de mons corps, ni les perceptions purement intellectuelles" (82/53).

22 Descombes describes the Cartesian Cogito as the "most subjective of all subjects." "Since Descartes, the most subjective of all subjects is the one which is certain of its identity, the ego of ego cogito." See Vincent Descombes (1981:76).

23 "à savoir que le discours et la communication philosophiques (c'est-à-dire le langage lui-même), s'ils doivent avoir un sens intelligible, c'est-á-dire se conformer à leur essence et vocation de discours, doivent échapper en fait et simultanément en droit à la folie. Ils doivent porter en eux-mêmes la normalitié."

24 This is, according to Derrida, not only a Cartesian problem. The simultaneous requirement and impossibility of escaping madness is a vulnerability from which no discourse can be protected. At best a de facto deferral of madness can be worked out by violently imposing form and then pretending that this is for keeps, thereby standing by decisions and nondecisions unflinchingly.

25 "Et paradoxalement, ce que je dis ici est strictement foucaldien" (83/54).

26 "Et si la folie, c'est, en général, par-delà toute structure historique factice et déterminée, l'absence d'oeuvre, alors la folie est bien par essence et en général, le silence, la parole coupée, dans une césure et une blessure qui *entament* bien la vie comme *historicité en général*."

27 There are at least three different phrases to notice in this passage: madness in general lies outside all structure (facts, history, you name it); madness in general is silence (because it lies outside all names, all discourse); and madness in general is located in a perpetual opening up (read dissension) of life as historicity in general.

28 ". . . la dimension de l'historicité en général . . . ne se confond ni avec une éternité anhistorique, ni avec quelque moment empiriquement déterminé de l'histoire des faits" (84/54).

29 This is Pocock's (1970:153–65) sense of historiography.

30 Just as healing is deferred, so is death. Everything definitive is necessarily postponed. What Bataille calls the "open wound" ("une blessure qui saigne") draws discourse close to death, allowing it

pathos. For a provocative inquiry into the relation of death and the affirmation of life in sensuality, see Georges Bataille (1957).

31 Read Jacques Derrida's (1981:330–39) "The Time Before First."

32 "Bien que le silence de la folie soit l'absence d'oeuvre, il n'est pas le simple exergue de l'oeuvre, il n'est pas hors d'oeuvre pour le langage et le sens. Il en est aussi, comme le non-sens, la limite et la ressource profonde" (84/54).

33 "*Il fait seulement semblant de l'exclure dans la première phase de la première étape, dans le moment non-hyperbolique du doute naturel*" (86/55–56).

34 "Que je sois fou ou non, *Cogito, sum*" (86/56).

35 ". . . point-zéro où le sens et le non-sens déterminés se rejoignent en leur origine commune" (86/56).

36 Hence the praise for the recovery of the negative.

37 Here, in a note of his own, Derrida says that it is less of a point than the origin of temporality in general (86/309).

38 "Il est le point de certitude inentamable où s'enracine la possibilité du récit foucaldien, comme le récit, aussi bien, de la totalité, ou plutôt de *toutes* les formes déterminées des échanges entre raison et folie. Il est le point où s'enracine le projet de penser la totalité en lui échappant. En lui échappant, c'est-à-dire en excédant la totalité, ce qui n'est possible—dan l'étant—que vers l'infini ou le néant."

39 Imagine having all of life's possibilities locked in your brain but being able to speak only by inserting an empty pen cartridge in your throat; your statements, however sublime, reasonable and orderly, would always carry the trace of the violence that made them possible. Whenever you pull out the pen, everything is once again possible. Just as, in this hypothetical example, your speech would carry traces of the violence that made it possible, so all writing carries the trace of violently laying waste to all that is not carried by the signs used. The history of Western metaphysics is, according to this view, an effort to pretend that the difference between the totality imposed through logos (reason and order) and the excess which necessarily overflows its bounds is a matter of their own (economical) decisions about which problems to solve first. They pretend to be in charge of economizing themselves rather than confessing that there is an economic relation between reason and extravagance which they cannot control.

40 History is over only in the sense that its totality must be overcome; it is over every time a space is encountered "anywhere."

41 It is not surprising that most social scientists might be closer to

Derrida than, for example, Husserl on the certainty of the foundations of the world. They are too religious about method, however, to celebrate the extremities of extravagance.

42 "J'entends bien qu'il n'y a pas seulement, dans le mouvement qu'on appelle le *Cogito cartésien*, cette pointe hyperbolique qui devrait être, comme toute folie pure en général, silencieuse."

43 "Dès qu'il a atteint cette pointe, Descartes cherche à se rassurer, à garantir le Cogito lui-même en Dieu, à identifier l'acte du Cogito avec l'acte d'une raison raisonnable. Et il le fait dès qu'il *profère* et *réfléchit* le Cogito. C'est-à-dire dès qu'il doit temporaliser le Cogito qui ne vaut lui-même que dans l'instant de l'intuition, de la pensée attentive à elle-même, dans ce point ou cette pointe de l'instant."

44 So this critical level is only Derrida's exaggeration of a place—no, a moment—in which to observe Descartes's exaggeration of a God and temporalized logos. While Derrida can only wish to speak but cannot speak at this stage, he wants to equate Foucault's remark, "madness is the absence of a work," with Descartes's temporalized discourse. Watch:

> And the reading of Foucault seems to me strong and illuminating not at the stage of the text which he cites, and which is anterior and inferior to the Cogito, but starting with the moment which immediately follows the instantaneous experience of the Cogito at its sharpest point—where reason and madness are not yet separated, when to side with the Cogito is neither to side with reason as reasonable order nor with disorder and madness, but is instead to grasp the source again, to start with the point at which reason *and* madness are empowered to make up their minds and to relate themselves. Foucault's interpretation seems illuminating to me starting with the moment when the Cogito must think itself and proffer itself in an organized philosophical discourse. That is *nearly all the time.* (91/58)

All of this says that Derrida admires the insight but wishes to apply it starting from the zero-point (the point at which temporalization begins, so to speak). Once again, the three levels of inquiry (phases within stages) are very important. The most far out (closest to the silent monstrosity of pure madness) is willed by the extravagant Derrida, a double agent attempting to stay alive and also to report the violence of the coming of time. Coming closer to order and reason (in a kind of twisted purgatory)—in phase two of the lower level—is the reassured believer Descartes, a metaphysician attempting to inaugurate linear time. Ignoring, if not scorning,

God and the beginning of time, but risking by his presupposition of linear time an abettal of the metaphysician's totalizing project (at phase one of the lower stage) is the naive genealogist, Foucault.

45 "Dès son premier souffle, la parole, soumise à ce rythme temporel de crise et de réveil, n'ouvre son espace de parole qu'en enfermant la folie. Ce rythme n'est d'ailleurs pas une alternance qui serait de surcroît temporelle. C'est le mouvement de la temporalisation elle-même en ce qui l'unit au mouvement du logos."

46 So temporalization itself is just another name for historicity in general for Derrida. It can be united with the movement of logos to produce historical structures, or it can disengage from its subordinate position in the speaking relation, refuse to be reduced to marginal existence, and live in the Cogito as hyperbole (in silence, to the demise of speech acts) before the first polar distinctions are imposed. One must will to speak the demonic hyperbole before the Cogito reassures itself, to sense the very possibility of temporalization, or historicity.

But Derrida is not about reassuring readers, who must therefore always be on their guard. The slumber of madness is perhaps uninterrupted but silence can sometimes sign on as muffled noise. The prisoners of madness can attempt to right their situation. There are always traces of the violent imprisonment of madness which liberates speech. Historicity is itself a trace of violence. Derrida gives an account of this, apprising, if not accosting, readers:

> But this violent liberation [from the undifferentiated Cogito to the unity of temporalization and logos] of speech is possible (and could not otherwise be continued) only up to the point where it guards itself (where it is the trace of this original violence) and up to the point where it resolutely holds fast, in conscience, as close as possible to the abuse which is the use of speech: just near enough to state the violence [in hyperbole], to speak of it as an irreducible violence; just far enough away to live and live as speech.

> Mais cette libération violente de la parole n'est possible et ne peut se poursuivre, que dans la mesure où elle se garde, où elle est la trace de ce geste de violence originaire, et dans la mesure où elle se tient résolument, en conscience, au plus proche de l'abus qu'est l'usage de la parole, juste assez près pour *dire* la violence, pour dialoguer avec soi comme violence irréductible, juste assez loin pour *vivre* et vivre comme parole. (94/61)

Derrida insists on this uncertain doubleness: the original violence, which requires hyperbole to speak it and which cannot be reduced to a finite structure; and also the guarded forgetfulness which is the use of speech. The use of speech is the abuse of madness. Historical structures forget hyperbole until crises come to a head. Then, at these certain hyperbolic points, madness is reawakened in statements of excess. And then all is again forgotten. If temporalization and the histories it permits were removed speaking philosophy would die as thought in the undifferentiated Cogito.

47 In this situation of confession the tables are turned against logos:

> In the crisis of confession Reason is madder than madness because it is nonmeaning and forgetfulness, and madness is more rational than reason because it is nearer to the source where it lives as silence or murmuring as meaning, this crisis has always already begun and is interminable.

> Mais cette crise en laquelle la raison est plus folle que la folie—car elle est non-sens et oubli—et où la folie est plus rationnelle que la raison car elle est plus proche de la source vive quoique silencieuse ou murmurante du sens, cette crise a toujours déjà commencé et elle est interminable. (96/62)

48 "Dans le moment où le doute abordait ses périls majeurs, Descartes prenait conscience qu'il ne pouvait pas être fou—quitte à reconnaître longtemps encore et jusqu'au Malin Génie que toutes les puissances de la déraison veillaient autour de sa pensée."

49 There is still confusion about how to use *defer* in *différance*. It has nothing to do with deferring to authority; such a use stems from a different root. For a contrary view, see Allen Thiher (1984:87).

50 "L'économie de cette écriture est un rapport réglé entre l'excédant et la totalité excédée: la différance de l'excès absolu" (96/62).

9 Redrawing the Lignes de Bataille

1 See Foucault (1977:29–52) on transgression.

2 The supplement of this book can be read as an attempt to draw some attention back to everyday practice without sacrificing the extravagance of Derridian reading.

3 This chapter is part of an effort to think about community without unity to avoid playing into both hands of the good Professor Dumm's (1988:209) bon mot, "deconstructing monades to establish nomads." While unities are displaced by my work, this is because I stress the impossibility of the dyad. Rather than launch a

fin de siècle Normandy invasion to liberate Paris from its captors—
which this time around is not worth the trouble because the forces
of deconstruction are doing better in America than in France—I
shall rearrange such couples inside/outside, individual/collective,
man/woman, old/young, and gain/loss, and attempt to observe
dyadic tension close up.

4 I will mention early Foucault (1970:387) here, but much of what
he says about the death of the subject is being erased like a face
drawn in sand at the edge of the sea, by admirers. See Bernauer
and Rasmussen (1988).

5 Derrida (1967/1978:51–97/31–63) provides a good example of
such a reversal. The above style of citation will continue throughout this chapter. Dates and page numbers to the left of the slash
refer to French texts; those to the right of the slash refer to English
texts.

6 Connolly (1987;1988) is engaged in projects to avoid reducing difference to opposition, but seems to come closer than Derrida to
endorsing Foucauldian transgression.

7 See Foucault (1988:3ff.) for a definition that does not throw out
power with domination. My task here is not to see how to reconcile
his art of the self with, or to distinguish it from, radical liberalism.
Rather, it is to explore whatever possibilities exist for an affirmation of community that is neither individualist nor collectivist.

8 There are readers who read the first fifteen words of this and leave
Bataille as quickly as possible. I read Bataille not to establish his
phallocentrism beyond a shadow of a doubt, but to explain why
one might expect to find phallocentrism in his shadows and his
doubts.

9 Foucault (1977:33–38) finds future possibilities in this transgressive fluctuation.

10 ". . . how could . . . a God or what resembles God, still be accept-
able?" (554/236).

11 Even one of her most disagreeable critics agrees with Dworkin
that Bataille may well stand in "a relation of complicity rather than
in a relation of rupture vis-à-vis dominant ideologies" (Suleiman,
1986:128).

12 Of course, no writing succeeds in illustrating deconstruction; but
some is more self-conscious than others. Derrida, for example,
spends the most time possible trying to preclude the establishment of new hierarchies by deconstructing the most critical texts.
A danger of deconstruction is that it will be elevated to the top
or bottom of a new academic hierarchy. Perhaps the only way to
avoid this is to politicize the effort to preclude new syntheses, to
take deconstruction—as a certain way of reading—to the streets in

a celebration of difference. Until then it will, at best, only succeed in interpreting the world.

13 See Foucault (1977:139–64).

14 See Kroker et al. (1986).

15 Derrida (1967) gives a similar reading to Foucault's work on madness.

16 A dictionary might allow this: "sommeil" is the "assoupissement naturel de sens."

17 It is important to notice that "déraison" is sovereign either way; for Bataille it is the "other," outside the LAW; for Derrida it is the play that precedes the law and order of inside/outside opposition.

18 We shall explore how Bataille's notion of monstrous savage expenditure—nonproductive excess—might be reread within the spaces and margins of significative discourse, and encourage replacing his remunerative "potlatch" with the communitarian free gift.

19 Discursive difference is Derrida's way of indicating how arbitrary signs establish meaning by not being identical: that is, the letter z is not a through y.

20 This is the death of the subject that worries critics of postmodernism; we shall see that this worry is somewhat premature.

21 "The sovereign operation [of Bataille] is not content with neutralizing the classical operations in discourse; . . . it transgresses the law or prohibitions that form a system with discourse, and even with the work of neutralization" (Derrida, 1967:403/274).

22 Perhaps seeking "the common ground and the . . . irreducible difference" (428/293) of reassurance and extravagance.

23 Derrida shows elsewhere that interpretation can be interpreted as an infinite play of signification in the absence of a transcendental signified, or message. The signs or codes and messages one uses in discourse to indicate the human being (soul, man, woman, child) only defer that presence infinitely; therefore their substitution is inevitable.

24 See Derrida (1987) on why this is not a triad standing in for a dyad.

25 While Berry is clearly warning of ecological disaster, there can be no disguising the fact that the largest unseen pattern one can respect, if not yet damage or destroy, is just another name for God.

26 I am, of course, interested in the difference between using community in less reassuring and more extravagant ways.

27 This progression is an attempt to connect Derrida (1967/1978) and Derrida (1987).

References

Alexander, J. 1982. *Theoretical Logic in Sociology*. Berkeley: University of California Press.

Allen, D., and G. Butterick, eds. 1982. *The Postmoderns: The New American Poetry Revised*. New York: Grove Press.

Allison, D., ed., 1985. *The New Nietzsche*. Cambridge, Mass.: MIT Press.

Anderson, P. 1984. *In the Tracks of Historical Materialism*. London: Verso.

Arendt, H. 1961. *Between Past and Future*. New York: Viking Press.

Aristotle. 1978. *The Politics of Aristotle*. Translated by Ernest Barker. New York: Oxford University Press.

———. 1984. *The Complete Works of Aristotle*. Edited by J. Barnes. Princeton: Princeton University Press.

———. 1985. *Metaphysics*. New York: Hackett.

Augustine. 1958. *City of God.* Translated by G. G. Walsh et al. New York: Image Press.

Barber, B. 1984. *Strong Democracy: Participatory Politics for a New Age.* Berkeley: University of California Press.

Barry, B. 1973. *The Liberal Theory of Justice.* Oxford: Clarendon Press.

Bataille, G. 1954. *L'expérience intérieure.* Paris: Gallimard.

————. 1957. *L'erotisme.* Paris: Minuit.

————. 1970. *Oeuvres Complètes.* Vol. 1. Paris: Gallimard.

————. 1985. *Visions of Excess: Selected Writings, 1927–39.* Edited by Allan Stoekl. Translated by Allan Stoekl et al. Minneapolis: University of Minnesota Press.

————. 1986. *Erotism: Death and Sensuality.* Translated by Mary Dalwood. San Francisco: City Lights Books.

————. 1988. *Inner Experience.* Translated by Leslie Boldt. Albany: SUNY Press.

Bay, C. 1981. *Strategies of Political Emancipation.* Notre Dame: University of Notre Dame Press.

Bellah, R. 1975. *The Broken Covenant: American Civil Religion in a Time of Trial.* New York: Seabury Press.

————, et al. 1985. *Habits of the Heart.* Berkeley: University of California Press.

Benn, S. 1982. Individuality, Autonomy and Community. In Kamenka, 1982:43–62.

Berger, P. 1976. In Praise of Particularity. *Review of Politics* 38:399–410.

Bergmann, F. 1977. *On Being Free.* Notre Dame: University of Notre Dame Press.

Berlin, I. 1969. *Four Essays On Liberty.* Oxford: Oxford University Press.

Berman, M. 1982. *All That Is Solid Melts into Air: The Experience of Modernity.* New York: Simon and Schuster.

Bernauer, J., and D. Rasmussen. 1988. *The Final Foucault.* Cambridge, Mass.: MIT Press.

Bernstein, R. 1976. *The Restructuring of Social and Political Theory.* Philadelphia: University of Pennsylvania Press.

————. 1983. *Beyond Objectivism and Relativism.* Philadelphia: University of Pennsylvania Press.

Berry, W. 1983. *Standing by Words.* San Francisco: North Point Press.

————. 1987. *Home Economics.* San Francisco: North Point Press.

Boone, C. K. 1983. Privacy and Community. *Social Theory and Practice* 9:1–30.

Bowles, S., and H. Gintis. 1986. *Democracy and Capitalism.* New York: Basic Books.

Boyte, H. 1984. *Community Is Possible*. New York: Harper and Row.

Burke, E. 1902. *The Works of Edmund Burke*. 8 vols. London: Bohn.

———. 1958–71. *The Correspondence of Edmund Burke*. Edited by Thomas W. Copeland. Cambridge: Cambridge University Press; Chicago: University of Chicago Press.

Burke, K. 1935. *Permanence and Change*. New York: New Republic.

Calinescu, M. 1987. *Five Faces of Modernity: Modernism, Avant-Garde, Decadence, Kitsch, Postmodernism*. Durham, N.C.: Duke University Press.

Canavan, F. 1960. *The Political Reason of Edmund Burke*. Durham, N.C.: Duke University Press.

Capek, M. 1961. *The Philosophical Impact of Contemporary Physics*. New York: Van Nostrand Reinhold.

Cavell, S. 1969. *Must We Mean What We Say?* Cambridge: Cambridge University Press.

———. 1972. *The Senses of Walden*. New York: Viking Press.

———. 1979. *The Claim of Reason*. Oxford: Oxford University Press.

de Certeau, M. 1984. *The Practice of Everyday Life*. Translated by S. F. Randall. Berkeley: University of California Press.

———. 1986. *Heterologies, Discourses on the Other*. Minneapolis: University of Minnesota Press.

Chapman, J. 1956. *Rousseau—Totalitarian or Liberal?* New York: Columbia University Press.

———. 1980. Justice, Freedom and Property. In Pennock and Chapman, 1980:289–324.

Cochran, C. 1982. *Character, Community, and Politics*. University: University of Alabama Press.

Comte, Auguste. 1953. *A General View of Positivism*. Translated by J. H. Bridges. Stanford: Academic Reprints.

Connolly, W. 1981. *Appearance and Reality in Politics*. Cambridge: Cambridge University Press.

———. 1983a. *The Terms of Political Discourse*. 2d ed. Princeton: Princeton University Press.

———. 1983b. Discipline, Politics, and Ambiguity. *Political Theory* 11:325–41.

———. 1987. *Politics and Ambiguity*. Madison: University of Wisconsin Press.

———. 1988. *Political Theory and Modernity*. Oxford: Basil Blackwell Press.

Corlett, W. 1982. The Availability of Lincoln's Political Religion. *Political Theory* 10:520–40.

———. 1989. Pocock, Foucault, Forces of Reassurance. *Political Theory* 17:77–100.

Culler, J. 1982. *On Deconstruction: Theory and Criticism after Structuralism.* Ithaca: Cornell University Press.

Dallmayr, F. 1984. *Polis and Praxis.* Cambridge, Mass.: MIT Press.

Deleuze, G. 1988. *Foucault.* Translated and edited by Seán Hand. Minneapolis: University of Minnesota Press.

Derrida, J. 1967. *L'écriture et la différence.* Paris: Seuil.

————. 1974. *Of Grammatology.* Translated by G. C. Spivak. Baltimore: Johns Hopkins University Press.

————. 1978. *Writing and Difference.* Translated by Alan Bass. Chicago: University of Chicago Press.

————. 1981. *Dissemination.* Translated with an Introduction and Additional Notes by B. Johnson. Chicago: University of Chicago Press.

————. 1982. *Margins of Philosophy.* Translated by Alan Bass. Chicago: University of Chicago Press.

————. 1987. Women in the Beehive: A Seminar with Jacques Derrida. In Jardine and Smith, 1987:189–203.

Descartes, R. 1967. *Oeuvres philosophiques.* Tome II. Paris: Garnier.

Descombes, V. 1981. *Modern French Philosophy.* Translated by L. Scott-Fox and J. M. Harding. Cambridge: Cambridge University Press.

Dreyfus, H., and P. Rabinow. 1983. *Michel Foucault: Beyond Structuralism and Hermeneutics.* 2d ed. Chicago: University of Chicago Press.

Dumm, T. 1988. The Politics of Post-Modern Aesthetics: Habermas Contra Foucault. *Political Theory* 16:209–28.

Dworkin, A. 1987. *Intercourse.* New York: Free Press.

Eldridge, R. 1985. Deconstruction and Its Alternatives. *Man and World* 18:147–70.

Ellenburg, S. 1976. *Rousseau's Political Philosophy.* Ithaca: Cornell University Press.

Elshtain, J. B. 1981. *Public Man, Private Woman: Women in Social and Political Thought.* Princeton: Princeton University Press.

Felman, S. 1985. *Writing and Madness.* Translated by Martha Evans et al. Ithaca: Cornell University Press.

Fish, S. 1979. Normal Circumstances, Literal Language, Direct Speech Acts, the Ordinary, the Everyday, the Obvious, What Goes without Saying, and Other Special Cases. In Rabinow and Sullivan, 1979:243–66.

Flores, R. 1984. *The Rhetoric of Doubtful Authority: Deconstructive Readings of Self-Questioning Narratives, St. Augustine to Faulkner.* Ithaca: Cornell University Press.

Foucault, M. 1961. *Histoire de la folie.* Paris: Librarie Plon.

————. 1970. *The Order of Things*. New York: Pantheon.

————. 1971. Nietzsche, La Genealogie, L'Histoire. In *Hommage A Jean Hyppolite*. Paris: PUF.

————. 1972a. *Histoire de la folie a l'age classique*. 2d ed. Paris: Gallimard.

————. 1972b. *The Archaeology of Knowledge* (includes the author's *The Discourse on Language*). Translated by A. M. Sheridan Smith. New York: Pantheon.

————. 1977. *Language, Counter-Memory, Practice*. Translated by D. F. Bouchard and Sherry Simon. Ithaca: Cornell University Press.

————. 1979. My Body, This Paper, This Fire. Translated by Geoff Bennington. *Oxford Literary Review* (Autumn: 9–28).

————. 1980. *Power/Knowledge*. Edited by C. Gordon. Translated by C. Gordon, L. Marshall, J. Mepham, K. Soper. New York: Pantheon.

————. 1983. Why Study Power? (written in English). In Dreyfus and Rabinow, 1983.

————. 1988. The Ethic of Care for the Self as a Practice of Freedom. Translated by J. D. Gauthier. In Bernauer et al., 1988: 1–20.

Freeman, M. 1980. *Edmund Burke and the Critique of Political Radicalism*. Chicago: University of Chicago Press.

Gale, Richard, ed. 1967. *The Philosophy of Time*. New York: Doubleday.

Gaus, G. 1983. *The Modern Liberal Theory of Man*. New York: St. Martin's Press.

Geerken, J. H. 1979. Pocock and Machiavelli: Structuralist Explanation in History. *Journal of the History of Philosophy* 17:309–318.

Geertz, C. 1973. *The Interpretation of Cultures*. New York: Basic Books.

————. 1980. *Negara: The Theatre State in Nineteenth-Century Bali*. Princeton: Princeton University Press.

————. 1983. *Local Knowledge: Further Essays in Interpretive Anthropology*. New York: Basic Books.

Goodman, N. 1978. *Ways of Worldmaking*. New York: Hackett.

Gramsci, A. 1959. *The Modern Prince and Other Writings*. Translated by L. Marks. New York: International Publishers.

de Grazia, S. 1948. *The Political Community: A Study in Anomie*. Chicago: University of Chicago Press.

Green, P. 1981. *The Pursuit of Inequality*. New York: Pantheon.

————. 1985. *Retrieving Democracy: In Search of Civic Equality*. Totowa, N.J.: Rowman and Allanheld.

Gunnell, J. 1968. *Political Philosophy and Time*. Middletown, Conn.: Wesleyan University Press.

———. 1979. *Political Theory: Tradition and Interpretation*. Boston: Winthrop.

———. 1981. Method, Methodology, and the Search for Traditions in the History of Political Theory: A Reply to Pocock's Salute. *Annals of Scholarship* 1:26–63.

Gusfield, J. R. 1975. *Community: A Critical Response*. New York: Harper and Row.

Gutmann, A. 1980. *Liberal Equality*. Cambridge: Cambridge University Press.

———. 1985. Communitarian Critics of Liberalism. *Philosophy and Public Affairs* 14:308–22.

Halle, L. J. 1977. *Out of Chaos*. Boston: Houghton Mifflin.

Hayek, F. 1979. *The Political Order of a Free People*. Chicago: University of Chicago Press.

Heidegger, M. 1984. *Nietzsche*. Vol. 2. Translated by D. F. Krell. San Francisco: Harper and Row.

Heraclitus. 1979. *The Art and Thought of Heraclitus: An Edition of the Fragments with Translation and Commentary*. Translated by C. Kahn. Cambridge: Cambridge University Press.

Hesse, M. 1980. *Revolutions and Reconstructions in the Philosophy of Science*. Bloomington: Indiana University Press.

Hiskes, R. 1982. *Community Without Coercion*. Newark: University of Delaware Press.

Hobbes, T. 1968. *Leviathan*. Edited by C. B. Macpherson. New York: Penguin.

Hollis, M. 1982. The Social Destruction of Reality. In Hollis and Lukes, 1982.

Hollis, M., and S. Lukes, eds. 1982. *Rationality and Relativism*. Cambridge, Mass.: MIT Press.

Horkheimer, M. 1974. *Critique of Instrumental Reason*. Translated by Matthew J. O'Connell et al. New York: Seabury Press.

Hoy, D. 1985. Jacques Derrida. In Skinner, 1985.

———, ed. 1986. *Foucault: A Critical Reader*. Oxford: Basil Blackwell Press.

Husserl, E. 1970. *Logical Investigations*. Translated by J. N. Findlay. New York: Humanities Press.

Hyde, L. 1979. *The Gift: Imagination and the Erotic Life of Property*. New York: Doubleday.

Jacobson, N. 1978. *Pride and Solace*. Berkeley: University of California Press.

Jaffa, H. 1959. *The Crisis of the House Divided*. New York: Doubleday.

Jameson, F. 1972. *The Prison-House of Language: A Critical Account* of Structuralism and Russian Formalism. Princeton: Princeton University Press.

Jardine, A., and P. Smith, eds. 1987. *Men in Feminism*. New York: Methuen.

Jay, M. 1984. *Marxism and Totality: The Adventures of a Concept from Lukács to Habermas*. Berkeley: University of California Press.

Kamenka, E., ed. 1982. *Community as a Social Ideal*. New York: St. Martin's Press.

Kant, I. 1929. *Critique of Pure Reason*. Translated by Norman Kemp Smith. New York: Macmillan.

Kariel, H. 1969. Expanding the Political Present. *American Political Science Review* 63:768–76.

Kohak, E. 1984. *The Embers and the Stars*. Chicago: University of Chicago Press.

Kramnick, I. 1977. *The Rage of Edmund Burke: Portrait of an Ambivalent Conservative*. New York: Basic Books.

Kroker, A., and D. Cook. 1986. *The Postmodern Scene: Excremental Culture and Hyper-Aesthetics*. New York: St. Martin's Press.

Krupnick, M., ed. 1987. *Displacement: Derrida and After*. Bloomington: Indiana University Press.

Kuhn, T. S. 1977. *The Essential Tension: Selected Studies in Scientific Tradition and Change*. Chicago: University of Chicago Press.

Lincoln, Abraham. 1953–55. *The Collected Works of Abraham Lincoln*. 9 vols. Edited by Roy Basler. New Brunswick: Rutgers University Press.

Luther, M. 1960. *Three Treatises*. Philadelphia: Muhlenberg Press.

Lyotard, J. 1984. *The Postmodern Condition: A Report On Knowledge*. Translated by Geoff Bennington and Brian Massumi. Minneapolis: University of Minnesota Press.

MacIntyre, A. 1981. *After Virtue*. Notre Dame: University of Notre Dame Press.

———. 1984. *After Virtue*. 2d ed. Notre Dame: University of Notre Dame Press.

———. 1988. *Whose Justice? Which Rationality?* Notre Dame: University of Notre Dame Press.

Macpherson, C. 1973. *Democratic Theory: Essays in Retrieval*. Oxford: Clarendon Press.

———. 1980. *Burke*. New York: Hill and Wang.

Mandelbaum, M. 1984. *Philosophy, History, and the Sciences*. Baltimore: Johns Hopkins University Press.

Mansbridge, J. 1980. *Beyond Adversary Democracy*. New York: Basic Books.

Marx, K., and F. Engels. 1978. *The Marx-Engels Reader.* 2d ed. Edited by R. C. Tucker. New York: Norton.

———. 1985. *The German Ideology.* Edited by C. J. Arthur. New York: International Publishers.

Megill, A. 1985. *Prophets of Extremity.* Berkeley: University of California Press.

Merleau-Ponty, M. 1964. *Signs.* Translated by R. C. McCleary. Evanston: Northwestern University Press.

Miller, N., ed. 1986. *The Poetics of Gender.* New York: Columbia University Press.

Mischel, T. 1977. *The Self.* London: Basil Blackwell Press.

Neruda, P. 1977. *Memoirs.* Translated by H. St. Martin. New York: Farrar, Straus and Giroux.

Nietzsche, F. 1969. *On the Genealogy of Morals.* Translated by Walter Kaufmann. New York: Vintage.

Nisbet, R. A. 1969. *The Quest for Community.* New York: Oxford University Press.

Novak, M. 1982. The Communitarian Individual in America. *The Public Interest* 68:3–20.

Oakeshott, M. 1962. *Rationalism in Politics.* New York: Basic Books.

Ogilby, J. 1965. *The Fables of Aesop Paraphrased in Verse.* Introduction by Earl Miner. Los Angeles: William Andrew Clark Memorial Library.

Ovid. 1958. *The Metamorphoses.* Translated by H. Gregory. New York: New American Library.

Parenti, M. 1983. *Democracy for the Few.* New York: St. Martin's Press.

Pennock, J., and J. Chapman, eds. 1980. *NOMOS XXII: Property.* New York: NYU Press.

Pitkin, H. F. 1972. *Wittgenstein and Justice.* Berkeley: University of California Press.

———. 1984. *Fortune Is a Woman: Gender and Politics in the Thought of Niccolo Machiavelli.* Berkeley: University of California Press.

Plato. 1973. *The Republic.* Translated by G. M. Grube. New York: Hackett.

Pocock, J. G. A. 1970. Untitled. In *The Historian's Workshop: Original Essays by Sixteen Historians.* Edited by L. P. Curtis, Jr. New York: Knopf.

———. 1973. *Politics, Language and Time: Essays on Political Thought and History.* New York: Atheneum.

———. 1975. *The Machiavellian Moment: Florentine Political Thought and the Atlantic Republic Tradition.* Princeton: Princeton University Press.

————. 1980. Political Ideas as Historical Events: Political Philosophers as Historical Actors. In Richter, 1980:139–50.

————. 1981a. The Machiavellian Moment Revisited: A Study in History and Ideology. *Journal of Modern History* 53:40-72.

————. 1981b. Political Theory, Methodology and Myth. *Annals of Scholarship* 1:3–62.

————. 1985. *Virtue, Commerce, and History: Essays on Political Thought and History, Chiefly in the Eighteenth Century.* Cambridge: Cambridge University Press.

Popper, K. 1950. *The Open Society and Its Enemies.* Princeton: Princeton University Press.

————. 1957. *The Poverty of Historicism.* New York: Basic Books.

Rabinow, P., and W. Sullivan, eds. 1979. *Interpretive Social Science: A Reader.* Berkeley: University of California Press.

Rawls, J. 1971. *A Theory of Justice.* Cambridge, Mass.: Harvard University Press.

————. 1985. Justice as Fairness: Political Not Metaphysical. *Philosophy and Public Affairs* 14:223–51.

Richter, M., ed. 1980. *Political Theory and Political Education.* Princeton: Princeton University Press.

Rorty, R. 1979. *Philosophy and the Mirror of Nature.* Princeton: Princeton University Press.

————, et al., eds. 1984. *Philosophy in History.* Cambridge: Cambridge University Press.

Rosenblum, N. 1987. *Another Liberalism: Romanticism and the Reconstruction of Liberal Thought.* Cambridge, Mass.: Harvard University Press.

Rousseau, J.-J. 1964. *The First and Second Discourses.* Edited by Roger Masters. Translated by Judith Masters. New York: St. Martin's Press.

————. 1978. *On the Social Contract.* Edited by Roger Masters. Translated by Judith Masters. New York: St. Martin's Press.

————. 1979. *Emile.* Translated by Allan Bloom. New York: Basic Books.

Ryan, M. 1982. *Marxism and Deconstruction, A Critical Articulation.* Baltimore: Johns Hopkins University Press.

Sandel, M. 1982. *Liberalism and the Limits of Justice.* Cambridge: Cambridge University Press.

————. 1984. Morality and the Liberal Ideal. *New Republic* 7 May: 15–17.

————, ed. 1985. *Liberalism and Its Critics.* New York: NYU Press.

Saussure, F. 1966. *Course in General Linguistics.* New York: McGraw-Hill.

Schaar, J. 1983. The Question of Justice. *Raritan* 3:107–29.

Schoolman, M. 1984. *The Imaginary Witness*. New York: NYU Press.

Sennett, R. 1974. *The Fall of Public Man*. New York: Knopf.

Shapiro, M. J. 1981. *Language and Political Understanding: The Politics of Discursive Practices*. New Haven: Yale University Press.

———, ed. 1984. *Language and Politics*. New York: NYU Press.

Sherover, C. M. 1971. *Heidegger, Kant and Time*. Bloomington: Indiana University Press.

Shipley, J. 1945. *Dictionary of Word Origins*. New York: Philosophical Library.

Shklar, J. 1969. *Men and Citizens*. Cambridge: Cambridge University Press.

Simmel, G. 1963. How is Society Possible? Translated by K. Wolff. In *Philosophy of the Social Sciences*, edited by M. Natanson, 73–92. New York: Random House.

Skinner, Q. 1975. Hermeneutics and the Role of History. *New Literary History* 7:209–32.

———. 1985. *The Return of Grand Theory in the Human Sciences*. Cambridge: Cambridge University Press.

Smith, B. 1985. *Politics and Remembrance*. Princeton: Princeton University Press.

Spivak, G. C. 1987. *In Other Worlds: Essays in Cultural Politics*. New York: Methuen.

Stanlis, P. 1958. *Edmund Burke and the Natural Law*. Ann Arbor: University of Michigan Press.

Staten, H. 1984. *Wittgenstein and Derrida*. Lincoln: University of Nebraska Press.

Stoekl, A. 1985. *Politics, Writing, Mutilation: The Cases of Bataille, Blanchot, Roussel, Leiris, and Ponge*. Minneapolis: University of Minnesota Press.

Strauss, L. 1953. *Natural Right and History*. Chicago: University of Chicago Press.

Strong, T. 1976a. *Friedrich Nietzsche and the Politics of Transfiguration*. Berkeley: University of California Press.

———. 1976b. Language and Nihilism. *Theory and Society* 3:239–63.

———. 1983a. Nihilism and Political Theory. In *What Should Political Theory Be Now?*, edited by J. Nelson. Albany: SUNY Press.

———. 1983b. Review of Dreyfus and Rabinow (1983). *Political Theory* 11:478–81.

Suleiman, S. 1986. Pornography, Transgression and the Avant-Garde: Bataille's *Story of the Eye*. In Miller (1986:117–36).

Taylor, C. 1975. *Hegel*. Cambridge: Cambridge University Press.

————. 1977. What Is Human Agency? In Mischel, 1977:103–38.

————. 1979a. *Hegel and Modern Society*. Cambridge: Cambridge University Press.

————. 1979b. Interpretation and the Sciences of Man. Rabinow et al., 1979:27–72.

————. 1984. Foucault on Freedom and Truth. *Political Theory* 12: 152–83.

————. 1985. *Philosophy and the Human Sciences*. 2 vols. Cambridge: Cambridge University Press.

Taylor, M. 1982. *Community Anarchy, and Liberty*. Cambridge: Cambridge University Press.

Thiher, A. 1984. *Words in Reflection: Modern Language Theory and Postmodern Fiction*. Chicago: University of Chicago Press.

Thoreau, H. D. 1972. *The Maine Woods*. New York: T. Y. Crowell.

————. 1984. *Walden and Other Writings*. Edited by William Howarth. New York: Modern Library.

Thurow, G. 1976. *Abraham Lincoln and American Political Religion*. Albany: SUNY Press.

Tinder, G. 1980. *Community*. Baton Rouge: LSU Press.

Titmuss, R. 1971. *The Gift Relationship*. New York: Pantheon.

Tonnies, F. 1957. *Community and Society*. Translated by Charles Loomis. New York: Harper and Row.

Unger, R. M. 1975. *Knowledge and Politics*. New York: Free Press.

————. 1984. *Passion: An Essay on Personality*. New York: Free Press.

Walzer, M. 1983. *Spheres of Justice*. New York: Basic Books.

————. 1986. The Politics of Michel Foucault. In Hoy, 1986:51–68.

Warnock, M. 1976. *Imagination*. Berkeley: University of California Press.

White, J. B. 1984. *When Words Lose Their Meaning: Constitutions and Reconstitutions of Language, Character, and Community*. Chicago: University of Chicago Press.

Wilkins, B. T. 1967. *The Problem of Burke's Political Philosophy*. Oxford: Clarendon Press.

Wittgenstein, L. 1953. *Philosophical Investigations*. Translated by G. E. M. Anscombe. New York: Macmillan.

————. 1972. *On Certainty*. Translated by D. Paul and G. E. M. Anscombe. New York: Harper and Row.

————. 1980. *Culture and Value*. Translated by Peter Winch. Chicago: University of Chicago Press.

Wolin, S. 1960. *Politics and Vision*. Boston: Little, Brown.

————. 1969. Political Theory as a Vocation. *American Political Science Review* 63:1062-82.

————. 1977. The Rise of Private Man. *New York Review of Books.* 14 April: 19–26.

————. 1983. From Progress to Modernization: The Conservative Turn. *democracy* 3:4:9–21. Fall issue.

Wood, D., and R. Bernasconi, ed. 1988. *Derrida and Différance.* Evanston: Northwestern University Press.

Zolberg, A. 1972. Moments of Madness. *Politics and Society* 2:183–207.

Index

Metaphysics of presence, 221
n.13
Municipality, 18, 67, 201, 208,
210, 211

Nietzsche, F., 48, 56, 57, 73, 80,
87, 89, 199
Nihilism, 3, 37, 192, 193, 201
Nisbet, R., 25
Nonmeaning, 83, 146–149, 161,
176, 177, 195, 196, 231 n.12,
240 n.47
Nonpresence, 158, 159
Novak, M., 25

Oakeshott, M., 78
Ogilby, J., 120
Oneness, shared, 4, 19, 22, 152,
202, 203. *See also* Commu-
nion
Open wound, 158, 164, 174,
231 n.6, 236 n.30. *See also*
Rupture
Opposition, binary. *See* Binary
opposition

Parmenides, 180
Passion, 93, 100, 101, 110, 112,
113, 115, 185
Patterns of subjectivity, 3, 4,
22, 56, 59, 67, 68, 181, 185,
207, 208, 212, 214. *See also*
Binary opposition; Subject
Phallocentrism, 241 n.8
Plato, 224 n.5
Play: radical, 15, 38, 63, 148,
163, 179, 213, 216; safe play,
62, 63, 212
Pocock, J. G. A., 14, 67, 69, 72–
81, 84, 85, 87–89, 92, 96, 105,
110, 116, 117, 126, 148, 151,
152, 157, 159, 174, 179
Polarity, 75–77, 93, 137, 166,

167, 173, 174, 177, 190, 226
n.19, 228 n.37. *See also* Binary
opposition
Political discourse. *See* Discourse, political
Political religion. *See* Religion
Positivism in social science, 57
Post-enlightenment, 45–47, 54,
57
Postmodernism: as abandonment, 3; as perspective, 11, 37,
87, 145, 188, 231 n.6; versus
interpretation, 30, 50, 73, 123,
187
Power: and discipline, 58, 133;
and extravagance, 70, 90,
129, 172, 180, 201, 207; of
fear, 124, 125, 129, 136, 137,
139; Foucault on, 38–45,
69, 148, 222 n.6, 241 n.7;
and prejudice, 126, 134; and
reassurance, 79, 147; and reciprocity, 70, 201, 207, 214; and
the State, 97, 98, 128, 134; of
Thomism as explanation, 55
Primordial chaos, 77, 81, 86,
118, 123, 125, 137, 147, 231
n.8
Privacy, 23, 24
Proust, M., 228 n.39

Rabinow, P., 227 n.22
Rasmussen, D., 241 n.4
Rationality, 27, 41, 42, 45–47,
50, 54, 59, 104, 140, 167, 186,
197, 199, 203
Rawls, J., 21, 24, 31, 220 n.4
Reciprocity. *See* Remunity
Religion: as Christian liberal
theories, 25; as Christian will,
31, 53, 59; as Church, 26, 44,
131–133, 136; as faith and
reason, 50, 137; as God, 10,

William Corlett is Assistant Professor of Political Science, Bates College, Lewiston, Maine.